D1519708

FRENCH RESISTANCE

JEAN-PHILIPPE MATHY

❧ ❧ ❧

French RESISTANCE

THE FRENCH-AMERICAN CULTURE WARS

University of Minnesota Press
Minneapolis • London

A portion of chapter 1 originally appeared as "The Resistance to French Theory in the United States: A Cross-Cultural Inquiry," *French Historical Studies* 19, no. 2 (fall 1995): 331–47; reprinted by permission of the Society for French Historical Studies and Duke University Press. A portion of chapter 3 originally appeared as "Repli sur la République: La nouvelle donne des intellectuels français," in the special issue "The French Intellectual: New Engagements," *L'Esprit Créateur* 37, no. 2 (summer 1997): 41–55; reprinted by permission of *L'Esprit Créateur*.

Published by the University of Minnesota Press
111 Third Avenue South, Suite 290
Minneapolis, MN 55401-2520
http://www.upress.umn.edu

Printed in the United States of America on acid-free paper

Library of Congress Cataloging-in-Publication Data
Mathy, Jean-Philippe.
    French resistance : the French-American culture wars /
Jean-Philippe Mathy.
        p.   cm.
    Includes bibliographical references and index.
    ISBN 0-8166-3442-4 — ISBN 0-8166-3443-2 (pb)
    1. France—Intellectual life—American influences.
    2. United States—Intellectual life—French influences.
    3. United States—Relations—France.   4. France—Relations—
United States.   5. Politics and culture.   I. Title.

DC33.7.M285 2000
303.48'244073—dc21   99-057336

11 10 09 08 07 06 05 04 03 02 01 00   10 9 8 7 6 5 4 3 2 1

*For Gabriel, Patricia,
and Christopher*

Chaque sujet a droit à sa culture,
aucune culture n'a de droit sur le sujet.
ROBERT LAFONT

Contents

᠂᠊᠂᠊᠂

Acknowledgments

❧ ❧ ❧

*M*any friends, colleagues, and students have contributed ideas and suggestions for this book. I am particularly indebted to my colleagues at the University of Illinois, Geoffrey Bowker, Pradeep Dhillon, Blair Kling, Harry Liebersohn, and David Prochaska, for their encouragement and insightful comments at various stages of the project.

I have learned a great deal about national cultures East and West from conversations with Kevin Doak (who also provided invaluable editorial help when most needed) and Nicolae Popescu (who guided me through the complexities of Quebec's ethnic-linguistic issues). Herman Lebovics and Steven Ungar provided stimulating critiques of the manuscript.

I also thank Herrick Chapman, Eric Fassin, Denis Hollier, Thomas Pavel, François Rigolot, David Kennedy, Duncan Kennedy, Ieme van der Poel, and Sophie Berto for inviting me to share some of my reflections with faculty and students at New York University, Yale, Princeton, Harvard, and the University of Amsterdam, as well as Dominique Jullien for her support at an early stage of the project.

An appointment at the Center for Advanced Study at the University of Illinois enabled me to complete most of the manuscript. I am grateful to the director, Braj Kachru, and to the staff for making my semester at CAS both pleasant and productive.

Introduction

ᐒ· ᐒ· ᐒ·

Why then the split between the cultures, one I experience as wrenching,
given my own divided loyalties (bilingual since early childhood, educated
in French, raised in the United States, "in" French, and a feminist)?
If there is one difference between the two cultures that holds maximum
explanatory power in this context it is the significance in France of the
notion of the universal, and of France and its language as its measure, the
French nation as its embodiment, the French revolution as its praxis.
NAOMI SCHOR

*T*he present study has its source in
the final pages of a book I wrote a few
years ago on French literary representations of American culture and society. In the epilogue, I suggested that the most recent developments in
French-American intellectual relations involve both a rapprochement and
a distancing on a number of issues regarding literary theory, postmodernism, and popular culture.[1] I also argued that there was a definite convergence between postanalytical American philosophy (especially in its neopragmatist forms) and French poststructuralism. In the early 1980s, Richard
Rorty praised what he called the North Atlantic "post-philosophical culture" for questioning the traditional division of labor between continental and Anglo-American philosophical traditions.[2] American pragmatism
and the French deconstruction of "Western logocentrism" found common
ground in opposing the metaphysical quest for certainty.

The initial burst of enthusiasm for French philosophical products in the United States throughout the 1970s was followed by intense resistance to French theory from various quarters of the academic, and later journalistic, worlds. The cultural Right bemoaned the deleterious influence of French philosophical gibberish on the minds of the young, claiming that theory was infecting them with the virus of relativism. The French imports were said to have contributed their interpretive sophistry to the revolt against the American way of life that had rocked America's campuses in the sixties. The works of Foucault, Derrida, and Lacan, their conservative critics argued, were used by the academic Left to produce sophisticated versions of what Jonathan Yardley has called the "America Sucks Sweepstakes," whereby anything Western and American was vilified as hegemonic, oppressive, and hopelessly logocentric.[3]

Tradition-minded supporters of Western civilization were not the only ones dissatisfied with the influence of Gallic antihumanism on state-of-the-art academic research in the humanities and the social sciences. Voices from the Left also rose in opposition. Marxists, especially in Britain, lambasted the theoreticism of the new rhetoricians, deploring their tendency to reduce social forces to effects of language and elusive traces of Derridean *différance*.[4] Feminists and gay activists argued that a good deal of poststructuralist thinking was still complicitous with masculinist ways of looking at the world. Postcolonial critics, for their part, claimed that French theory, born with the crisis of the nation-state, was still privileging Eurocentric viewpoints, however subtly. The French theorists' widespread skepticism regarding the efficacy of any political mobilization against "discursive hegemony" and the web of "power-knowledge" seemed to be depriving colonial people of political agency at the very moment they had a chance of getting their voices finally heard.

As a matter of fact, one of the latest episodes of the theory wars ("the Sokal affair") started as a quarrel within the Left. In 1996, Alan Sokal, a New York University physicist, wrote a parody of a "postmodern" critique of science and sent it to *Social Text,* a prominent journal of critical theory and cultural studies. The paper, replete with postmodernist clichés and blatant scientific errors, was accepted, and its author revealed the hoax a few months later in an article published in *Lingua Franca,* a review for academics and education professionals with a wider readership than the avant-garde *Social Text.*[5] Sokal, who presented himself as hailing from the Left ("I am a leftist too: under the Sandinista government I taught

2

mathematics at the National University in Nicaragua"), said he had been motivated by anger at all the subjectivist "silliness" about scientific proto-cols of inquiry as the product of social convention emanating from "the self-proclaimed Left." "The recent turn of many 'progressive' or 'leftist' academic humanists and social scientists toward one or another form of epistemic relativism," he wrote in *Lingua Franca,* "betrays the worthy her-itage [of the Left] and undermines the already fragile prospects for pro-gressive social critique" (64).

In a response to the editors of *Social Text,* Sokal persisted in question-ing the progressivist credentials of "fashionable thinkers in 'science stud-ies,' literary criticism and cultural studies." His goal, he went on, "was not to defend science from the barbarian hordes of lit crit (we'll survive just fine, thank you) but to defend the Left from a trendy segment of itself. Like innumerable others from diverse backgrounds and disciplines, I call the Left to reclaim its Enlightenment roots" (57). The debate that followed the publication of Sokal's article involved positions that are central to my own argument, since the dispute soon focused primarily on the evaluation of the Enlightenment legacy and on the role of reason and universality in emancipatory politics then and now. The science wars are part of a larger struggle involving definitions of the nation and of universality, especially with regard to the relation between the rule of law and cultural pluralism.

Both sides hurled at one another accusations of anti-intellectualism, a notion that I believe to be crucial to the understanding both of the status of discursive knowledge in general and of the resistance to theory in par-ticular in American culture. Sokal invoked two characteristics of the "char-latanism and nonsense purveyed by dozens of prominent French and American intellectuals" that I have encountered time and again in my sur-vey of antitheoreticism in Anglo-American life, from the Renaissance to the present: stylistic and epistemic obscurity (the "pomo gibberish") and intellectual arrogance. Sokal quotes as an epigraph a passage from Larry Laudan's *Science and Relativism* (1990) that condemns "the idea that every-thing boils down to subjective interests and perspectives" as "the most prominent and pernicious manifestations of anti-intellectualism in our time" (cited in Sokal, 62).

In his "Reflections on the Sokal Affair," Andrew Ross, one of the edi-tors of *Social Text* taken to task by the physicist, countered that the dispute had demonstrated above all the intolerance of "those who had decided they belonged to the true Left" and were "morally authorized to punish the

3

backslidden."[6] "What made the Sokal Affair an unusual, but germane, event in the Culture Wars," Ross wrote, "was that it gave rise to an outbreak of old-style correctness, complete with impatient calls for purges of a faux Left. This is always a sad spectacle, especially when it features anti-intellectual sentiment masquerading as 'sufficient' political consciousness" (151).

Alan Sokal became an overnight celebrity, touring campuses and speaking to standing-room-only audiences, and thereby providing much evidence of the sensitivity of the academic community to issues of relativism and truth. He later teamed up with Belgian scientist Jean Bricmont, and the pair wrote a book that broadened the scope of Sokal's early articles in American journals. Copiously reviewed in the Parisian media, *Impostures intellectuelles* charged Lacan, Deleuze, Irigaray, Kristeva, Guattari, and Baudrillard with being scientific ignoramuses who improperly used mathematical references to legitimize what remained at bottom an antirationalistic philosophical enterprise.[7] The publication of the book in Paris brought the dispute back to where it had originated thirty years earlier, that is, at the former center of the theoretical empire now under siege.

The speed of translation of the controversy, in both linguistic and spatial terms, from one national field to the next (barely a year went by between Sokal's essay in *Lingua Franca* and the book publication in France, and the English version, entitled *Fashionable Nonsense: Postmodern Intellectuals' Abuse of Science,* is already available in the United States) attests to the integration of the new transatlantic ideological force field I examine in the following pages, as well as to the dominance of the American pole in the new intellectual world order. The American anti-postmodernists (and their French and European allies in the university, the publishing industry, and the media) initiated and framed the debate while their opponents found themselves on the defensive, compelled to position themselves within parameters defined elsewhere.

In the concluding remarks of *Extrême-Occident* I suggested that the success of French poststructuralism and the subsequent resistance to it were both grounded in characteristics of Anglo-American culture that preceded and shaped these developments. The antimetaphysical, antirationalist character of American pragmatism and British empiricism explained the early success of the French critique of Enlightenment foundationalism. Similarly, the antielitist thrust of the Anglo-American, liberal-democratic tradition accounted for the later resistance to what became yet another instance of the arrogant, pretentious, jargon-laden, hermetic prose of the Gallic avant-gardes. The fate of theory in the United States takes on added meaning when it is set within the larger context of the Anglo-American tradition and of the history of its conflictual relationship with French political culture at least since the French Revolution. One could make the case that the assaults on French theory are the latest skirmish in a long, protracted struggle against aristocratic intellectualism in the English-speaking world.

I subsequently came across several studies that supported my own interpretation. In his *Nationalism, Romanticism and the Revolt against Theory*, David Simpson covered similar ground since he too attempted to interpret recent transatlantic controversies in the light of earlier developments in the history of ideas.[8] Simpson uncovered striking rhetorical similarities between the disputes in Britain surrounding the French Revolution and current discussions of postmodernism and poststructuralism. Simpson was interested in finding out "why the British habitually and the Americans often have been hostile to theory . . . and how the anglophone national traditions have constructed and perpetuated this particular phobia" (3). In the course of his investigation, he went back further than the 1790s, grounding the antitheoretical propensity of the Anglo-American idiom in earlier critiques of Cartesian-Ramist method in seventeenth-century England.

By the mid-eighteenth century, apologists of English national culture contrasted British common sense and French excess, the latter a mixture of inhuman rationality and unbridled sentimentality later associated with the nefarious deeds of Rousseau's Jacobin disciples. Evidence from a variety of sources, from the Romantics' denunciation of the revolutionary Terror to contemporary critiques of the fetishism of method in French structuralism, led Simpson to conclude that "the 'theory wars' occurring in today's humanities departments are to some degree a mediated response to the tensions generated by the French Revolution and by the English Revolutions of the 1640s" (179).

Joan DeJean makes a similar case in her comparative study of the seventeenth-century French Battle of the Books and our current culture wars. She proposes to review the latter "in the light of issues and concepts that proved crucial in the seventeenth-century intellectual upheaval that began the revolutionary shift in *mentalité* upon which the Enlightenment was founded."[9] DeJean claims that in the course of the 1980s, the conflict between ancients and moderns "gradually disappeared as a factor in French cultural life—so much so that, in recent years, the only coverage of the

Culture Wars in the French press is devoted to the situation in America" (28). In fact, the French critique of political correctness and ethnic differentialism in the United States is often directed at those forces within France that champion American-style liberalism, culturalism, and relativism. In any case, the shift in the epicenter of the culture wars (from France at the onset of the Enlightenment to America at the end of the twentieth century) seems to support DeJean's national(istic) reading of the current Battle of the Books. Remarking that a new age of sentimentalism, echoing the French one but this time of American inspiration, is "moving onto our cultural horizon," she wonders whether this "new culture of emotionality would indicate that we should begin to prepare ourselves for what . . . will inevitably follow: a second Enlightenment, but this time an Enlightenment made in the U.S.A." (30).

Liah Greenfeld's genealogy of nationalism in Europe and the United States also provides useful insights in current cross-cultural disputes, especially between the French and Anglo-American traditions. Greenfeld shows how English specificity was from the start conceived in stark opposition to continental, and especially French, social and political developments.[10] As early as the sixteenth century, the main features of the English difference had already been delineated, and they all pointed to the superiority of homegrown institutions, from the political limitations of the Crown's prerogatives to the spread of biblical literacy in the vernacular to unparalleled achievements in science and technology. In his *Epistle on the Excellency of the English Tongue* (1595–96), Richard Carew exalted the magnificence of England's mother tongue when compared to that of its European neighbors. In a characteristic passage, the language of the French is disqualified as "delicate but ouer nice, as a woman scarce daring to open her lipps for fear of marring her countenance" (cited in Greenfeld, 69). This gendered characterization of French preciosity announces early nineteenth-century considerations on French excess as a feminine mixture of hysterical passion and weepy sentimentality as well as contemporary charges that poststructuralists are nothing but wimpish ninnies who hide the vacuity of their thought behind an impenetrable jargon.[11]

By the end of the seventeenth century, most features of the dominant image of English culture were already in place. Prominent among them was a mixture of "unaffected sincerity" and "sound simplicity" that distrusted the "fancy language," excessive refinement, and unfounded speculations often associated with intellectual imports. "The Temper of the English," Thomas Sprat declared in *Observations on Mons. de Sorbiere's Voy-*

age into England, "is Free, Modest, Kind, hard to be provok'd. If they are not so Talkative as others, yet they are more Careful of what they Speak" (171–72). On the contrary, a Frenchman, according to Samuel Johnson, "must be always talking, whether he knows anything of the matter or not." [12] In other words, the "Genius of the English Nation" was more conducive to the deliberate inquiry of science than to the verbose, high-minded, and deceptive lucubrations of continental *belles-lettres.* Henry Oldenburg was of the same opinion; he wrote in 1665 that "it must be said that England has a large number of learned and inquisitive men, a larger number than is found in all Europe; and what they produce is solid and detailed—the world has, for too long, been sufficiently entertained with general theories" (486).

The need to establish English literary credentials in a cultural universe (the Renaissance and the Baroque Age) dominated by Italian, and to a lesser extent French and Spanish, artistic productions led to a growing dissatisfaction with the "arrogance" of those foreigners who, according to Sprat, professed "that there is scarce any Thing of late written that is worth looking upon, but in their own languages. The Italians did at first endeavour to have it thought that all Matters of Elegance had never yet pas'd over the Alps" (*Observations,* 102). In his book, a passionately nationalistic response to the disparaging description of English life by a French aristocrat, Sprat argued that the apparent deficiencies of his native culture in "matters of elegance" were actually a sign of superiority.

What goes for art and literature is also true of *cuisine,* and Sprat went on to exalt the commonsensical virtues of Boil'd Beef and Roast over fancy, but unnatural, Gallic cooking. The simpler and more robust fare of his compatriots attested to the fact that "the English have the same Sincerity in their Diet which they have in their Manners; and as they have less Mixture in their Dishes, so they have less Sophisticate Compositions in their Hearts, than the People of some other Nations" (175). No matter that some of their neighbors think the English to be "a little defective in the Gentleness and the Pliableness of their Humour"; this lackluster modesty turns out to be an asset, for "that Want is abundantly supplied by their firm and masculine virtues: And perhaps the same Observation may be found true in Men which is in Metals, and that the Noblest Substances are hardest to be polished" (171–72).

Historical evidence points to continuities in the way the English have defined and celebrated their cultural exceptionality since the late Middle Ages and, all things considered, discussions of the ethos of the common man and the lack of social distinction in the United States since the 1800s are reminiscent of earlier considerations on English plainness of manner and speech in the Renaissance. As the celebration of common sense, experimental knowledge, and "leveling" aspirations crossed the Atlantic ocean, it formed the core of the national ideology of the American colonists, who often came from the most radical quarters of British religious and political dissent.

One of the claims of the present study is that irritations caused in the English-speaking world by French foppishness, weakness for abstractions, and absolutist proclivities in politics as in philosophy have survived to this day, lending their peculiar sort of energy to the most recent transatlantic controversies, whether they involve issues of national identity, individual rights, and computerization or conflicting interpretations of the legacy of the French Third Republic in matters of ethnic and linguistic diversity.

The passion for theory has largely subsided today, or rather it has taken on new forms, moving away from its initial association with the postwar French philosophies of meaning and desire into a decidedly more nativistic terrain, that of the culture wars involving issues of gender, sexuality, race, nationality, teaching, and canonicity that are distinctly American. Typically, many cultural studies theorists are as critical of the elitism and Eurocentrism of French theory as the poststructuralists were of Arnoldian or New Critical celebrations of literature as a transcendent aesthetic realm.

The electoral gains of Le Pen's Front National in the last fifteen years and the Socialists' ambiguous, often embarrassed position on immigration have confirmed the view that most of French culture, right and left, is still profoundly racist, illiberal, and conformist. Lawrence Kritzman links the current popularity of American and British cultural studies to recent France-bashing campaigns in the American academe that "characterize France (and French Studies) as politically retrograde, opposed to the discourse of empowerment and liberation" (18).

Authors whose work could be taken to contribute to the current anti-French mood in anglophone French studies scholarship have expressed similar concerns. In *French Literary Fascism,* David Carroll argues against the official French view that fascism was a foreign phenomenon, an imported ideology grafted onto a native intellectual tradition based on humanism and rational thought that would eventually reject it. Carroll contends, following other prominent students of the Vichy regime such as Robert O. Paxton, Zeev Sternhell, and Michael R. Marrus, that fascism in its popular and literary form was very much a homegrown phenomenon, its genealogy going back to the influential prewar writings of Barrès, Maurras, and Péguy.

Carroll is quite aware of the implications of his argument in the present climate, and he takes pains to dissociate himself from any reading of his book that would support the current demonization of French culture. "In the hands of some," he notes in his introduction, "both the rigorously documented analysis of the responsibility of the Vichy government and many French sympathizers for criminal actions taken against the Jews and the argument that insists on the indigenous roots of the fascism of various French intellectuals have been transformed into a general indictment of almost everything French" (95).

Blanket condemnations of *the* French ideology to be found in books by Bernard-Henri Lévy and others on both sides of the Atlantic end up replacing one myth with another, substituting unmitigated evil for the unequivocal goodness of French culture celebrated in the postwar Gaullist and *résistantialiste* official discourse.[13] Ironically, by painting a picture of modern French history as intrinsically evil, those critics take the literary nationalists at their word and accredit their view of a monolithic "eternal" French culture. This is precisely the kind of dehistoricizing essentialism the painstakingly detailed deconstruction of the metaphysics of presence in cultural studies and postcolonialism was supposed to steer us away from.

At any rate, Carroll's disclaimer attests to the pervasiveness of anti-French sentiment in the current interpretive climate and points to a need to reassert the diversity and complexity of ideological and political struggles in twentieth-century France:

> What interests me, is neither the innate goodness nor the evil of French society or French culture. Like all societies, France has just and unjust, benevolent and criminal, and democratic and antidemocratic moments in its long social and political history. Like all cultures, both homogenizing, hegemonic, xenophobic, and racist traits and heterogeneous, decentralizing, and antiracist elements can be found in its cultural and political history. (5)

France-bashing is not limited to the halls of academia, however. Not a week goes by, it seems, without some article in the mainstream press in America taking on the French for being incapable of worthwhile aesthetic creation, for foolishly refusing to get on the Internet, or for persisting in defending outdated conceptions of the welfare state in the age of capitalistic global competition. The new public discourse on Gallic weaknesses echoes postwar descriptions of France as the sick man of Europe.[14] In the sixties and seventies, "the French miracle" made the label unseemly and Britain became everyone's favorite European basket-case economy. Today, the British are said to be more prosperous than ever, and London's cultural renaissance is ritualistically hailed in American magazines. Chronic unemployment, repeated strikes, and technophobia have made France once again the laughingstock of the American media, even though it still ranks fourth in worldwide exports.

In *The New York Times* Alan Riding chronicles the passing of the "glory that France was," ascribing the waning of French creativity in arts and letters to a complex of familiar flaws: snobbery, which scorns commercial success in the arts; excessive state centralization, a sure way to smother initiative and creativity; a Cartesian intellectualism that kills spontaneity ("death by theory"); an elitist, backward-looking arrogance that fosters a fateful ignorance of popular entertainment and new technologies; a cultural protectionism that encourages a navel-gazing obsession with native ways of doing things; and last but not least, "fear and loathing of Americanization." No wonder nobody pays attention any longer to what's going on in the cafés, lecture halls, and art studios of the Left Bank!

A *Los Angeles Times* article dated 7 January 1997 explored the various reasons "Why the French Hate the Internet" and concluded, quite predictably, that they "are wary of being wired because of fears of cultural pollution and a strong tradition of centralization." Even those who acknowledge the many examples of successful modernization and technological achievement in Mitterrandian France, with some of these developments quite friendly to American businesses (six hundred McDonald's restaurants peppered all over the country), argue, like Roger Cohen, a frequent critic of things French, that the "very public French stand against the harsh capitalism of America's boom and the dangers of a world driven by the American quest for profit" is highly hypocritical, a way for duplicitous politicians to sugarcoat the bitter pill of downsizing and global competition. Eventually, the French won't be able to have their cake and eat it too, and modernize while preserving their imagined community. Cohen puts it in a nutshell:

France has become America's favorite European basket case. With its socialist government trying to create state-sector jobs by the hundreds of thousands, its record unemployment, its diatribes against globalization, its quaint plans for 32-hour work weeks and its defense of an apparently unaffordable welfare state, France has taken over Britain's role as the faintly risible archetype of the failed European economy. It is the Titanic-with-piano-still-tinkling adrift on a sea of global competition.[15]

All of this accounts for the crepuscular mood that surrounds recent ruminations on the decline of the demand for French culture and society on American campuses. Those whose role it is to pass on to younger generations of educated Americans the awareness of the glory that France was, that is, professors of French literature and history, are quite despondent about the bleak future of French studies in the United States. Reviewing *Realms of Memory*, the monumental collection of essays prominent French historians and critics have devoted to the memorable sites of French collective identity *(les lieux de mémoire)*, David A. Bell deplores, while deeming it inevitable, the lack of attention paid to the book in the United States. "There was a time, not too long ago," he writes, "when France gazed fixedly at its own navel, and the rest of the world gazed with it. Now this is clearly no longer the case. And this fact testifies to what is, in a way, *Realms of Memory*'s real subject: the decline of France" (32).

Bell shares to a certain extent some of the quasi-Spenglerian pessimism he sees at work in many of the essays in the collection. Clearly, the quality of what is still coming out of French universities and research institutes will not reverse the trend. No one has time any longer for the brilliance of the French interpretive industry. "The irony," Bell concludes, "is that the same developments that allowed [the Parisian Cultural Mandarinate] to write such a powerful work will also ensure that the world gives it less consideration than it has given to many lesser pieces of Parisian wisdom in the past" (36). There is a sense in Bell's account that the French had it coming all along, given their refusal to acknowledge the limitations of their national idea (obsolete in a postcolonial world) and of their elitist, bookish conception of the unexamined life (doomed by the triumph of electronic culture). For all his admiration for the achievements of French scholarship, Bell ultimately joins the ranks of all those who think there is something deeply amiss in contemporary French culture. Its thick arteries, he argues, would benefit from a dose of diversity and decentralization.

A few months earlier, Bell had likewise chastised fellow historian Gérard Noiriel for the "strong enthusiasm" he expressed for the national model of ethnic and racial integration in his book *The French Melting-Pot: Immigration, Citizenship and National Identity* (7). Noiriel was wrong, Bell writes, to downplay the heavy price paid by descendants of immigrants as a result of the Jacobin model of assimilation that "ruthlessly suppresses all trace of their ethnic identities" (7). Americans, by contrast, are not forced like second- or third-generation French people to "repress pride in their origins in return for social and material success." The American historian concludes with some friendly advice to his insufficiently pluralistic colleagues overseas, tying in the theme of multiculturalism with that of the fear and loathing of the American linguistic juggernaut: "French intellectuals might do well to attend a few more ethnic festivals, and not merely in the guise of social scientists conducting field-work. It might lead them to realize that a renewed appreciation of France's immigrant heritage . . . could make for a better defense of French culture against the dreaded American 'invasion' than any number of laws banning the use of English" (7).

As I started looking at recent opportunities for friction between French and American cultures, I could not help but notice the same complex patterns of rapprochement and distancing that structured the theory debates of the 1970s. The North Atlantic drift in intellectual and cultural matters is moving apart as much as it is coming together. On the one hand, the "liberalization" of French society in the last two decades, illustrated by such seemingly unrelated developments as the decline of French communism, the end of government monopoly in the electronic media, the growing independence of the judiciary, and the new consensus on leveling the playing field between "public" and "private" (i.e., mostly religious) schools, has aligned France more than ever with its European neighbors to the north and with North American democracy. The rise of a pluralistic consumer-oriented France has impacted the intellectual community in such a way that some of its most prominent representatives, from Lyotard to Baudrillard, have been instrumental in providing well-circulated descriptions of the postmodernization process itself. Formerly fashionable models of political *engagement* have been discarded along with the Marxist views that often accompanied and legitimized them, and many 1968 militants have gone back to the ivory tower, much like their American counterparts, the controversial "tenured radicals."

Concurrently, intellectual activities in France have been resorting increasingly to Anglo-American philosophical products. Richard Rorty, John Rawls, Michael Walzer, and Charles Taylor have replaced German philosophers as some of the Parisian intelligentsia's favorite foreign imports. The content of public debate in France has also undergone considerable

change. In the fifties, sixties, and seventies, intellectual journals were replete with discussions of alienation, revolution, and transgression. The last
two decades have taken the conversation away from questions of existential
or libidinal emancipation toward a less exhilarating reexamination of the
democratic process and of the role of individualism in French life. The
American experience loomed large in this reevaluation, both as an example of a freer, more tolerant society and as a reminder of all that had
gone wrong in the overly centralized French road to democracy. As for
the American Revolution, it was hailed by some as a countermodel to the
French one, and it became a central reference in the debates surrounding
the Bicentennial of 1789.

All of this has led to a paradoxical situation: while a new generation of
French intellectuals was busy renouncing (and denouncing) Marxism,
existentialism, and poststructuralism, turning instead to the idiosyncrasies
of their national past in relation to a rehabilitated liberal tradition, French
theory was still alive and well, if under siege, in prominent quarters of the
American academic Left. American proponents of French poststructuralism were quite nonplussed by the turn to the right of their former theoretical mentors, and dismayed at the new Zeitgeist abroad in the land that
had given Zola, Sartre, de Beauvoir, and Foucault to the progressive camp.

While France seemed to have fallen back into line with other European
liberal-democratic societies, the United States was entering a particularly
contentious phase of its social and cultural history. As Eric Fassin put it in
an essay devoted to the culture wars in America: "At a time when France
is becoming more Americanized and when many fear or wish that French
exceptionalism might fade away, it is strange to see the rise of an America
altogether more French than France, a country where people tear each
other apart over issues of culture and education, where the teaching of literature and history is part of a wide public debate, and where the crisis of
the model of the intellectual enjoys a lasting success" (301).[16]

This contrasted picture of a post-68 subdued, consensual France and
of a vocal, polarized America adds a further twist to the already complex
set of relations between the two countries. There is yet another side to
this multifaceted configuration, however. While recent converts from the
Left discovered the charms of philosophical liberalism, extolled the virtues
of democratic individualism, and celebrated the new limitations of state
power, whether in the media, the school system, or international trade, the
value of America's assets as a model of what *libéralisation* had to offer went

up as the value of the Soviet Union's assets collapsed at the stock exchange of ideas.[17] For a while, it looked as though the long history of French hostility toward liberalism in general and its American incarnation in particular might be finally over.[18] In fact, the social tensions ushered in by the prolonged crisis of the French economy, the requirements of European integration, and the issue of immigration in a country racked by a two-digit unemployment rate led many to question the fashionable modernist discourse on *libéralisation* and rekindled the flames of anti-Americanism.

The sixties were an exciting time for those French people who reaped the benefits of modernization following what some economists dubbed the postwar French miracle. The downturn of the economy and the loss of confidence following the so-called energy crisis of the mid-seventies put a damper on the self-congratulatory celebration of national prosperity. It transformed the volatile debate over *la société de consommation* into more sober, and somber, ruminations on the place of France in the world (once again!), and on the fate of *l'exception française* in the age of transnational corporations, global capitalism, and increased postimperial migrancy. While France sank deeper into *la morosité,* as the disenchanted public mood came to be known, many voices in the intelligentsia rose in opposition to *le libéralisme,* the many-headed hydra responsible for all the problems the country was now facing, from immigration and urban unrest to high crime rates and chronic unemployment.

The old divisions of the intellectual world resurfaced in the form of a struggle between "neoliberals," who welcomed the collapse of France's absolutist legacy, and "neorepublicans," who clamored that the national idea was gradually being undermined by the spread of Image and Capital in a new postcommunist world order dominated by the United States. America found itself once again at the core of impassioned disputes covering anything from the degrading philistinism of EuroDisney (described by right-wing journalist Jean Cau as "a cultural Tchernobyl") and the linguistic hegemony of the World Wide Web to the destruction of French cinematic creativity by the General Agreements on Trade and Tariffs. Simply put, liberalism sounded the death knell of the French difference, threatened by the evils of African and Asian immigration, European integration, and Americanization. Multiculturalism and globalization, as related manifestations of transnational capitalism, combined to undermine the national idea, the one from within and the other from without.

The news coming from the other side of the Atlantic did nothing to alleviate the fears of the self-appointed guardians of republican civic virtues.

The American people, it seemed, had simply gone mad. They were quarreling over sexual harassment, ethnic diversity, and gay rights, and their puritanical obsession with sex spread into the remotest corners of an individual's privacy. Every day the French media reported new horrors from the politically correct front that only confirmed what was in store for France as the deleterious influence of American society became more and more prevalent.[19] Two elements of the new transatlantic developments went to the heart of the French malaise: the canon wars and multiculturalism.

The critique of the Western canon of great works in the humanities departments of major American universities was seen as going against what the French national mythology held dearest: the sacredness of high literature and fine arts as collective treasures from the country's glorious past, revered vectors of its cultural identity throughout the ages. Powerful historical forces are at work behind these contemporary contentions. The manufacture of the national memory by the French republicans relied heavily upon the tradition of state sponsorship of high aristocratic culture initiated by the monarchy. Literature and the arts were made into canonical expressions of what the *mission civilisatrice* was all about. American society, on the contrary, was steeped from the start in petty bourgeois, egalitarian values, and the national culture became more and more associated with mass consumerism, economic mobility, and popular forms of entertainment.

The theme of American cultural relativism dovetails nicely with the preservation of republican rationalism: to defend the canons of classicism and high modernism against postmodern relativism is at the same time to safeguard the French model of cultural identity. To cite one example among many, an article in *Le Monde* (17 February 1994) entitled "French Trapped in American Multiculturalism" deplored that "on some campuses, the study of French is censored by the 'politically correct' wave imposed by ethnic and sexual minorities." The author of the article reported in disbelief that books from African authors that "are practically impossible to find in France" have become classics in English translation. The benighted attempts by some American teachers of French to replace Racine and Rabelais with contemporary Francophone African and Caribbean authors or "obscure" eighteenth-century women writers is described as one more example of what goes wrong when demagoguery and consumerism carry the day.

Not surprisingly, the notion of universalism is often associated with the French dismay at the American culture wars. The article points out that the "compartmentalization of studies" and the "ghettoization" of literary authors induced by the competing agendas of various academic pressure groups imply a refusal "of the universal scope of a given text beyond the minority supposedly represented by the author" (12). To top it all, a sacrilegious student of comparative literature at Columbia is quoted as saying that the Universal Declaration of the Rights of Man and Citizen was nothing but "a text written by men for other men."

The anti-American thrust of the French neorepublican discourse conveniently brings all these issues together: the critique of American individualism hooks up with attacks on relativism and pragmatism as the ideologies of late liberal capitalism, and on multiculturalism as yet another product of pluralism gone awry. Americanization, then, threatens French society on all fronts: philosophically, it undermines the metaphysical foundations of the republican project; economically, it turns citizens into individualistic consumers and subjects the national economy to the whim of transnational corporations; culturally, it debases the high standards of the indigenous aesthetic canons, substituting soap operas for the classical plays of the *Comédie Française,* displacing Versailles with Disneyland; politically, it dissolves the shared values of citizenship into a neoromantic celebration of diversity.

As racial tensions rose in France and as the anti-immigration agenda of the National Front gained more and more currency, major intellectual figures from the Left, such as Alain Touraine, Régis Debray, Alain Finkielkraut, and Julia Kristeva, voiced their concern over the way ethnic and sexual minority claims were couched in the United States.[20] Multiculturalism was denounced as a consequence of the hardening of tolerance into an absolutist cult of difference for its own sake. If France were to adopt what Socialist leader Lionel Jospin called "the Anglo-Saxon model of the communities," the French ideal of republican integration would give way to an ethnic war of all against all.

The persistence of anti-Americanism in post–Cold War France points to the resiliency of traditional views of the Anglo-American tradition. Although the words may be different ("liberalism" and "differentialism" have replaced "capitalism" and "imperialism" as the labels of choice to stigmatize all that is wrong with the American way of life), the complaint remains generally the same: the Anglo-American obsession with individual rights has finally reached a point where it undermines liberal society, threatening individual freedom itself. Private concerns and entitlement claims ("the culture of victimization") are chipping away at what once was a public culture. The dialectics of individualism are seen as having the same unintended consequences on the modernist project as the Frankfurt School theorists' dialectics of Reason, albeit for different reasons. It ends up destroying what it purported to promote, that is, the peaceful negotiation of individual and group interests within the framework of a democratic polity.

These concerns are not limited to French observers of the American scene. They will have a familiar ring to readers informed of recent debates in the United States between defenders of the "procedural Republic" and communitarian critics of self-indulgent acquisitive individualism.[21] In the following pages I repeatedly point to the structural homology between public disputes in France and the United States on issues of theory, individualism, nationalism, rights, and liberalism. The lines of contention are often drawn in similar ways, and comparable arguments are advanced on both sides of the continental divide, admittedly with variations and differences in emphasis due to the specificity of each ideological context. The acceleration in the traffic of ideas is such that foreign authors are often enrolled in domestic disputes, as when cultural conservatives in the United States use Alain Finkielkraut's works or when French neorepublicans borrow communitarian arguments made in America.

The response of American liberals and multiculturalists to the latest forms of French anti-Americanism also testifies to the lasting influence of the cultural lenses through which both countries have been observing each other for the past two hundred years. In his book on the romantic critique of theory, David Simpson voices his frustration at seeing "so much evidence of how direct and uncritical the reproduction of the rhetoric of the 1790s can be" in today's transatlantic controversies (172). While the French have lamented the atomistic nature of American life ever since Tocqueville, contemporary Anglo-American critics level charges at French cultural and political centralization that often do little more than update the liberal critique of Rousseau's legacy from Burke and Constant to Isaiah Berlin. Tony Judt, to give a recent example, describes totalitarianism as "a logical and historical derivative of precisely that universalistic vision of republican democracy that still bedazzles so many French thinkers."[22] He also argues that "of all the enemies of liberalism and rights," the French Republicans proved to be the most "deadly" because they managed to stay in power for so long, replacing the ideal of liberty with the unfortunate notion of "a universal and undifferentiated democracy" (240). The manner of their success, Judt concludes, "placed the final nail on the coffin of liberal thought in France" (238).

Meanwhile, multiculturalists have lost no time in relating what they describe as a neoracist consensus in contemporary France to the long history of disregard for minority rights and linguistic diversity that is, in their view, endemic to French national culture.[23] Postcolonial theory has made its way into French studies, and the recent Anglo-American historiography of modern France has tended to focus on moments of acute identity crisis, widespread racism, and xenophobia, namely, the Dreyfus affair, the interwar years, and the rise of the National Front.[24] The importation of the trilogy of race, class, and gender into the discipline of French studies in Britain and the United States has shaken the profession, prompting anxious questions on the future of the teaching of French literature and culture in the English-speaking world.

Adding insult to injury, the combined assaults on French colonialism, national-republican mythologies, and the Eurocentrism of theory have coincided with a dramatic drop in undergraduate enrollments in French language and literature in the United States. Fears of a decline in the intellectual community's interest in French cultural products are seemingly confirmed by the harsh reality of statistical trends in the classroom. The downturn in the numbers of French, German, and Russian majors, coupled with the domination of Spanish and the rise of Asian languages, is often construed as yet another indication that multicultural America is turning its back on its Old World roots and its gaze toward its own neocolonial backyard in Latin America and its new commercial partners in the Pacific Rim, both those areas now purveying the bulk of its recent nonwhite immigrants.

Here again, interesting crosscurrents are at play. The continental drift takes America farther and farther west and south, away from the historical moorings of its intellectual and political origins, at a time when the triumph of post–Cold War capitalism spreads American consumer culture northeastward, turning Europe into what some describe as a simulacrum of the American experience. While American teachers of French studies chafe under the tutelage of Francocentric imported notions of what the teaching of culture and literature should be, French intellectuals again sound the alarm of American cultural imperialism, each camp accusing the other of hegemonic intents and colonizing practices.

Liberal and multiculturalist critics of Gallic universalism do agree on one thing: French culture is incompatible with a tolerant multiracial liberal democracy of the kind that is currently being experimented with in Britain and in the former settler colonies of the British Empire (the United States, Canada, and Australia). While Anglo-American critics believe the French inability to think in pluralistic terms stems from basic flaws in the local culture (universalism, stato-centrism, and a monolithic concept of the nation, for starters), French neorepublicans see the national model of integration as the only defense against boundless liberalism, hyperindividualism, the dissolution of the social fabric, and the wholesale destruction of civic virtues.

In an essay on the "political correctness" controversy, Eric Fassin uncovered the series of misunderstandings and the play of inverted mirror images that make up the French-American culture wars.[25] While the American opponents of "political correctness" saw it as a particularly noxious cultural virus imported from France, its French critics described PC as a distinctly American phenomenon, the product of egalitarianism gone mad. On the one hand, in an essay attacking multiculturalism, Richard Rorty wrote the word in French to better underscore the foreignness of the concept; on the other, François Furet called multiculturalism "a democratic utopia *à l'américaine*," arguing that it was nothing but the return of the good old egalitarian individualism of American democracy dressed in new clothes.[26] In Fassin's words, "French for the Americans, American for the French, political correctness is always essentially foreign. It always represents the figure of the other intellectual."[27]

In fact, political correctness never gave rise to a debate in France, at least in its initial phase, since the condemnation of American practices was unanimous among leading intellectuals and media personalities. The discussion brought about unexpected realignments among the various camps that had just finished feuding over the interpretation of 1789 as compared to 1776. The same people who had been arguing for a reevaluation of the American Revolution as a positive counterpoint to the Jacobin Terror and advocating a return to civil liberties, political pluralism, and human rights after years of structuralist and Marxist rhetoric, were now saying that America suffered from a strong case of puritanical neo-Stalinism ("a McCarthyism of the Left"). The country that had produced a tolerant, liberal-minded, and god-fearing alternative to the Jacobin road to democracy, the well-behaved child of 1776, was suddenly indulging in the worst excesses of dogmatic intolerance, bringing back memories of 1960s cultural revolutions in France and abroad that everyone wished to forget.

The novelist and essayist Pascal Bruckner expressed a widely shared feeling among the post-68 French intelligentsia when he declared that "we've already had sixties radicalism ['le gauchisme'], which is a rehash of these movements [PC and multiculturalism], and we know what it's all about."[28] America was once again failing those who had put their hopes in her as an alternative to the radicalism of the French Left in 1793 as well as in 1968. Liberalism gone mad was giving birth to its opposite, a wave of unprecedented tyranny (Jean-François Revel went so far as to talk about "concentration campuses"). This sudden reversal could only rekindle the flames of French antiliberalism: the Gulf War, GATT negotiations, the U.S.-led NATO campaign against Serbia, and, more recently, American trade barriers against French agricultural products ensured that the fire of anti-Americanism was properly stoked.

The overnight transformation of the American model as guarantor of civic liberties into its opposite, a countermodel that forcefully suppressed freedom of speech, did pose a theoretical problem. How could a society based on liberty secrete the poison of intolerance? American anti-multiculturalists like Rorty had their answer: the poison came from outside, it was a French import, the belated effect of French poststructuralism on American campuses. French admirers of the American liberal tradition like François Furet did not see the multiculturalist agenda as a break in the tradition caused by external factors. On the contrary, they interpreted sexual codes of behavior and the apology of cultural separatism as a result of the radicalization of the deep-seated egalitarianism of American culture.

The multiculturalism debate is frustrating in more than one way, if only because of the semantic vagueness in which it is currently couched. Multiculturalism means different things to different people. For some, it is purely descriptive and points to the empirical reality of a society made up of a variety of social groups, however defined. The word is also used prescriptively as a cure for the ethnic and racial divisions that continue to plague American society. Most multiculturalists advocate the toleration of a plurality of identities based on race, ethnicity, religion, national origin, gender, and sexual orientation. Others, who should be called *mono*culturalists, insist that entire sections of the American population, say African Americans or Native Americans, share a common mode of being distinctive from that of "white Americans" as a whole.

The confusion is just as widespread when one turns to the political consequences of multiculturalist claims. In a recent article in the *New York Review,* Anthony Appiah tries to bring some amount of order and clarity to the current confusion surrounding the multiculturalist misunderstanding. Appiah proposes to distinguish two kinds of multiculturalism. The good, liberal kind advocates the respectful recognition of the plurality of collective identities that make up our common civic life, while the bad, illiberal brand "wants to force children to live within separate spheres defined by the common culture of their race, religion, or ethnicity." [29] The first type of multiculturalism is compatible with what Appiah calls the dream of an immigrant society that "people of many kinds should share the public sphere on equal terms" (35), while the kind of cultural nationalism that informs illiberal multiculturalism is not.

Appiah makes the point that illiberal multiculturalism leads to a phantasmic identity formation, since it is based on the nostalgic reinvention of religious and cultural differences that have been systematically erased by the socialization of all Americans, blacks and whites, natives and immigrants, to the same political civic religion (democratic liberalism) and the same consumer culture extending "eclectically from *Seinfeld* to Chinese takeout." For all the talk of diversity, what strikes the foreign visitor or the alien resident in America is the "broad cultural homogeneity" of a country in which everyone speaks the same language; celebrates the same sport, television, and movie stars; shops American style; and "knows a good deal about the same consumer goods: Coca-Cola, Nike, Levi-Strauss, Ford, Nissan, GE" (31).

The multiculturalist politics of nostalgia run up against inescapable social processes: immigrants and rural folks are ruthlessly captured, as they are all over the world, in the web of a U.S.-driven urban consumer modernity, whether they like it or not.[30] Appiah rightly reminds his readers that the much-touted resistance of Hispanic immigrants to the English language is largely mythical. He cites a Florida poll that shows 98 percent of Hispanics want their children to speak English well, and a recent U.S. Census figure that reveals only 1.9 million Americans over five speak no English, a number proportionately only a quarter as high as it was in 1890, in the heyday of eastern and southern European immigration. Similarly, most mainstream religions in the United States, from Catholicism and Judaism to Islam, have been thoroughly "liberalized" as a result of the dominance of Protestantism in the national culture.

Appiah concludes from the cultural homogeneity and the assimilation-ist nature of immigration patterns in the United States that "culture is not the problem, and it is not the solution." "It is not black culture," he writes, "that the racist disdains, but blacks. . . . No amount of knowledge of the architectural achievements of Nubia or Kush guarantees respect for African-Americans. No African-American is entitled to greater concern be-cause he is descended from a people who created jazz or produced Toni Morrison" (36). Appiah sees individualism, not group consciousness, as the engine of the politics of recognition. "The growing salience of race and gender as social irritants, which may seem to reflect the call of collective identities, is a reflection, as much as anything else, of the individual's con-cern for dignity and respect" (35).

Appiah's liberal argument against ethnic separatism draws support from one of the books reviewed in his essay, Michael Walzer's *On Toleration,* a plea for the peaceful management of identity politics in a pluralistic de-mocracy.[31] In his book, Walzer offers his own version of the specificity of American liberal multiculturalism relative to the various other historical "regimes of toleration" that have attempted to deal with the challenge of difference in various parts of the world, from the Ottoman Empire to the Swiss Confederation. The distinctiveness of the American model lies in the fact that the United States is an immigrant society in which cultural claims based on territorial autonomy are impossible. Liberalism as the dominant political idiom, the civil religion (in Rousseau's sense), the official culture in which all newcomers are socialized, ensures that children are taught respect for others.

Contrary to ethnic separatists who view American majority culture as an oppressive system imposing white values and categories of taste and be-havior on nonwhite communities, Walzer argues that cultural diversity is compatible with a civic definition of the nation based on equal access to the public sphere. His brand of multiculturalism aims "to recognize [chil-dren] as the hyphenated Americans they are and to lead them to under-stand and admire their own diversity. There is no reason to think that this understanding or admiration stands in any tension with the requirements of liberal citizenship—though it is important to stress again that liberal citizenship is more relaxed than that of a republican nation-state" (75). France obviously belongs to this last category: while in an immigrant soci-ety such as the United States there is "no group whose culture is the offi-cial culture, whose language has special pride of place" (Appiah describes

America as the nation-state without the majority), in France "everybody but the dominant group is treated as a minority [and] the only publicly celebrated identity is that of the dominant culture: tolerance and full civic rights may be extended to minority groups but the national history is the history of the majority" (34).

The term "minority groups" applied to the French case might be a useful descriptive empirical term, but it does not have any conceptual place in the republican discourse. Indeed, the republican doctrine has no room for such a thing as a minority (and consequently no official concept of a majority) since newcomers and people living in spaces incorporated into the Republic are expected to become individual members of the national community without ever being granted any kind of group rights. French republican discourse (as opposed to the differentialist rhetoric of the Action française, for example) has constituted the population living within the spatial boundaries of the state according to legal-political criteria, that is, as made up of citizens and noncitizens, or nationals and *ressortissants étrangers,* a distinction that is not, at least theoretically, predicated upon ethnic differences, place of birth, size of the immigrant population, or length of residence in the country (once the probationary period before one can apply for citizenship has elapsed).

Besides, France is also an immigrant society and has been for over a hundred years, even though the role of immigration in the shaping of late modern and contemporary France has always been minimized both in official discourse and in mainstream historiography (in contrast to America's self-description as "a nation of immigrants"). While Walzer concedes that France is "one of the world's leading immigrant societies" (which complicates the nation-state vs. immigrant society model and makes of France an "anomaly" combining "the physical presence and conceptual absence of cultural difference"), he nevertheless argues that "it isn't a pluralist society—or at least it doesn't think of itself, and isn't thought of, as a pluralist society" (*On Toleration,* 38). The distinction is important, since what nations think of themselves rarely coincides with what they are. In fact the unitary aspect of French republicanism (the fact that it does not think of the nation as a culturally pluralist society) is partly a response to the actual diversity of regions and peoples that have historically been incorporated into the nation while retaining their linguistic and cultural particularisms long after the Revolution of 1789.

Rather than oppose France and the United States as historically distinct regimes of toleration, which they are, I want to argue that France as a civic (immigrant) nation based on the principle of the equality of all citizens before the law is now confronted with similar challenges as the United States when it comes to closing the gap between democratic principles and the historical reality of oppression and persecution of certain groups on the basis of race, ethnicity, religion, national origin, and past colonial status.[32] Despite the obvious differences in their respective histories of nation formation and in the conceptions of the relationship between unity and difference, the two countries are more comparable than the current polarized rhetoric of tolerance and exclusion, pluralism and centralization, would lead us to believe. What I call in this book *la troisième voie,* the middle way between assimilation and exclusion that many French intellectuals and public figures are trying to imagine today (they call it *intégration*), seems to me quite akin to Walzer and Appiah's attempts to preserve the plurality of accepted social identities and individual behaviors in a democratic society while preserving a common, cohesive public culture that is the cornerstone of a republican form of government.

In the final chapter of this book, I contend that the strictly dichotomized opposition between an Anglo-American pluralist and a French unitary model of national integration, while not without any ground or merit, especially at a somewhat generalized level of ideological debate or philosophical discourse, is overly reductive when it comes to the particular history of localized developments. Such an opposition is not mindful enough of the complexities of the respective histories of immigration and nation formation in France and the United States. The rest of the book aims at making sense of the conflicting currents that have contributed to the North Atlantic drift, and to shed some light on that most ironic of postmodern ironies: it is precisely when French and American societies have come to display similar patterns of economic behavior, cultural consumption, and political practice that their intelligentsias and public opinions are most divided, within and across national boundaries, as to the proper responses to the challenges of "the new world order."

Chapter 1 revisits the issue of French theory, replacing contemporary debates in the *longue durée* of a remarkably resilient philosophical quarrel. For at least two centuries, the Gallic and Anglo-American traditions have looked askance at each other, and there is no sign of change on the horizon, wishful claims about the normalization of French intellectual life notwithstanding.

Chapter 2 moves on to the interminable controversy surrounding the Bicentennial of the French Revolution and suggests that it laid the groundwork for the subsequent French debate on the place of liberalism and individualism in the country's rocky road to democracy and for the subsequent rise of a "neorepublican" discourse aimed at countering the effects of post–Cold War liberalization.

In chapter 3 I interpret this return to la République as a retreat to a fallback position on the part of a generation of progressive intellectuals nonplussed by the demise of the emancipatory narratives they had championed in more idealistic times and fearful of the consequences of an amoral, relativistic capitalist culture made in America but turned irresistibly global.

Chapters 4 and 5, finally, examine how some of the most recent historiography of France in the English language has popularized a view of the French mind as utterly unable to conceive of a tolerant pluralistic post-imperial society. The 1989 affair of the veil, which focused the country's attention on a handful of students insisting on wearing Islamic headdress in the public schools, serves as an entry point into the ensuing transatlantic disputes on the relative merits of the French and American responses to the challenges faced by multiethnic societies.

I

French Theory in the United States

꩜ ꩜ ꩜

I have been too long a farmer to be governed by any thing
but events; I have a constitutional abhorrence of theory,
of all trust in abstract reasoning.

ARTHUR YOUNG

The Example of France as a Warning to Britain (1793)

⟡he Britons who "removed to America" in the seventeenth and eighteenth
centuries took with them the most radical elements of the idea of Englishness. During the two centuries following the Puritans' landing at Plym-
outh Rock, they never ceased to consider themselves full-fledged members
of the English nation. As late as 1765, Daniel Dulany insisted that "the subjects of the British empire in Europe and America are the same" (Greenfeld, 649). It was precisely because one could not speak of Britons and
Americans, but rather of the Europeans and Americans of Britain, that the
denial of all the rights and privileges of British subjects to the colonists was
so intolerable, and ultimately justified the rebellion against and eventually
separation from the "mother country."

The specific conditions of the establishment of the American colonies

27

(what Daniel J. Boorstin has called the circumstances of a New World) encouraged the radicalization of the English national idea into its most democratic and egalitarian implications. In *Nationalism: Five Roads to Modernity,* Liah Greenfeld notes that outside of British settlements in America the new liberal-democratic principles had been imported "into social environments whose reality stood in flagrant contradiction" with them. "But in America," Greenfeld goes on, "there was almost no social reality other than the one the settlers brought with them in their own minds . . . While in older societies the novel idea was acting upon the obdurate reality, in America the new reality acted upon the stubborn inherited idea" (402).

In 1765, Lord Adam Gordon, a British visitor to America, noted that although the inhabitants of Massachusetts looked a lot like the people of Old England, "the leveling principle here operates strongly and takes the lead" (cited in Greenfeld, 408). In many ways the Americans of Britain saw themselves as "better English than the English" since there was no question for them that the ideals of political freedom, scientific inquiry, and economic prosperity were more satisfactorily realized in their midst than anywhere else in the world.

In his well-known study of the genesis of the "American Frame of Mind" in colonial times, Daniel Boorstin singled out four decisive facts about the new culture of provincial America: regression (to the conditions of an earlier age), versatility (required by the unexpected), the scarcity of institutions, and a mixture of labor scarcity and land plenty (*The Americans,* 218–19). The last factor played a major role in the radicalization and democratization of the idea of Englishness that came to dominate the colonists' self-understanding. The scarcity of labor tended to remove social prejudices, strengthening the leveling tendencies the newcomers had inherited from their dissenting British forefathers. There was also a dearth of literati, scholars, and men of learning. There was simply not enough of them to form a new monopolistic caste of *cognoscenti,* wresting power and knowledge away from the people. As a consequence, control of the new institutions of higher learning "inevitably fell to representatives of the community at large."

The colonists transposed into their new surroundings the suspicion of the professional clerics that had been the hallmark of sectarian Protestantism, with its militant conception of the priesthood of all believers.[1] The most important innovation of the New World lay for Boorstin not in the material environment of the British settlements, but in the new concept of knowledge made possible by the regression to an earlier age and the challenges of the unknown. The Britons of America brought with them from the metropolis the ideology of common sense that formed the core of English national self-identification. But the appeal to self-evidence and the empiricist regard for facts and experience, like the rest of knowledge, was wrested from the professionals and handed over to the ordinary folk, becoming, in Boorstin's phrase, "a philosophy which had no philosophers" (175).

In the new setting of the settlements, the antischolasticism of the English reformers was profoundly democratized, its egalitarian logic pushed to limits unconscionable in the old world of orders, hierarchies, and monopolies. The Baconian cult of experience took a more militant turn in America: the practical was preferable to the theoretical because popular common sense was naturally superior to the ratiocination of the cultivated elites. The new pragmatism implied a profound distrust of pure reason, as academic disputations in the scholarly tradition were deemed incapable of solving anything of relevance. To argue was to waste one's time since human beings were not persuaded by reasoned argument, but by concrete evidence. Antitheoreticism was at the core of what Boorstin describes as an "anti-aristocratic way of thinking about thinking" (177).

ANTI-INTELLECTUALISM THEN AND NOW

In the introduction to his own historical account of America's "national disrespect for mind," Richard Hofstadter argued that "anti-intellectualism, though it has its own universality, may be considered a part of our English cultural inheritance, and that it is notably strong in Anglo-American experience" (20). The historian went on to quote Leonard Woolf ("no people has ever despised and distrusted the intellect and intellectuals more than the British"), proposing that perhaps Woolf had not given "sufficient thought to the claims of the Americans to supremacy in this respect" (20). Writing, like his colleague Louis Hartz, at a time when eggheads were the targets of a powerful coalition of "cultural vigilantes, suspicious Tories and militant philistines," Hofstadter added that those who had made their case against intellect had "not found it necessary to originate a single new argument," since the mythology of the noxious intellectual "is deeply rooted in our historical experience" (45).

In many ways, the postwar historian's genealogy of American anti-intellectualism is as timely as ever today and as relevant to the debates surrounding the fate of French theory in the United States as they were to

McCarthy's crusade against another species of what Hofstadter called "the fatal foreign isms." In both cases, the various contenders went back to time-tested rhetorical devices, spontaneously and, I will argue, often unconsciously borrowing from the battery of ready-made arguments made available to them by the anti-intellectualist mythology.

To compare the present culture wars to the 1950s red scare will sound to many as both misguided and malevolent, since intellectuals can hardly pass today for the victims of an ideological witch-hunt. Quite the contrary, the argument goes, they presently enjoy a level of prestige, influence, and social power never attained by their peers in previous American history. Conservatives routinely complain that leftist scholars and critics are ubiquitous in the electronic and print media, that they are truly the darlings of the "liberal press." They write for the op-ed pages of the national dailies, appear regularly in the top 100 lists of the cultural elite, are featured in fashion magazines, interviewed on radio talk shows, and portrayed in television profiles. Not a day goes by without a writer, artist, or critical theorist being given a chance to enjoy Andy Warhol's fifteen minutes of fame. America, the argument goes, loves its cultural producers. The explosion of higher education in the sixties, the central role of research and technology in a postindustrial economy, the growing cosmopolitanism of the culture industry—all have helped to give the intelligentsia, provided they are willing to play the game of notoriety, an enviable place at the table of America's celebrated tastemakers.

And yet, references to McCarthyism abound in the midst of the canon and culture wars, with the difference that this time it is the Left that is accused of trying to silence dissenting opinions. The debates on political correctness have afforded observers and participants from the whole political spectrum with numerous occasions to attack what they see as the totalitarianism of the avant-garde, from *Newsweek*'s thought police to Rush Limbaugh's feminazis. For many, the whole controversy brought back unpleasant memories from the fifties. In his review of Dinesh D'Souza's *Illiberal Education: The Politics of Race and Sex on Campus,* Eugene Genovese denounced the new McCarthyism of the terrorists of sensitivity. "As one who saw his professors fired during the McCarthy era, and who had to fight, as a pro-Communist Marxist, for his own right to teach," Genovese wrote, "I fear that our conservative colleagues are today facing a new McCarthyism in some ways more effective and vicious than the old" (30).

Others have denounced the anti-intellectualist bent of the new cultural studies paradigm. In an open forum devoted to the conflictual relationship between cultural studies and the literary in *PMLA,* the journal of the Modern Language Association, Kathy Trumpener and Richard Maxwell argued that the new academic populism has "served mainly to confirm a long national tradition of philistinism; the American bourgeoisie, after all, affirms itself by ridiculing art and the aspirations of intellectual life, attitudes now replicated within the academy."[2] In other words, the anti-elitism of the new academic elites, far from subverting prevalent (petty) bourgeois aesthetic categories, in fact reinforces the most deeply ingrained tendencies of American middle-class culture. Academic radicals and *nouveau riche* philistines may seem to be strange bedfellows at first; for Maxwell and Trumpener, their unholy alliance accounts for the widespread disparaging of "elite" literary theory and of literary studies in general in America.

THE STRANGE FATE OF FRENCH THEORY

A striking feature of the controversy surrounding French theory is that it came under attack from every political quarter. Why this consensus, which, among other things, has helped to give the saga of French theory in America a strange, unexpected turn? By strange, I mean that what was originally a corpus of very demanding, and more often than not arcane, philosophical and critical texts from a foreign culture has given rise over the course of the last decade to one of the most hotly debated domestic issues in recent American history, carrying in its wake debates on multiculturalism, the state of the nation's universities, and the very future of the American moral and social fabric, all topics which have far exceeded the initially rather limited impact of structuralism and poststructuralism on literary studies.

French theory was imported to the United States following a two-step process: the dazzling success of the French philosophies of desire and of the sign during the first ten or fifteen years that followed the International Conference on Structuralism at Johns Hopkins in 1967 gave way to increasing resistance from various quarters of the American intellectual, journalistic, and even political fields. It was during this second reactive phase that the social and cultural construction of the meaning of "France" and "French culture" played a crucial role in drawing lines of contention, filling what had hitherto been mainly a theoretical and largely academic dispute with a powerful emotional charge.

31

This set of cultural representations, "France in American eyes," is a symbolic matrix that is rarely thematized explicitly in the arguments advanced on all sides of the issue, but that nevertheless accounts for a great deal of the form and direction of the debate. I propose to look at the fate of French theory in the United States as the latest chapter of a long history of conflictual cross-cultural relations between the French and Anglo-American intellectual traditions.[3] In this view, French culture figures both as a historical context-bound set of representations and practices specific to a given geographical and national area and as the various (mainly culturalist) perceptions and descriptions of it by foreign intellectuals.

The underlying assumption here is that *longue durée* has some heuristic value in these matters, that there does indeed exist something like a French intellectual tradition and an Anglo-American intellectual tradition, even as one must be careful not to reify those notions and unduly generalize their use. One of the ways to achieve this type of understanding is by historicizing those traditions, by showing how they change in time, constantly reworking, while maintaining, the differences in their philosophical outlook and in the values they express. The problem with culturalism is not that it takes culture seriously, as a set of representations and practices that frames ideologies, but that it often absolutizes the differences between national traditions, romanticizing the *Sprachgeist* of a particular national or ethnic community, turning the accidents of history into an unchanging, eternal nature.

I will concern myself here less with the philosophical and theoretical arguments over the place and value of French poststructuralism (the literature on the subject is already enormous, and growing) than with, first, the institutional contexts of the production in France and the transference in the United States of French theory and, second, the underlying, resilient cultural perceptions that have shaped the reception of French theory in America.[4] The subterranean, latent character of these widely shared views of things French in the United States, and the fact that they are often the unacknowledged basis for nobler, more sophisticated philosophical or political considerations, makes looking for them somewhat similar to the search for clues in a detective story.

Because cultural assumptions are largely implicit, they often surface when and where the constraints of philosophical or social scientific discourse are relaxed, when the control of expression and thought and the imperatives of objective detachment give way to social passions and ideological prejudices. Interviews and polemical articles are more likely to reveal culturalist biases than carefully crafted and controlled academic expositions, which is why I often use documents of the former kind. When the dispute over French theory spilled out of the narrow confines of critical circles into the public sphere, all sorts of familiar descriptions of French intellectual culture cropped up in accounts written by professors and journalists of widely diverging political persuasions.

The vast corpus of works devoted to French structuralism and post-structuralism in the United States in the past twenty years oscillates, as most studies of the intellectual world usually do, between two opposite and incompatible interpretive polarities. On the one hand, we have count-less critical examinations of the tenets and limits of French theory, from a variety of feminist, pragmatist, Marxist, or humanistic viewpoints. Paying lip service to the "materiality of discourse," most of these studies do not ex-plore all the consequences of the fact that French theorists are the product of a particular national self-understanding and set of educational institu-tions, and of a highly specific kind of literary and linguistic culture.[5] The obsession with the question of the subject and the anti-authoritarian tone of most of French poststructuralism, for example, has a lot to do with the role of the state in modern French history and with the traditionally contentious relation of intellectuals to the Jacobin version of centralized political power, a situation which differs greatly from that of British or American cultural producers, who must write and act within the confines of a quasi-hegemonic liberal political environment.

On the other end of the interpretive spectrum, we have a growing body of polemical essays focusing on the self-interested nature of what they de-scribe as "the deconstruction craze," jeremiads on the hostile takeover of the humanities by "barbarians in tweed" and other "tenured radicals." Under the cover of objective social science, this type of analysis reduces in-tellectual activities to promotional strategies centered around faculty ten-ure and the establishment of new programs in critical theory and Conti-nental philosophy, or the creation of entire departments of women's or cultural studies. To reduce the study of ideas to the description of academic power games—self-interested struggles for promotion, publication, and publicity—is a little like writing a history of the coal industry without ever mentioning coal, to quote from French historian François Dosse.

This is not to say that such considerations are not part and parcel of the practice of academic intellectuals, in the United States as elsewhere. But many critics of French theory attribute its continued success in the United States and, to some extent, in Britain, Italy, and Latin America, *solely* to the traditional fascination for French cultural products in Euro-American interpretive communities. In this view, familiarity with the imported theoretical fashions from the Left Bank grants foreign intellectuals both status and legitimacy, and signals sophistication of thought, fostering a sense of belonging to what Alvin Gouldner has called an international culture of critical discourse. The problem with this view is that it denies any other value to the ideas it opposes than that of intellectual status bearers and trendy markers of in-group belonging. While it delegitimates the relationship of individuals to the discourses they imitate and/or appropriate, it also reduces intellectual activities to the mere pursuit of academic prestige or peer recognition.

Intellectual history must avoid the twin pitfalls of the history of ideas, which often forgets that the autonomy of the symbolic sphere is only at best *relative,* and a (cynical) sociology of intellectuals that reduces their writings to being mere tools in a struggle for political power and social recognition. I am suggesting that cultural assumptions, prereflexive mental habits or *mentalités* (what Roland Barthes has called "the discourse of others" within each of us), are precisely what mediates between the purified and abstract realm of ideas and the practical empirical field generated by the social and political struggles of intellectuals.

NATIONAL CONTEXTS OF RECEPTION AND REJECTION

The initial success of French theory is not only a consequence of the traditional role of the French literati as trendsetters and purveyors of renewed topics for high-brow cocktail party chatter. It rests at a deeper level on epistemological changes having to do with the social and political developments loosely referred to as postmodernism. Briefly put, the globalization of consumerism and of the media, the collapse of socialism, and the growing indifference on the part of the intelligentsia and the educated public of postindustrial nations toward the emancipatory "grand narratives" of the Enlightenment have all contributed to the diffusion of relativistic, antifoundationalist, and neopragmatist views in academic communities worldwide.[6]

These developments prompted Richard Rorty some years ago to speak of a convergence between postanalytical American philosophy (especially in the form of the current revival of pragmatism) and French poststructuralism.[7] What goes today under the name of postmodernism is indeed a transatlantic intellectual movement, and one finds traces or varieties of pragmatism in the works of many French theorists.[8] Rorty's line of argument may provide us with one key to understanding the success of this kind of philosophy in the New World. Some sectors of the American academy gave poststructuralism such a warm welcome because the ground had been prepared by the native pragmatic refusal to think of truth as correspondence to reality.[9]

This complicity between some literary and social critics in France and the United States can be described as a kind of pragmatization of a French tradition long dominated by rationalist and universalistic models of intelligibility.[10] It is not purely epistemological but is rooted as well in a shared social situation among academics in the new transatlantic post-Enlightenment culture. The professionalization of the French life of the mind in the past twenty-five years has accompanied the demise of the Voltairean model of the intellectual *engagé,* with Sartre perhaps its last incarnation. The French master-thinkers of the sixties were almost all professors, like their American supporters and disciples, and no longer *Freischwebenden* artists, publicists, and novelists, as Hugo, Zola, or de Beauvoir had been. This convergence of professional interests and academic practices could only facilitate the importation of French theories, and French visiting professors, to America.

At the same time, the rapid institutionalization of poststructuralism in American departments of French, English, and comparative literature was facilitated by the presence of a large (relative to France) population of students in the humanities, a guarantee that there would be a market for the translation and publication of French theory. Ironically enough, the autonomy of American academic life (itself a product of its high degree of professionalization), which has often been blamed by radical critics on both sides of the Atlantic for the political impotence and cultural marginality of American intellectuals, is precisely what allowed literary theory to weather attacks both from within and without the university throughout the Reagan years.

In France, where intellectual life is much more dependent on the public sphere, the media, and the state of enlightened public opinion, the philosophies of the sixties did not survive the rise of neoliberalism, the recent turn to pragmatism, and the concurrent demise of Marxism and radical feminism in the last twenty years. In other words, the very mechanisms that had propelled the French structuralists, almost overnight, to the forefront of the national (and later international) intellectual scene precipitated their downfall in the same expeditious manner.[11]

Ideas have a much shorter shelf life in France than in the United States. It takes longer for them to take root in American soil, but once they are established, the size of the intellectual market and the relative autonomy of the various theoretical subcultures allows them to flourish long after they have wilted on the Left Bank, soon to be replaced by another crop of "new" philosophies that are often nothing more than fifty-year-old ideas everyone had been busy forgetting.

A comparative study of the influence of poststructuralist theory in France and the United States shows a marked difference in intellectual rhythms, a sort of disjointed temporality. There is a time lag between the two periods of infatuation with things undecidable on each side of the Atlantic. Michèle Lamont's study of the annual distribution of Derrida's publications in both countries shows that whereas the diffusion of deconstruction decreased sharply in France after a 1972–73 boom, it rose steadily in the United States from 1973 to 1984 (when Lamont's study ends), with a particularly sharp increase after 1982.[12] Translation played a major role in the dissemination of imported French theoretical products.[13] Derrida and Foucault's major works started appearing in English in the late seventies, occasioning a plethora of comments and citations at a time when *la pensée 68* was already under attack in France.

Lamont rightly points out that French theory was not a homogeneous product: there were differences in the rate and rhythm of reception of the different authors (Derrida and Foucault, for example), not only in the national contexts of appropriation. She notes that the diffusion of Derridean deconstruction was relatively weak outside of the United States and France. In Britain, books and articles on Lacan and Foucault outnumbered those on Derrida eight to one and five to one, respectively. Lamont attributes the resistance to what she calls Derrida's "nihilism" to strong leftist intellectual traditions in Britain, Italy, and Latin America, all contexts in which Foucault's appeal has remained strong (606–7). This may also be true to a certain extent of American academia in the 1980s: a lot of the criticism directed at literary theory for not being political and emancipatory enough came from a cultural Left, partly influenced by Foucauldian and Deleuzian views.

These differences in the national institutional contexts of the production/reception of contemporary theory and in the relationship between the academic field and the rest of society on both sides of the Atlantic explain the paradox of the current situation: the radicalism of French theory (albeit in reappropriated, indigenized forms) is part and parcel of a national debate over the future of American education and moral values, while it has lost much relevance to ideological developments in the land of Sartre, Voltaire, and Foucault.

There are a number of endogenous factors accounting for the fit between French theory and the intellectual and institutional climate in American humanities departments in the early seventies. New Criticism had prepared the ground by promoting theoretical approaches to literature as a legitimate alternative to traditional textual exegesis. Moreover, the new imports from Paris provided a long-awaited response to the disciplinary crisis opened up by the postwar ascendancy of the empirical and social sciences in the university, and by the related pressure to make academic research "relevant" to social needs.

As Michèle Lamont puts it, humanities departments saw in literary theory a way to "reaffirm 'the distinctive features' on which their prestige was based, that is, high culture" (614).[14] At the same time theory gave comparative literature the unifying paradigm it had been searching for (a set of interpretive operations readily transferable to any kind of text regardless of its geographical origin), it also "offered American humanists a criticism of science that was much needed to promote their own intellectual products" (616).

A commonly held view of the success of French theory in America is that it provided a new generation of young professors and graduate students radicalized by the political upheavals of the sixties on campus and elsewhere with an interpretive method that infused the canonical reading protocols of the New Criticism with the ideological dimension it had lacked in the conformist campus atmosphere of the Eisenhower era. In the late sixties, the new imports from Paris met a strong social demand for politically informed and politically relevant methods of reading. They enabled a generation of students and critics of literature and culture to combine the profits of theoretical sophistication with those of ideological critique, temporarily resolving the dilemma of the oppositional, but powerless, ivory tower intellectual confined to the gilded ghettoes of academia.[15]

In *The Eye of Prey,* Herbert Blau has argued that seventies theory was the French contribution to a revolutionary dynamics that originated in the United States but did not find its ideological expression until it crossed the Atlantic, igniting social upheavals throughout European campuses and later coming back to America in the form of a sophisticated, theoretical account of the American students' unreflective practices:[16]

What I am suggesting is that when the radical activism of the sixties abated or went underground, it surfaced again in *theory* as the new erotics of discourse. The lifestyles and polymorphous desires which were celebrated at Woodstock and seemed to be savaged at Altamont also went under, retreating across the Atlantic, and entered the high intellectual traditions of continental thought, given the *ideology* they were charged with *not* having in the sixties, and are being recycled, biodegradably, as an assault on the phallogocentric structure of bourgeois power, with its invisible ideology (7).[17]

Michèle Lamont and Marsha Witten note that the members of the new theory community or interdisciplinary subculture often "consumed French theory as a genre or a style of intellectual work" (20). They used the French imports as a form of cultural capital in their struggle to gain prominence within their respective disciplines, from comparative literature to communications and anthropology. But the profit was not only academic, it was also existential. The future "tenured radicals" found in the lifestyle of the French oppositional intellectuals a powerful antidote to the middle-class philistinism and political quietism endemic to liberal-democratic society.

The French theorists were not only writers and thinkers, they were also charismatic public figures who provided, as Lamont puts it, a "role model" for young French and American aspiring intellectuals via updated descriptions of the traditional notion of *engagement.* The romantic-Nietzschean theme of "life as a work of art," of the practice of philosophy as the construction of the self and the invention of a stylized (and stylish) existence was later to become the basis of Foucault's rereading of the Greek culture of subjectivity.

THE FRENCHNESS OF THEORY

Although the gradual integration of academic research worldwide pulls French and American intellectual cultures together, powerful forces on both sides of the Atlantic also tend to reactivate older sources of tension between the two countries. In the United States, the anxiety generated by the consequences of contemporary antifoundationalism has recently taken the form of a growing resistance to French theory, both in intellectual circles and in the educated public at large. The convergence between some aspects of these imported philosophical discourses (the deconstruction of the notion of origin, the questioning of established epistemological traditions, the problematization of history) and the American imagination as a radical break with the past may help explain the initial success of French theory. However, other, more subliminal considerations eventually worked against its reception by mainstream American intellectual culture.

And that is where the "French" in French theory comes into prominence. The diverse connotations attached to the adjective by the various participants in the debate over poststructuralism illuminate the general conditions of the reception of theoretical imports from France in the United States. The use of "French theory" in the singular is questionable in that it conjures up the notion of a highly homogeneous philosophical corpus, while in fact the various species of *la pensée 68* were often very critical of one another, and even sometimes incompatible.[18]

The adjunction of a marker of nationality, that is, *French,* to this corpus of critical thought raises further questions by suggesting an unproblematic, direct relationship between ideas and the national culture in which they are produced. Besides, the label is paradoxical in that most of so-called French theory engaged the works of *German* thinkers, from Hegel, Marx, and Nietzsche to Freud, Husserl, and Heidegger.

There is a sense, however, in which the French philosophies of the sixties were unmistakably French. They were themselves the product of a form of theoretical import-export business, the result of an extremely successful reappropriation of German philosophy within the discursive and institutional constraints of the French intellectual field. The scholastic, academic, some would say ponderous, developments of German post-Enlightenment thought were given an undoubtedly French flavor, most apparent in the literary, allusive, highly metaphorical style in which they were refashioned. The use of a specifically literary style in French philosophy and the human sciences, and its relation to the status of belles lettres in the native culture has received a lot of attention lately from intellectual historians and sociologists of culture.[19]

In America, this culturally specific feature of the French style of philosophizing operated at first solely within the confines of the academic community. Even there, its introduction met with a strong resistance on the part of disciplines dominated by analytic or Chomskyan paradigms.[20] Many departments of philosophy and linguistics refused to make room for the new semiotic and Freudian-Marxist imports from Paris, rejected as softheaded, "fuzzy," amateurish, and unscientific.

Once the reputation of French theory went beyond the limits of academia and once its merits were publicly debated in the marketplace of ideas, more widely shared views on France and the French crept into the debate, displacing earlier considerations on the style, content, and value of theory. Behind the façade of highly technical professorial polemics over the meaning of Derrida's *différance* or Foucault's power-knowledge syndrome, older, broader cultural forces were set into motion, reviving long-held myths, prejudices, and even sometimes truths about French literary culture, its inherent elitism, and the illiberal and antidemocratic proclivities of most of its intellectual heroes. Beyond considerations of style, it is the aristocratic and authoritative *tone* of French theory that was ultimately to inspire most of the attacks mounted against it.[21]

The very qualities that had contributed to the appeal of French theory in critical circles, that is, its conceptual *hauteur,* its hermetic style, and the subtle exegesis it applied to the most difficult of the tradition's sacred texts, were equally responsible for its fall from grace in the larger cultural opinion. For the esoteric writings of the French critics soon aroused in this country the same ambivalence toward European sophistication that can be found in American attitudes toward *haute couture* or *nouvelle cuisine,* a fascination that conceals a deep resentment, which can surface at any moment, on the part of a fiercely democratic and egalitarian culture.

Rejection of French philosophical "jargon" was not limited to literary traditionalists. In an article partly devoted to the influence of French theory on American academics, Elaine Showalter argued that "feminist criticism has worried too much already, in my opinion, about communicating with the white fathers, even at the price of translating its findings into the warp of their obscure critical language" (119).[22] In a similar vein, Winnie Woodhull remarked that American feminists tend to regard the "linguistic games" of their French counterparts as mere "virtuoso exhibitionism."[23]

Tony Judt has noted that the mixture of amusement and irritation with which many Anglo-American intellectuals view the verbosity, hyperbole, and discursive pyrotechnics of their French counterparts has a long history. More than two centuries ago, Dr. Samuel Johnson poked fun at the French pretension of having an opinion on just about everything under the sun. Judt himself devotes a substantial part of his recent study of postwar French intellectuals to what he calls "the local cultural habit of rhetoric and abstraction," following Durkheim's well-known observations (in *L'Evolution pédagogique en France*) about the close relation between the tendency toward the impersonal and toward analogical reasoning in Gallic thought and the pedagogical habits of the Jesuits, who educated generations of French literati and left a lasting imprint on the French school system (252).

In the course of his discussion of "the inherited characteristics of the French intelligentsia," Judt repeatedly contrasts the status of literary language in France and Britain. Béat-Louis de Muralt's remark, in an early eighteenth-century book comparing French and English customs, that in most countries "expressions are born of thought" while in France "it is the reverse; often it is expressions that give birth to thoughts," prompts the following comment from Judt:

> This is more than a witty aphorism; the importance of rhetoric and style in France are incontestable, shaping thoughts and ideas under an unquestioned discursive authority, in contrast with England, for example, where the vernacular and the literary had merged into a rich but open, almost anarchic language. With rhetorical primacy, there came abstraction, a power attaching to language and concept independently of the thing they thought to express or describe. (249)

This performative function of rhetorical style, which can make the most abstract speculations seem convincingly real, was also diagnosed as a specific trait of French culture by Julien Benda, who complained that his compatriots too often "treat as genuine forms of philosophy the rattling of 'intuitions,' flung down with no order, no cohesion, no critical apparatus, a sort of verbal action and sometimes very seductive" (316).

For Judt the unfortunate tendency of the French to favor reasoning by way of metaphor and analogy over the principles of identity and contradiction has moral consequences when applied to political issues such as those raised by postwar Stalinism. The off-handed way French thinkers have had of brushing aside objections based on fact, their disregard for empirical inquiry, and their predilection for self-contained and self-validating philosophical systems authorizes for Judt all manners of denegation and obfuscation of reality. "This genius for abstracting, reifying, and generalizing is what made it possible for perfectly peaceable and gentle men to advocate violence, for persons of moderate personality to see nothing amiss in an admiration for excess, and for clear-headed and gifted thinkers to ignore (or 'overcome') simple rules of coherence and logic" (253).

THE LOCALITY OF RESISTANCE

The critics of French theory in the English-speaking world often revive the traditional opposition between Gallic abstruse skepticism and Anglo-American common sense. Displacing the site of the debate from the epistemological to the aesthetic, from questions of truth to issues of taste, David Lehman, for example, has described the growing influence of Gallic intellectual imports on American campuses in the following terms: "The American lit-crit profession slowly but steadily shed its tweedy English image in favor of foppish French fashion" (48).

The dominance of empiricism in Anglo-American philosophy and the relative ideological consensus achieved through the extension of the culture of liberalism gave intellectual life in Britain and in the United States, at least up to the 1960s, a genteel, level-headed, and "civilized" patina in sharp contrast with the virulence and radicalism of the literary politics Tocqueville held responsible for the fall of the old regime and the excesses of the French Revolution. Edward Shils has remarked that British intellectuals, who were as revolutionary and antibourgeois as their Continental counterparts in the first half of the nineteenth century, later joined the civil service, the church, parliament, the press, and the leadership of political parties. This participation of intellectuals in civil society, achieved "through the ancient universities primarily, but also through kinship and through the social and convivial life of London upper-class, constituted a bond from which few could escape and which no other country could then and has since been able to match" (139).

British intellectuals, integrated as many of them were in the Establishment, never harbored as a group the same feelings of alienation and *ressentiment* as the most militantly radical members of *la république des lettres* or *le parti des intellectuels*. In the United States, the dominance of liberal-democratic principles, the ascendancy of petty-bourgeois egalitarian values and tastes, and the pervasiveness of anti-intellectual antielitism contributed (at least until the New Deal) to the relative marginalization of intellectuals, who were never as accepted as their British colleagues or as revered as their French counterparts.

The existence of a strong liberal-democratic consensus within the postwar American intellectual community explains why French theory found opponents on both the Right and the Left, a fact often noted by observers of the current culture wars in academia. Beyond their disagreements, both literary traditionalists and progressive cultural critics have been uncomfortable with the epistemological and political radicalism of poststructuralism, as well as with its illiberal consequences, a claim reinforced by the periodic reexamination (in the form of so many "affairs" disclosed by literary journalists) of the close ties between the most prominent figures of philosophical modernity, such as Heidegger, Blanchot, or de Man, and fascism/Nazism. Early nineteenth-century French liberals, who saw in Rousseau's writings the prefiguration of Robespierre's Terror, would have heartily concurred. Similarly, the *nouveaux philosophes* of the 1970s drew a direct line between Hegel's philosophy and the Soviet labor camps.

Richard Rorty reflected on these suspicions in an 1988 essay written in response to the controversy that had erupted in Paris over the publication of Victor Farias's *Heidegger and Nazism*. "Many people think," Rorty wrote, "that there is something intrinsically fascistic about the thought of Nietzsche and Heidegger, and are suspicious of Derrida and Foucault because they owe so much to these earlier figures. On this view, fascism is associated with 'irrationalism,' and decent democratic outlook with 'confidence in reason.'"[24]

Although Rorty goes on to refute such attempts at "simplifying" the thought of original thinkers by "reducing them to moral or political attitude," he nevertheless elsewhere chastises his French colleagues for their "anti-utopianism" and their "apparent lack of faith in liberal democracy." "Even those who, like myself, think of France as the source of the most original philosophical thought currently being produced," he writes, "cannot figure out why French thinkers are so willing to say things like 'May 68 refutes the doctrine of parliamentary liberalism'" ("Cosmopolitanism," 220).

The appropriation of French theory within the liberal culture of American academia has often resulted in erasing its most radical and illiberal elements, notably all that it owed to the culture of transgression of the interwar period and its fascination for death and violence as catharsis and salvation (Bataille, Blanchot, Artaud, and so on).[25] A few years ago, Vincent Descombes distinguished between an "Anglo-American Foucault," the historian of cultural practices who figured so prominently in academic debates throughout the English-speaking world in the last years of his life, and a "French Foucault," the Nietzschean, radical, "inhuman" iconoclastic philosopher eulogized by, among others, Gilles Deleuze and Maurice Blanchot. "The American Foucault," Descombes wrote, "may take our concerns and practices very seriously. Yet it may be the 'anarchist' Foucault who keeps fascinating his readers" (210). The widespread liberalization (de-radicalization) of Foucault's thought in America (the same is true of Nietzsche) recalls the process Lionel Trilling described as the "legitimization of the subversive" resulting from the inclusion of the major texts of critical modernity in the literary canon for American undergraduates (23–24).

The new critical academicism fostered by French theory looked to many American observers like yet another expression of a demagogic, intolerant mandarinate. *Plus ça change, plus c'est la même chose*, as Americans are fond of saying about France and the French. One of the most damaging criticisms from the Left presented poststructuralist theory as a sophisticated version of the traditional *commentaire de texte*—a brilliant example of continuity within change and a means of rejuvenating classical academic studies of canonical texts. After all, the French critics applied their interpretive skills to the consecrated authors of the national and continental traditions, seldom, if ever, dealing with nonwhite, non-European, or female writers, let alone with popular culture: Derrida deconstructed Valéry, Nietzsche, or Lévi-Strauss; de Man wrote on Proust, Rousseau, and the Romantics; and Barbara Johnson's early studies focused on Baudelaire and Mallarmé.[26]

THE SUBALTERNS TALK BACK

With the recent arrival on the American critical scene of new multicultural actors advocating the study of non-European texts and cultures and questioning the centrality of the Western canon, discussions of poststructuralism from the Left have increasingly focused on its ethnocentric, even Gallocentric character. During a discussion recorded in *The Post-Colonial Critic*, Gayatri Spivak, who was born in India but teaches in the United States, was faulted by a group of young Indian academics for her excessive reliance on what they described as "First World elite theory" (69). Soon, even the most revered figures in the theory constellation would be subjected to the probing gaze of the postcolonial critics.

In a special issue of *PMLA* devoted to the emerging field of colonial discourse analysis, Rosemary Jolly took Derrida himself to task for what she described as his highly ambiguous position on apartheid in South Africa in his 1985 essay "Racism's Last Word." Derrida's characterization of apartheid as "the ultimate racism in the world" ended up, according to Jolly, exonerating Western nations from their historical responsibilities in colonial exploitation.

The founder of what Russell Jacoby has derisively dubbed "Complicity Studies" was in turn found to be highly complicitous with the hegemonic discourse of colonialism. "Derrida's identification of South Africa as the most spectacular criminal in a broad array of racist activities," Jolly argues, "turns the reader's critical gaze away from American and European colonialism and thus displaces the actions of the colonizer countries both geographically and chronologically onto the colony—South Africa . . . [which] becomes the 'last' place where the racism of the imperial West, assumed to be past, still flourishes" (21–22).

Jolly uses deconstruction to deconstruct the father of deconstruction in yet another attempt to use the master's tools to dismantle the master's house. Derrida's duplicitous condemnation of apartheid, she claims, ends up reactivating the very ideological mechanisms his philosophy was purported to uncover, starting with hierarchized binary oppositions. Consequently, Derrida's text is guilty of shoring up "the authoritarianism of the Western subject-object binarism that is an integral part of the imperialist history of the Western academy" (20). In other words, French theorists, for all their transgressive rhetoric, are still master-thinkers of the less reputable kind.

Similarly, Anne McClintock and Rob Nixon emphasize the high degree of abstraction and the fetishization of language inherent in Derrida's brand of dehistoricized idealism, a common complaint among critics of the depoliticizing effects of deconstruction: "Is it . . . the word, apartheid, or is it Derrida himself, operating here in 'another regime of abstraction' . . . removing the word from its place in the discourse of South African racism, raising it to another power, and setting separation itself apart? . . . The essay's opening analysis of the word apartheid is, then, symptomatic of a severance of word from history" (140–41).

This and other accounts of the duplicity of French theory may have been prompted by Derrida's own evolution away from what had been (hastily?) construed as a blanket condemnation of Western civilization. In *The Other Heading,* his own contribution to the debate on the new Europe emerging from the ashes of Stalinism, the philosopher attempted to counter the dispersion of the "European Idea" and to move beyond "all the exhausted programs of *Eurocentrism* and *anti-Eurocentrism,* these exhausting yet unforgettable programs" (13).

Joining many of his countrymen, Derrida even cast doubts on the desirability of differentialism (my word, not his), especially in the former colonies of the Soviet empire freed from Communist rule but now open to the double threat of capitalism and tribalism. "If it is necessary to make sure that a centralizing hegemony (the capital) not be reconstituted," he writes, "it is also necessary, for all that, not to multiply the borders, i.e., the movements and margins. It is necessary not to cultivate for their own sake minority differences, untranslatable idiolects, national antagonisms, or the chauvinisms of idiom" (44).

The growing impatience with the Eurocentric, elitist character of French theory in postcolonial circles is partly responsible for the present malaise in the discipline of French studies in the United States. While French departments undoubtedly benefited greatly in the 1970s and 1980s from the theoretical turn in terms of the visibility of some of their faculty on the critical scene, the current mood is less euphoric, in part because all brands of literary criticism, whether traditionalist or deconstructionist, are now on the defensive, increasingly challenged by the new interpretive paradigms (multiculturalism, New Historicism, colonial and postcolonial discourse analysis, cultural studies, etc.), all of which privilege the social and ideological production of literary texts and harbor some measure of anti-aestheticism.

In addition to an intellectualist tendency to privilege discourse over practice, French theory, especially in its postmodern forms, is also faulted for the detached cynicism of many of its representatives, who are said to view any kind of political action as one more way of reproducing the status quo. The intellectual Left both in Britain and the United States has always been wary of the politically demobilizing and some even say reactionary effects of authors who stress the indeterminacy of meaning or the ubiquity of simulacra, when they do not, like Paul de Man, view political activity as a burden rather than an opportunity (293). The French intellectual propensity for universalizing specific cultural forms or behaviors is also responsible, in the eyes of many American feminists, for the inherent essentialism, idealism, and aestheticism of what came to be known as *French* feminism.

Although I cannot here go into detail regarding the complex relationship between poststructuralism and radical feminism, it is safe to say that what attracted some feminists to French theory at first was the strategic use by its proponents, whether male or female, of the notion of "the feminine" (*le féminin*, incidentally a masculine substantive in French). For the anti-Hegelian, anti-Platonic French philosophers of the sixties, the feminine did not refer to the biological or existential situation of being a woman, but to the movement by which being, or writing, escapes "the totalization of dialectics" or "the closure of metaphysics." In Elaine Showalter's words, "the alliance of feminism and deconstruction is not new; male theorists such as Derrida and Lacan have for some time used woman as the wild card, the joker in the pack who upsets the logocentric and phallocentric stack of appellations" (124).

I offer this example of the ubiquitous use of the category of the feminine in poststructuralism to illustrate the point I made earlier about the reluctance of many literary critics to address the question of the specificity of French theory and of its relation to the national academic and intellectual fields at large. In this particular case, it may not be enough to invoke a general European or even worse, Western (male) literary tradition of representing woman as the dark continent of culture, as a natural, demonic force always ready to subvert and/or engulf the precarious arrangements of civilization. How can one account for the prevalence of the notion of the feminine in *French* philosophical circles? One may have to look outside of poststructuralism, or even outside the philosophical tradition per se for an answer.

Alice Jardine, drawing on the work of Julia Kristeva, suggested in *Gynesis* that the poststructuralists' obsession with the feminine may have something to do with Catholicism and the role the figure of the Virgin Mary plays in the French cultural imaginary. For Jardine, "the history of France is the history of monarchy—the determination of alliance and filiation through the father within the Judeo-Christian tradition at a very symbolic level . . . The history of the United States . . . has a very different symbolic matrix: that of Protestantism and democracy." Jardine goes on to contrast this situation with "the absence of the Virgin Mother as sacred object in the Protestant tradition." "Is it not possible," she asks, "that feminism has a longer and more vocal tradition in Anglo-Saxon countries because the Virgin Mother is not taken into account within the dominant symbolic economy of Protestantism?" (232).

The extent to which the secularizing effects of Protestantism and liberalism have eroded the Marian cult, the ideology of courtly love, and their attending idealization of women and mothers might explain the misogynist character of American literature and the resistance of many American feminists to the French notion of *le féminin,* as well as the amused bafflement with which French intellectuals, both men and women, have chronicled the war of the sexes in America and the controversies involving sexual harassment in the workplace and codes of erotic conduct on American campuses. Whatever the validity of these interpretations, they have the merit of trying to come to terms with the historical genealogy of national traditions, and to show how literary themes, religious symbols, and social practices (in this case gender relations) interact within a common symbolic matrix.

Pursuing a somewhat similar line of inquiry as Alice Jardine, although with different conclusions, Elizabeth Badinter and Michèle Sarde have argued that gender relations are much less contentious in France than in the United States, and consequently feminism less vocal, because of the importance of the tradition of courtly love in French culture. The institutionalization of court culture and later of the salons is said to have enabled elite women to gain influence and to civilize, in Norbert Elias's sense, social relations with men to their own benefit.

Michèle Sarde devotes almost a third of her study of the (self)representations of French women since the tenth century to what she calls *la matrice courtoise,* a cultural matrix rather limited in scope both socially and temporally but critical to the subsequent struggles over the definition of women's role and image in French society. Her book, *Regard sur les Françaises,* follows in the steps of the French Annales School's *histoire des mentalités.* Sarde is concerned with the "ancestral mechanisms" that inform people's actions and reactions over time, arguing that contemporary women's struggles are rooted in a historical "substance" *(matière)* where "ancient operations reproduce, sometimes without their knowledge, the behaviors of their mothers or great-grandmothers" (647).

For Sarde, the specific discourse on love that originated in twelfth-century Southern France was highly subversive, giving rise to a new ethics of gender relations more favorable to the emotional and pulsional interests of women. The new erotic code required reciprocity and exchange, separated sexuality from reproduction, legitimated female adultery, and answered women's aspirations to dignity and social recognition by "integrating feminine Desire and making woman the mistress of her own pleasure" (138).

This view of the social, ethical, and libidinal radicalism of the courtly ideal is still the object of much controversy, since for many historians the impact of the new vision on medieval society was highly limited. Sarde's point, however, is that a seed was planted in the French cultural compost, a seed that would continue to grow despite subsequent setbacks and that would have a lasting legacy in French letters, from the husband/wife/ lover triangle of medieval farce, classical comedy, and nineteenth-century *théâtre boulevardier* to the genteel *commerce* of gender-mixed Enlightenment salons.

The discourse of courtly love transferred to aristocratic women the freedom and the power their husbands enjoyed as a result of the institution of feudal vassalage. The ladies became both consumers and producers of romance and in the process found their own voice. Female sovereignty became "the keystone of a code of relations between men and women based on verbal exchange, *mixité* and intersexual *métissage*," defined as "the implicit acceptation of the feminization of men and of the masculinization of women within intersexual union" (137).

This issue of intersexual *métissage*, which its critics, especially in the United States, describe as a form of class collaboration with the enemy, is what distinguishes many French and Anglo-American conceptions of gender relations as well as brands of feminist theory. For Sarde, French feminists have traditionally centered their analysis of alienation on the repression of voice and body, while American feminists have insisted on social and economic oppression.[27] This difference in emphasis ultimately refers to distinct national histories and, unsurprisingly, to the prominence of courtly love in the French tradition: "These two conceptions of the liberation of women reflect exactly national *mentalités* as we see them at work since the time of the cathedrals when French women, proud of their femininity, sought to impose its sovereignty rather than claiming man's power for themselves" (645).

Following in Michèle Sarde's footsteps, Mona Ozouf also highlights the French difference in gender relations, although she focuses less on the courtly tradition than on literary salons and the role of the republican state as decisive milestones along what Michèle Perrot has called the French way to feminism.[28] France in the eighteenth century was, according to David Hume, a country of women. By this, the Scottish philosopher meant that men and women were more "mixed," more closely associated in all the circumstances of life than in Britain. The ancien régime was congenial to women in a way that the Jacobin republic or the British constitutional monarchy could never be: in a world of difference such as eighteenth-century France, sexual difference was only one among many, quite unimportant when compared to differences in birth and social rank.

In an absolutist state, aristocratic men are deprived of their ancient political, judicial, and military functions; they are free to join women in the games of social figuration. Court culture, as Norbert Elias has so persuasively demonstrated, imposed an extremely complex set of psychological constraints on individuals as they competed for social visibility and royal favors. What ensued was a subtle, "civilized" struggle for status in which women would excel. As Ozouf puts it, "In a monarchical society, every man's passions are exerted in defending his privileges, holding and marking his place, which opens a wide field of action for women's savoir faire, the sureness of their psychological sense, the fertility of their social imagination" (230). Montesquieu and Voltaire celebrated French *politesse* as a unique form of refinement, unparalleled in the whole world, the product of the reciprocal education of men and women.

Ozouf, like Sarde, also stresses the role of the republican schools in advancing the rights of women. The rationalist vision of the Republicans implied that men and women equally shared in the natural lights of Reason, even if social conditions and the weight of history still accounted for empirical inequalities between them. As a consequence, both genders were, at least in principle, submitted to the same educational requirements. The principle of equal training meant that the school system became the main avenue of integration and promotion for women,[29] and the figure of the salaried *institutrice,* often married to a schoolteacher, embodied a syncretic ideal of maternity, as Ozouf puts it. Again, cultural factors come to the fore in the French case. Although the political emancipation of French women (suffrage, elective positions) has always lagged far behind that of Americans and northern Europeans, the ratio is inverted in terms of access to education. In 1963, 43 percent of French students were women, as opposed to 32 percent in Britain and 24 percent in Germany (Ozouf, 267).

The egalitarian character of French republican rationalism explains both the advances in women's education and the stagnation of their political rights. French women were considered as individuals first, and women second. While Anglo-Saxon democracies are inclined to grant rights to individuals as members of specific groups, the abstract individualism of the French revolutionary tradition is suspicious of any claim based on gender, ethnic, racial, or other particularities.[30] Paradoxically, French women were excluded from political rights precisely because their actual dependence on their husbands and the church made them unworthy of the privileges they were ideally entitled to as the autonomous individuals they were yet to become in the eyes of the male legislators. Meanwhile, as Pierre Rosanvallon has remarked, British women were called to the voting booth as women, not as individuals (268).

Ozouf's main point is that the long tradition of *commerce* between the sexes going back to the medieval courts and the salons of early modern France was reinforced by state-driven educational reforms inspired by republican egalitarianism. The French mind, she writes, is decidedly rebellious toward communitarianism because of the original alliance in France "between the memory of the aristocratic world, which initiated happy exchanges between the sexes, and the reality of an 'extreme democracy' which places no limit on the idea of egalitarianism" (281). As a consequence, French women have always had a hard time conceiving of themselves as minorities and have rejected the "feminism of difference" advocated by radical theorists on both sides of the Atlantic.

Ozouf's study of prominent French women from Manon Roland to Simone Weil is inseparable from her quarrel with American differentialism in matters of gender and sexuality. French exceptionalism in these matters is contrasted, not with German or Russian practices, but with American ones. Ozouf's discussion includes the obligatory quote from Tocqueville's famous pages on the sexual division of labor in American gender relations (as opposed to the *mixité* of French salon culture):

> The Americans have applied to the sexes the great principle of political economy which governs the manufacturers of our age, by carefully dividing the duties of man from those of woman in order that the great work of society may be the better carried on. In no country has such constant care been taken as in America to trace two clearly distinct lines of action for the two sexes and to make them keep pace one with the other, but in two pathways that are always different. (212)

Ozouf, following many French commentators, sees in the "valorization-segregation" of the American woman suggested by Tocqueville the source of the early development of radical feminism in the United States. Michèle Sarde, for her part, notes that Tocqueville's surprise that a beautiful woman could cross America by boat and stagecoach without ever encountering a mark of disrespect from men portended complaints from twentieth-century French women visiting the United States that gender relations are depressingly de-eroticized in the New World. Describing a French friend's reaction upon visiting America, Sarde writes that "what depressed [Françoise] above everything was the lack of interest in women displayed by men in public. No man would look at her when she walked down the street, even less talk to her" (21).

Ozouf's book begins and ends with a critique of an Anglo-Saxon gender particularism based on "radical alterity" that ends up replacing the right to difference with demands for different rights. The somewhat idyllic picture of a French culture happily combining universalism and particularism, where women, because they see themselves first and foremost as free and equal individuals, can "experience sexual difference without resentment, can cultivate it with joy and irony, and can refuse to essentialize it" (274), is contrasted with the threat of "the America of minorities" where politically correct academics teach "ovulars" instead of seminars. The last pages of the essay resort to the vocabulary of cultural struggle, as do so many other contemporary French observations on the passing of the great national tradition. "Is it possible to imagine," Ozouf wonders, "that women's demands, instead of subordinating particularist attachments to universalist values as they have spontaneously done, may sink into particularity? Can we expect the perversion of French egalitarianism? Must we believe that America is shaping the future of feminism?" (396).[31]

NEOROMANTICISM AND THE FRENCH CORTEX

The national(istic) rhetoric of Mona Ozouf's final remarks shows how much the transatlantic dispute is embedded in nativistic celebrations of cultural superiority. The mixture of pedantic jargon and intellectualism usually associated with French high culture not only precipitated an unexpected alliance between the cultural Right and the critical Left in the United States. French theory also came under fire from other quarters, from neoromantics such as Camille Paglia, for example, who likes to contrast the liberating and liberated sixties with what she calls the "French seventies," which she describes as a "panic reaction by headlocked pedants unable to cope with the emotional and sensory flux of the iconoclastic sixties" ("Ninnies," 33), a paradoxical statement when one considers that poststructuralism was in some of its manifestations a philosophy of desire, heir to a culture of transgression and eroticism going back to Sade and Baudelaire, all the way down to Artaud and Bataille.

Paglia's views, because of their extremism and the acerbic and vindictive rhetoric in which they are couched, are generally discounted in serious academic circles. Their very radicalism and extravagance seem to me to be useful and worth mentioning here precisely because, like any caricature, they accentuate by distortion the essential features of the American romantic rejection of (French and European) high culture. I take these features to be present in one form or another in many contemporary discourses that aim at rehabilitating popular culture by contesting the privilege of elite categories of judgment and taste.[32]

Paglia's views are simply an extreme case of the way French culture, reduced to its classical and high modernist components, is constructed time and again by the American imagination through a simple opposition between (cerebral) elitism and (corporeal) populism. The second term of the dyad, that is, the true nature of American culture, is said to reside in mass-mediated, popular forms of entertainment that "leaped far beyond European thought the moment we [Americans] invented Hollywood" (29). The elitist views of the French theorists are rejected because they are incompatible with American pop culture; they constitute in themselves a form of un-American activity: "In the United States, deconstruction is absurd, since we never had a high culture of any kind. Far from being illiterate, we are still preliterate, accentuated by an image-dominated popular culture that was the all-embracing educational medium of my generation" (33).

A hundred and fifty years ago, America was in the eyes of the French literati the land of uniformity, boredom, and sexual repression, a country that managed to worship both the Puritan God and the Almighty Dollar. "Washington would bore me to death," Stendhal wrote, "and I would much rather be in the same salon as M. de Talleyrand." Today, the roles are reversed: the culture of fun and sun, the promised land of *Baywatch* and *Beverly Hills 90210* is made in the U.S.A. Europe, by contrast, seems a little timid, a little reserved, slightly quaint, even prudish. Paris is no longer a movable feast, but California is.

As Régis Debray puts it, "the old foe of individual happiness has become the embodiment of universal happiness. 'The libertine and insolent cheerfulness' that in 1840 was thought of as *l'esprit français* has crossed the Atlantic, thanks to Hollywood, *Holiday on Ice,* aerobics and the Academy Awards being beamed all over the world. The spirit of the shopkeeper, Stendhal's 'stupid and selfish mediocrity' are back in the old world. When it wishes to escape from them and have a little fun, Europe turns to the pop and the tag, hip-hop preachers, sex-shops, fast-food and video-clips. The propelling force of the 'American dream' is sensorimotor: it moves across our bodies and *through them*" (*Contretemps,* 86).

The "image-dominated" world of Hollywood and MTV evokes by contrast the concept-dominated universe of the French tradition. The emphasis on the abstract, bookish, and cerebral character of imported theory leads naturally to a lyrical celebration of America as a culture of the body and of physical and sexual prowess (as in break dancing). The combination of cultural nationalism and of a romantic exaltation of feelings, passions, and unrestrained sensuality, as opposed to the repressed, sublimated, "civilized" eroticism of the courtly tradition, is reminiscent of the struggle of dominated literatures against the cultural hegemony of European imperial powers. The German romantics, for example, opposed the robust nature of the German folk to the effeminate decadence of Voltairean France.

Paglia exhorts her compatriots who worship at the altar of poststructuralism to free themselves from this "rigid foreign ideology," a "French fad" that is nothing but "a grotesque head trip" imposed on American minds from the outside ("Junk Bonds," 180, 179). In typically nativistic manner, the foreign threat is said to be aimed at the very heart of American identity: "One of the most unpalatable aspects of the French fad is the way it has shown ambitious academics drifting from and selling out their own cultural identity" (198). The French occupation of the mind threatens to turn American ethnic diversity into the repressive cultural monolith that is France: "America . . . by virtue of its overlapping and competing ethnicities—Jewish, Italians, Greek, Puerto Rican, Chicano, Irish, Swedish, German, Polish, Russian, Chinese, Japanese—had intrinsic to its character as an immigrant nation a multiplicity of perspectives on life, language, and behavior that snobbish, homogeneous France, suppressing its resident Algerians, lacks" (183).

Again, Paglia's views are hyperbolic expressions of ways of looking at French culture that are shared by many in America today, as the following chapters will make clear. In many ways, the current battles over the Western canon in colleges and multiculturalist curricula in secondary schools echo earlier denunciations of imperialism and celebrations of native worldviews and folkways by German romantics, Russian Slavophiles, Asian and Arab traditionalists, and Pan-Africanists.

Within the system of ideological positions that define the parameters of the current culture wars, the poor French theorists can never win: too iconoclastic and transgressive for the conservatives, too illiberal for the liberals, and too ethnocentric for the multiculturalists, they are also too square for the hip devotees of popular culture such as Paglia.

Let me conclude by stressing that the interplay between traditionalist, multiculturalist, populist, and radical views in the contentious construction of French intellectual culture is not the whole story. I have deliberately chosen extreme positions, and, as I said in my introductory comments, favored polemical texts and interviews in order to dramatize the stakes of recent disputes over contemporary theory. Many American scholars and critics have benefited from French theories in their own work without either endorsing them wholesale or rejecting them altogether. A whole range of opinions spans the divide between Rorty's postmodern convergence and the diatribes of cultural conservatives or radical populists. Besides, the debates over deconstruction or French feminism constitute only one strand in the complex texture of recent French-American cultural relations. Other publics and other demands need to be examined if one is to make a fair assessment of these relations.

While some may rejoice over the demise of French theory, others lament the disappearance of the French difference. The best-selling success of Peter Mayle's books on Provence shows that what the educated readers of the *New York Times Book Review* expect from France and the French is not any kind of philosophical *aggiornamento* or yet one more description of the postmodern apocalypse they are routinely reminded they live in, but precisely the opposite, a reprieve from modernity, the eternal unchanging values of a rural, aristocratic, premodern *civilisation*. The very radicalism of French theory is what prompted many Americans to reject it, another apparent paradox since American culture has been since World War I the symbol of modernity for French intellectuals and their readers.

Books like *A Year in Provence* and *Toujours Provence* address this nostalgia for a precapitalist, bucolic, small-town France that is said to survive (however precariously) on the slopes of the Cévennes and the Lubéron, the very areas Parisian technocrats were accused a quarter of a century ago of callously turning into a desert. Richard Bernstein, who spent many years in France as the *New York Times* cultural correspondent, concludes his portrait of France and the French, significantly entitled *Fragile Glory,* with something like an obituary, a belated version of Heidegger's crepuscular darkening of the Spirit:

The French will be like us, and as they become like the rest of us— Americanized, prosperous, modern, complacent—a great historical epoch will vanish from the earth, the epoch of Frenchness . . .

Perhaps, as you hold this volume in your hands, we will be experiencing the last few minutes of the existence of the French difference . . . You can be sure that when the urge to be different fades and the need to make that difference a common property disappears, the world will feel a bit relieved and deprived as well. For, as Victor Hugo said, without the French we will be alone. (334)

Here, melancholy American Francophiles join ranks with those who, in France, led the revolt against EuroDisney or recently took up arms to defend the French cinematic *exception culturelle* from the competition of the American entertainment industry. The fate of Mickey, Donald, Goofy, and the others on the plains of Ile-de-France helped shift the French-American debate from the questions of taste and style that were at the heart of the resistance to theory toward more pressing, and in many ways more emotional, issues, those of cultural identity, national unity, and "global competition." Many French people feel they are losing ground in all those areas and that American models of economic behavior and interethnic relations have something to do with the crisis of national confidence they are experiencing.

Mona Ozouf draws a parallel between the feminist debates of the sixties and the multiculturalist misunderstandings of the nineties, presenting them as two examples of the confrontation between divergent conceptions of group relations based on universal principles on the one hand, and particularistic ones on the other. Both controversies involve competing ways of dealing with diversity, both touch on volatile issues of self and group identity, both engage diverging definitions of what the national community, as a contested space between various groups somehow condemned to live together, is all about. Before examining whether the French historian's rapprochement between feminist and multiculturalist debates is legitimate, one needs to address the recent transatlantic controversy surrounding the one historical event that embodies the universalist principles Ozouf had in mind, namely the Revolution of 1789.

2

The French Revolution at Two Hundred

THE BICENTENNIAL AND THE RETURN
OF RIGHTS-LIBERALISM

❧ ❧ ❧

> French thought, by and large, eschewed the recourse to the notion that
> there is a final harmony of interests, and that particular conflicts will
> benefit the common good. Even in devising a liberal economic system
> such as physiocracy, it felt the need to embody society in a unified
> image—the rational authority of legal despotism.
>
> FRANÇOIS FURET

> The French regard time in a sense which differs wholly from the German
> point of view. The French live more deeply in remembrance and
> in the past than we do. For us the past is the story of a growth, for the
> French it is the vivid and vital realization of a tradition.
>
> ERNST ROBERT CURTIUS

The passing of the postwar philosophies of suspicion from the French
intellectual scene has taken transatlantic debates away from the uses of theory to diverging conceptions of liberalism, nationhood, and individual
rights, especially in the wake of the Bicentennial of the French Revolution. While the resistance to poststructuralism revealed the strength of the
antitheoretical slant in Anglo-American thought, debates about the new
developments associated with the "globalization" of cultures mobilized another side of the liberal tradition: the critique of French political and cultural centralization. As in the case of theory, this critique has roots in the
history of literary relations between the two traditions for the past two
hundred years.

FRENCH RESISTANCE

EDMUND BURKE AND THE FETISH OF COMMON SENSE

In 1665, Henry Oldenburg voiced the typical British distrust of the theoretical excesses of Continental scholars. "It must be said that England has a large number of learned and inquisitive men, a larger number than is found in all Europe; and what they produce is solid and detailed—the world has, for too long, been sufficiently entertained with general theories" (cited in Greenfeld, 486). A century later, the increasing international competition between Britain and France and the shock waves the French Revolution was sending throughout Europe made it politically expedient to stick some national labels on the still unspecified targets of Oldenburg's impatience with the outside world's general theories.

English conservatives had no qualms about making the French philosophers' propensity for *l'esprit de système* responsible for the bloody mess the French Revolution had made of the Continent. In well-known pages of his *Reflections on the Revolution in France,* Edmund Burke denounced the revolutionaries' "geometrical policy," which made it an absolute necessity that "the whole fabric should be at once pulled down, and the area cleared for the erection of a *theoretic* experimental edifice in its place" (141, my emphasis).

The cardinal sin of the French metaphysical heresy was its fundamental antihistoricism, its arrogant belief in the possibility of starting from scratch, of remaking society from top to bottom, of applying to matters of human government the Cartesian principle of the tabula rasa, which should have been limited to philosophical speculation.[1] "The French builders," Burke fulminated, "clearing away as mere rubbish everything they found, and, like their ornamental gardeners, forming everything into an exact level, propose to rest the whole local and general legislature on three bases of three different kinds; one geometrical, one arithmetical, and the third financial. For the accomplishment of the first of these purposes they divide the area of their country into eighty-three pieces, regularly square, of eighteen leagues by eighteen" (188–89).

The analogy between the systematic nature of the revolutionary reordering of social space and the art of French gardening calls to mind the conventional opposition between the neoclassical, domesticated symmetry of the French ornamental gardens *(jardins à la française)* and the carefully arranged disorder of their English counterparts. The Jacobins wanted to shape human nature just like their royal predecessors had trimmed physical nature, following the same laws of logic and symmetry that govern the landscape architecture of their princely chateaux, from Chenonceau to Versailles. To understand decrees and policies, one has to look at flower beds and bowling greens too.

By transferring the argument from political philosophy to aesthetic doctrine, Burke's analogy testifies to the comprehensive scope of his ideological critique: it aimed at French civilization as a whole, treating it as a system of symbolic structures that produce homologous effects in various closely interrelated domains of practice. The same wrongheaded principles guiding the perception and organization of reality operate in all aspects of French culture, from metaphysics to landscaping to territorial administration.

The central argument of *Reflections* is that the Republicans would have been well advised to look at the English example before turning the world upside down. The revolutionary experiment was doomed to fail because it was contrary to "the pattern of nature" and to the lessons of history the English had drawn from their own ill-advised tinkering with the original contract between king and people. In their wisdom, they had made sure that a second revolution would never be necessary.

The glorious Revolution had done away with the very possibility of revolution, rendering it "almost impracticable for any future sovereign to compel the states of the kingdom to have again recourse to those violent remedies" (39). The sense of historical continuity (Burke's "tradition") was precisely what distinguished the British character from the utopian radicalism of the revolutionary bushwhackers who gleefully cleared away, "as mere rubbish," the generous profusion of the natural world, turning it into the artificial, frozen landscape of a methodically redesigned environment.

The critique of the "drunken delirium" that was the French Revolution has for its counterpart the celebration of the genius of English politics, of the superiority of a people wise enough to complement "the fallible and feeble contrivances of reason" with the preservation of "the method of nature." The practical conservatism of the English mind should have been a lesson to its fickle, speculative neighbors across the Channel: "Thanks to our sullen resistance to innovation, thanks to the cold sluggishness of our national character, we still bear the stamp of our forefathers" (99).

For Burke, the "noble freedom" of the English rested on a deep respect for "a patrimony derived from their forefathers," sole guarantors of "the rights of Englishmen." While the "rights of men" were based on abstract principles and "general theories," English centenary franchises were rooted in the inheritance of tradition: "For reasons worthy of that practical wisdom which superseded their theoretic science, [the members of Parliament] preferred this positive, recorded, *hereditary* title to all which can be dear to the man and the citizen, to that vague speculative right, which exposed their sure inheritance to be scrambled for and torn to pieces by every wild litigious spirit" (44).

In his *Nationalism, Romanticism and the Revolt against Theory*, David Simpson documents the remarkable continuity with which "the British tradition of fetishizing common sense" has defined itself time and again in opposition to the twin perils of emotionalism and abstract systematic thinking evidenced by the Jacobins' destruction of the old order. The French worshipers of Reason were prone to the most irrational fits of Gallic frenzy. Rousseau exhibited to the highest degree this combination of psychosocial pathologies so abhorrent to what Burke referred to as "our wishes and temperament."

Burke portrayed the author of *The Social Contract* and *The New Eloisa* as addicted to metaphysical speculation and the coarsest sensuality, his works a "ferocious medley of pedantry and lewdness." Jean-Jacques's life itself had shown to what abysses of debauchery and "disgustful amours" the doctrine of libertine materialism could lead the Gallic intelligentsia. The demonization of the French character served to highlight the superiority of the English one. The British newspaper *The Anti-Jacobin* opined that the example of Rousseau's life and works, a mixture of personal immorality and misguided political views, only enhanced by contrast "the solid, strong understanding, the power, and habits of cool and profound investigation which distinguish the British philosophers" (cited in Simpson, 72–73, 80).

The rhetoric of the happy medium, of the tempered middle ground, generated a wide range of cultural judgments directed first at the French, and later at the Germans. Both peoples were similarly guilty of an excessive love of system *and* an unbounded sensibility that shaped collective *mentalités* in all sorts of areas, from political philosophy to architecture and literature. The revolt against theory meant that the rhetoricians of the English national idiom found in the Romantic sublime a welcomed antidote to the dry abstraction of the general theories of the rationalist camp. At the same time, however, the "cold sluggishness of the national character" prevented them from indulging in the immoderate transports of German emotionalism.

The result was a compromise, the adoption of what Simpson calls a domesticated and nationalized sublime, which formed the centerpiece of a conception of English literature as "the avoidance of excess of any sort: political, sexual, or stylistic" (131). Literature was therefore defined as a gentleman's activity, the art of the amateur and the connoisseur rather than of the professional critic, or worse, of the philosopher of aesthetics. This type of aristocratic practice was informed "less by form than humor"; it enticed a "measured disorder," as spontaneous and free as an English garden, precisely. The business of literature was to be as distant from what the Earl of Shaftesbury had stigmatized as the "methodic or scholastic manner of the precise and strait-laced professor in a university" as it was from the delirious hyperbole of the continental Romantics (47).[2]

LIBERALISM AS UNCONSCIOUS

A half-century ago, Louis Hartz argued that American political culture was mostly scripted in the liberal idiom. Lockeanism was the natural ideology of the New World, and its invisible, taken-for-granted naturalness was a direct result of the absence of feudalism in the primitive setting of the American experience.[3] "America represents the liberal mechanism of Europe functioning without the European social antagonisms, but the truth is, it is only through these antagonisms that we recognize the mechanisms" (16). By crossing the Atlantic, the liberal creed lost both its enemies and the institutional structures against which it had defined itself in the Old World. Consequently, it went underground and lived a secret, subterranean existence, becoming invisible to those who embraced it and put it into practice. "The submerged and absolute faith" in natural liberalism turned it into "a psychological whole, embracing the nation and inspiring unanimous decisions" (14).

The very absence of a liberal movement or party was for Hartz further evidence of the overwhelming force of the liberal ethos in American history. Anticipating some of the critiques of contemporary communitarians, the historian agreed with Tocqueville that the tyranny of the majority was a permanent temptation of the American experiment, the dark underside of freedom, the result of consensus gone awry. In the course of his demonstration, Hartz also referred to the ideological controversies of the 1790s. British society, he said, with all its Old World social inequalities and cultural hierarchies, had paradoxically been more able to preserve the pluralistic nature of the liberal project by keeping together the two sides of the liberal coin, the conservatism of Burke, holding the radicalism of Paine in check:[4]

> Freedom in the fullest sense implies both variety and equality; but history, for reasons of its own, chose to separate these two principles, leaving the one with the old society of Burke and giving the other to the new society of Paine. America, as a kind of natural fulfillment of Paine, has been saddled throughout its history with the defect which this fulfillment involves, so that a country like England, in the very midst of his ramshackle class-ridden atmosphere, seems to contain an indefinable germ of liberty, a respect for the privacies of life, that America cannot duplicate. (57)

There lay at the bottom of the American experience of freedom, Hartz felt, some "inarticulate premise of conformity." Writing in the midst of McCarthy's red scare, the historian argued that in moments of intense national crisis, the liberal credo had taken on ominous hegemonic proportions, hardening into a divisive brand of nationalism: "We have only had the American Way of Life, a nationalist articulation of Locke which usually does not know that Locke himself is involved . . . Locke has a hidden conformitarian germ to begin with, since natural law tells equal people equal things, but when this germ is fed by the explosive power of modern nationalism, it mushrooms into something quite remarkable. One can reasonably wonder about the liberty one finds in Burke" (11).

Many have since qualified Hartz's contention, and numerous studies have attempted to show that American political thought was never as consensually Lockean as his concept of the liberal society had implied. Some have stressed the importance of the classical republican or civic humanist tradition in shaping political ideologies in the eighteenth and early nineteenth centuries. Admittedly, the consensus was never perfect, and competing versions of the most desirable polity, from Southern conservatism to socialism and present-day communitarianism, have always been there.[5] Nevertheless, it seems right to assert that Americans even today, in the words of Gillis J. Harp, "continue to enjoy greater agreement about political and economic fundamentals than do Western Europeans" (4).

In fact, in the eyes of many of those western Europeans, the current public debate in America is entirely framed within the parameters of the liberal consensus. To the foreign observer raised in the northern European social-democratic fold or in the southern European "Jacobin" tradition, both conservative Republicans and left-leaning Democrats are but various kinds of liberals. The former are *economic* liberals in the nineteenth-century classical sense of the term, even if their apology of free-market forces has been tempered, at least since the New Deal, with a modicum of acceptance of the basic outlines of the modern welfare state (with the exception of the libertarian wing of the conservative camp). As for left-wing, New Deal Democrats, they are in the eyes of many Continental socialists nothing more than *social* and *cultural* liberals who attempt to correct, through government intervention, the most glaring inequalities and social pathologies generated by a capitalist economy none of them is prepared to live without.

Even the most radical forms of militancy in the contemporary United States, from multiculturalism to women's or gay rights movements, are often derided in Europe for their undue concern with the superstructural aspects of power inequalities (discrimination, prejudice, intolerance, unethical conduct, etc.) while they remain quite uncritical of capitalism itself, sometimes openly celebrating consumerism as liberation. At best, the claims of all those radical movements are nothing but a call for the *extension* of the franchises of the liberal project to individuals and groups heretofore excluded from full participation in an open, egalitarian, democratic society. In no major way do they call into question the basic tenets of the liberal program. More than ever, for foreign (and domestic) critics of liberalism, American political life today, in the absence of any viable alternative to liberalism, seems to be driven by the need to narrow the gap between liberal theory and liberal practice, between the ideals of the democratic project and their imperfect realization in society. In this view, the difference between the literary traditionalists and the radicalized liberals currently enlisted in the culture wars is little more than the contemporary transcription of old liberal positions; the difference, say, between the liberal conservatism of Burke and the liberal radicalism of Paine, or between Hamiltonian Whigs and Jeffersonian Democrats.

A TALE OF TWO REVOLUTIONS

The French Revolution did have a profound effect on the politics of the early Republic. The storming of the Bastille and the tumultuous events that followed had as deep and lasting an impact on American public opinion as it did on British political culture, creating similar divisions among ardent supporters of the sister Republic and horrified opponents of the politics of Terror. In their introduction to a collection of selected letters and papers on the French Revolution by major American contemporaries, Jean-Pierre Dormois and Simon P. Newman write that it was probably the topic in foreign policy that divided American opinion the most until the Vietnam War (18).

America, like Britain, soon had its own homegrown brand of Jacobins, who participated from 1793 to 1795 in dozens of patriotic clubs or "societies" dedicated to the propagation of the transatlantic republican ideals of liberty, equality, and anti-aristocratism. Members organized regular meetings and banquets celebrating the festivals of the French and American revolutionary calendars, commented on recent events in Europe, planted trees of liberty after the French manner, proudly sported the tricolor, drank to the health of the heroes of both revolutions, and sang revolutionary songs in the tongue of Rousseau and Robespierre.

Their Federalist opponents witnessed with increasing trepidation the unfolding of this "Jacobin Phrenzy," the unraveling of the implacable logic of external war and internal terror by which the Revolution, as the phrase goes, ended up devouring its own children. The writings of the most prominent witnesses of these events display a range of opinions and arguments strikingly similar to those advanced by contemporary French historians during the Bicentennial dispute. The central questions of the 1989 debate ("Was 1789 already fraught with 1793?" and "Do the circumstances of the moment [the foreign and civil wars] explain, and to a certain extent excuse, the Terror?") similarly divided the American interpreters of the Jacobin Revolution in the 1790s.

In the spring of 1789, Gouverneur Morris still assured George Washington, from Paris, that the United States had "every reason to wish that the [French] Patriots may be successful . . . I say that we have an Interest in the Liberty of France. The Leaders here are our Friends. Many of them have imbibed their Principles in America and all have been fired by our Example" (60). At the time Jefferson also was confident that the King and his ministers were prepared to grant the French nation the constitution bearing the stamp of the balance of powers that the people expected. A few months later, Franklin still hoped that the flames of freedom that were spreading across Europe would "act on human rights like fire on gold," purifying without destroying them.[6]

By August 1790, however, the *Gazette of the United States* expressed doubt about who was governing France—the Assembly, the people it represented, the National Guard, or the Parisian mob? The Revolution may have instituted a democratic government, the newspaper wrote, but certainly not a regime of freedom.[7] The King's beheading dealt a violent blow to the French cause in America. William Bentley noted in his journal on 25 March 1793 that the French had just lost the ascendancy they had held for so long over the hearts of all Americans.

Jefferson persisted in his support of Jacobin politics, writing to William Short on 3 January 1793 that he would rather see the earth devastated than witness the failure of the cause. He had been deeply saddened, he wrote, by the tragic deaths of people he knew and admired ("In the struggle which was necessary, many guilty persons fell without the form of trial, and with them some innocent") but he mourned them "as I should have done had they fallen in battle." Not only was the Revolution necessary, but it meant war, and as such produced unavoidable casualties. "It was necessary to use the arm of the people," he contended, "a machine . . . blind to a certain degree . . . My own affections have been deeply wounded by some of the martyrs to this cause, but rather than it should have failed I would have seen half of the earth desolated; were there but an Adam and an Eve left in every country, and left free, it would be better than as it now is" (10).

The pro-Jacobin faction put forward some of the same arguments used by those who, in France and elsewhere for the past two hundred years, have explained, if not justified, the excesses of the Terror by "exceptional circumstances," both internal and external: the reactionary coalition of kings and *émigrés* besieging the new nation, the counterrevolutionary upheavals in Brittany and Vendée, the corruption and treachery of those former revolutionaries who put their personal interests before the common good and undermined the cause. In February 1794, in the midst of the terrorist period, Nathaniel Cutting rejoiced in the sudden military reversal that gave the army of the Great Nation a sudden advantage over the forces of European reaction. Although he claimed not to overlook the crimes of the ruling party in France, no doubt motivated by what he called too great a desire for freedom, Cutting believed nevertheless that isolated and temporary calamities are sometimes needed to achieve the common good.[8]

Hamilton objected, denouncing "the horrid and systematic massacres of the 2.d & 3.d of September," thundering against Marat and Robespierre, "the notorious prompters of those bloody scenes." Any comparison between the cause of France and that of America during its revolution, he argued in 1793, was totally unwarranted:

> Would to Heaven that we would discern in the Mirror of French affairs, the same humanity, the same decorum, the same gravity, the

same order, the same dignity, the same solemnity, which distinguished the cause of the American Revolution . . . I own, I do not like the comparison . . . When I observe that Marat and Robertspierre [*sic*] . . . sit triumphantly at the Convention . . . I acknowledge that, I am glad to believe, there is no real resemblance between what was the cause of America & what is the cause of France—that the difference is less great than that between Liberty and Licentiousness. (475–76)[9]

Hamilton, echoing Burke, argued that the political theories of the French radicals were opposed to human nature and oblivious to the lessons of experience, and bemoaned the fact that the convulsions on the other side of the Atlantic exerted such a fascination on those of his compatriots who should know better than to be fooled by the revolutionary mystique. Noah Webster, for his part, ascribed "the political madness and barbaric fury" of the revolutionaries to the ideological hubris of their abstract utopianism, their arrogant belief in the possibility of legislating human minds. As long as "the legislators of France confined themselves to a correction of *real evils,* they were the most respectable of reformers: they commanded the attention, the applause and the admiration of surrounding nations. But when they descended to legislate upon *names, opinions* and *customs,* they could have no influence upon liberty or social rights, they became contemptible" (21).

The political disaster that was the French Revolution was rooted in long established features of the French character, a mixture of conceptual arrogance, love of abstraction, and disregard for the teachings of experience that Webster called "the system of reason." John Adams wrote in 1811 that "the philosophers of France were too rash and hasty":

They understood not what they were about. They miscalculated their forces and resources: and were consequently overwhelmed in destruction with all their theories. The precipitation and temerity of philosophers has, I fear, retarded the progress of improvement and amelioration in the condition of mankind for at least a hundred years. The public mind was improving in knowledge and the public heart in humanity, equity, and benevolence. . . . But the philosophers must arrive at perfection *per saltum.* Ten times more furious than Jack in the Tale of a Tub, they rent and tore the whole garment to pieces and left not one whole thread in it. What an amiable and glo-

rious Equality, Fraternity and Liberty they have now established in
Europe! (cited in Boorstin, 178)

THE ROOTS OF FRENCH ILLIBERALISM

Tony Judt's study of postwar French intellectual life is predicated upon a
deeply held (and widely shared) belief in the moral shortcoming of the
French intelligentsia going back to the days of Burke and John Adams. In
Judt's view, the moral failure of the French men of letters explains why the
most prominent among them turned a blind eye to, or found every possible excuse for, the violence of Stalinism: "At the heart of the engagement
of the 1940s and 1950s there lay an unwillingness to think seriously about
public ethics, an unwillingness amounting to an incapacity" (229).

In the introduction to *Past Imperfect,* Judt disparages the kind of intellectual history that looks for a *longue durée* in the realm of ideas and explains
specific developments in terms of influences going back hundreds of years.[10]
He nevertheless proceeds to discuss "the Frenchness of French intellectuals" and other "peculiarities of French political thought" based on cultural
continuities that predate the modern era. The specific words and actions of
the postwar leftist intelligentsia are thus interpreted within the context of
an age-old tradition that encompasses the medieval doctrines of French letters as the continuation of Greco-Roman antiquity *(translatio studii)* and
of the manifest destiny of the French nation as the privileged expression of
God's Kingdom *(gesta Dei per Francos).* These cultural continuities are presented as the outcome of centuries-old sociological developments that have
also made intellectuals so prominent in French life and that account for
other specific "inherited characteristics" of the French intelligentsia: "Ever
since the eighteenth century, the French intellectual (to employ a convenient anachronism) has displayed certain distinctive traits" (248).

Beyond the play of cultural factors harking back to medieval Catholicism and ancien régime absolutism, the ethical shortcoming of the intelligentsia is said to have more immediate, middle-range sources. The singular weakness of the French liberal tradition is critical to the country's
political inadequacy (when compared, of course, to Britain and the United
States). The moral deficiency of the postwar intellectuals was due in large
part to "the widely held belief that morally binding judgments of a normative sort were undermined by their historical and logical association
with the politics and economics of liberalism" (229).

The paradoxical outcome of such a belief system is that a prosperous country with a large educated elite and a long history of enlightened philosophical views, a country that can be said to have grounded modern politics on the collective assertion of human rights, harbored such a long-lasting hostility toward the traditional questions of the liberal worldview. What sets France apart from Britain and the United States is that its popular classes have looked for the theoretical legitimization of their struggle against the bourgeoisie *outside* of the liberal tradition, which explains why there never was in France a viable left liberalism akin to British or American radicalism. In France, as in much of Continental Europe, liberalism came to mean something rather different, since "it connoted a social arrangement where a new secular ruling class availed itself of the former language of opposition to secure its own status against the claims of the revolutionary class below" (232).

For Judt, the riddle of the French Revolution lies in this, that rights lost their extrapolitical status, became an object of suspicion, and ceased to be taken seriously (233). He revisits here the central issue of the French Bicentennial debate: how did 89 turn into 93, when and how did the revolutionary process drift away from the discourse and practice of rights (the theme of the *dérive totalitaire*) or, more dramatically, skid off the liberal road into the abyss of Terror (Furet's *dérapage*)? Judt's argument, although in keeping with a long line of liberal theorists, from Burke and Constant to Tocqueville and Isaiah Berlin, interestingly parts company with the Tocquevillean emphasis on the role of the centralization of the state in the failure of the liberal principles of 1789.

The roots of the failure of liberalism are not to be found in the legacy of a *dirigiste* Colbertist tradition, but in the internal contradictions of the liberal project itself (233). For reasons having to do with the immediate political context, the discourse of rights was used to legitimize the new power, to replace the royal sovereign with a national-democratic one. But with this new, positive role, rights lost their earlier "negative" function, that of limiting government and protecting the individual against the encroachments of public power.

It is at this point of the argumentation that the reference to the American revolution as a counterexample to the French one, as an instance of successful safeguarding of the central tenets of the liberal program, becomes strategically important. The contrast between 1789 and 1776, between the two competing and incompatible models of the Age of Democracy, helps illuminate the paradoxes of modern French political culture and points to its endemic pathology. Contrary to their American counterparts, who had been protected from the abuses of absolutism by the very political system against which they rebelled, the French revolutionaries were unable to proclaim without being challenged the "self-evidence" of the popular will or their own "natural" authority as self-appointed representative voices of that same collective will.

Although Judt claimed earlier in *Past Imperfect* that the French liberal only had themselves, and their immediate situation, to blame for their failures, he reintroduces at this point in his argument the weight of history and the imprint of tradition. If the revolutionaries wrongfully used the rights of the people as "an incantation in defense of a claim to authority that was otherwise extremely unsteady and fragile," it is because they were "burdened by centuries of monarchical and clerical authority" (234). And so it happened that, very early in the course of the Revolution, the language and practice of rights underwent a considerable transformation, described, in classical liberal fashion, as the passage from a conception of the natural, individual *rights* of man as predating the social contract to a statist and oppressive notion of the collective *duties* of the citizen, "from a device with which to defend the individual person against the overpowerful ruler [to] the basis for advancing the claims of the whole against the interests of its parts" (234).

From this point on, the emancipatory program of the revolutionaries was irremediably vitiated. The only legitimate source of law being the government, "the idea of rights in France became dependent upon the superior claims of the all-powerful authority of the Assembly . . . The very rights of the people that gave the revolutionary governments their legitimacy also gave them the authority to restrict the practice of rights and liberties by that same people" (235). The Jacobins and their republican disciples no longer asked for whom they should govern but to what end, substituting positive entitlements to Mill's negative liberties as the goals of their ambitious program of social engineering.

The pathology of the French political culture rests in its fateful tendency to subordinate the individual to the collectivity, a tendency that found a lasting theoretical expression in the holistic categories of positivism, taken to be the overarching philosophical framework of French political discourse whether in its progressive (Saint-Simon) or reactionary (Maurras) versions. Saint-Simonian theory, developed by Comte as a historicist philosophy of human development, "nullified any concern for the isolated individual" (235).[11]

Judt's point here is that French culture *as a whole,* regardless of the obvious diversity of aesthetic sensitivities and political affiliations that make up its postrevolutionary history, is allergic to pluralism and ambiguity, a view shared by many Anglo-American critics of the French character. Even the French liberals of the Guizot generation came to support a strong executive for fear of popular unrest, renouncing the utilitarian or ethical individualism of their British counterparts (240).

The French hostility to the open society has its roots in a fondness for abstract universalism that cuts across political divisions: "Left and Right alike shared a vision of the intellectual as someone defined by a search for truth in abstractions; distaste for the confusions and realities of public life; and fascination with the exotic, the aesthetic and the absolute" (242). In Anglo-American eyes, the archetypal French theorist combines a doctrinaire love of abstraction with a strong commitment to communitarian values, a mixture of abstract principled rationalism and emotional, often irrational, attachment to the national community that early nineteenth-century British conservative opinion, as we have seen, found realized to the highest degree in the life and works of Rousseau and, by extension, in the behavior of his most zealous disciples in the revolutionary vanguard.

Sunil Khilnani's study of the intellectual left in postwar France, *Arguing Revolution,* shares this distaste for the utopian propheticism of the Gallic literati. Khilnani sees the need to belong to a larger community both as a central component of the notion of intellectual commitment and as a structural feature of the French life of ideas. To be an intellectual in France, he argues, is to share in a collective identity. The Dreyfus affair saw the emergence of "the intellectuals" as a distinctive social category in large part because it was a struggle over "the fundamental political character and identity of France: over whether that identity was best represented in the form of the Republic, an institutional form of the universal and universalizing project begun by the French Revolution, or by a more local (racial) definition of the nation" (12).

For Khilnani, the link between the definitions of political community and intellectual identity became a constant feature of the self-definition of the French intelligentsia. It accounts for the fact that "one important source of authority for intellectuals in the postwar decades was their ability to claim experience of or participation in collective political activity"

(13). The dialogic practice of "arguing revolution" answered the intellectuals' need to inscribe themselves in a particular community. For Sartre, Althusser, and others on the Left, the language of revolution was, as Khilnani puts it, "a resource with which to construct both an image of the political community, and of the role of the intellectual in relation to it" (15).

Judt, for his part, argues that the rhetoric of commitment among postwar existentialists had everything to do with the need to feel like a part of the movement of history and to exchange the anxieties of Cartesian doubt and critical distance for the certainties of shared collective action with the proletariat and colonized peoples. The virulent anti-individualism that is endemic to French cultural identity informs the Constitution of 1848, which does away with all reference to the rights of man (forever discredited as "bourgeois") and endorses instead "the collective rights of socially determined units of people (citizens, workers, children, families, and so on)," that is, "claim rights" or entitlements, "charges upon the community in return for the performance of social and political duties" (237). The shift from rights to duties to entitlements illustrates the dominance of collectivistic and organicist representations of the social in the French imagination.

FRENCH REPUBLICANS AND THE LIBERAL ETHOS

The real thrust of Judt's critique, however, is not so much directed at the 1793 Jacobins or even at the 1848 Democrats and Socialists, but, strangely enough, at the more moderate, liberal-minded, compromise-inclined leaders of the Third Republic. What their predecessors failed to do, in part because of their radicalism, the opportunistic Republicans successfully brought about: the marginalization of liberalism (in Judt's sense of the word) as a viable political force, and the elimination of individual rights language in constitutional documents and courts until at least after the end of World War II. "Of all the enemies of liberalism and rights," the Republicans proved to be the most "deadly" because they managed to stay in power for so long, replacing the ideal of liberty with the unitary notion of "a universal and undifferentiated democracy" (240). "The manner of their success," Judt concludes, "placed the final nail on the coffin of liberal thought in France" (238).

Such an assertion is paradoxical, even bewildering at first, since the Third Republic, as Judt himself acknowledges, ended up granting its citizens many of the rights that had been at the core of the liberal program since the days of Locke, Hume, Kant, and Spinoza: right to a free press, to an elementary education, to property. Despite their obsession with reuniting the nation, avoiding social tensions, and shunning any association with the Socialists, the *Opportunistes* even accorded the people the right to strike and form unions. Many histories of Western political thought, even in the English-speaking world, readily include some members of the French republican family as representatives of the liberal ethos.

In *French Political Thought in the Nineteenth-Century,* R. H. Soltau writes that during the early years of the Third Republic, middle-class liberals "had really very little to complain from the Government and the majority of cabinets in office during those years were, under various labels, composed of representatives of the Liberal tradition" (295). E. K. Bramsted and K. J. Melhuish concur with Soltau in their anthology, *Western Liberalism,* remarking that "the loose dividing line between liberals and *radicaux* in France is often difficult to discern" (70). They go on to quote Jules Simon, the first genuinely republican prime minister of the new regime, who expressed the hope in his *La politique radicale* that "power, if it is faithful to his mission, must work with persevering energy toward its own elimination" (73).

More recently, William Logue devoted a whole book to the rise of what he calls a new liberalism in republican circles during the years preceding World War I. Many of the new liberal theorists he includes in his *From Philosophy to Sociology: The Evolution of French Liberalism, 1870–1914* are indeed Republicans, from Simon and Renouvier to Durkheim. Logue goes so far as to speak of "a Jacobin strain in French liberalism"! (3). Far from being a marginal phenomenon, a carryover from an earlier, happier, liberal era, the new liberalism is described as "the most significant aspect of French political and social thought in the period 1870–1914" (11). Opposed to the "selfish individualism of the earlier part of the century," the new liberalism stressed the social as well as the individual and "admitted a role for the state that was not merely one of necessity but one justified by liberal theory" (2).[12] It was clearly a phenomenon of the Left, since most of its representatives belonged to the petty bourgeois *centre-gauche,* "the vital pivot of political life in the Third Republic" (16).

The paradoxical fact that the new ideology has been neglected by Anglo-American scholarship is not a reflection of its marginality, but rather of its prevalence: middle-of-the-road, centrist ideas were the main current back then, and students of ideas are more attracted to the extremes, such as socialism or right-wing nationalism (Logue, 1). Obviously, the definition and scope of what Logue calls liberalism are quite different from Judt's, for whom there is no such thing as a liberal brand of French republicanism before 1945. Logue himself remarks that one major "obstacle to any comprehensive study of French liberalism is the difficulty in agreeing on which thinkers should be considered liberals . . . No more than in other places, no more than in other times, no more than other political terms, did the word 'liberalism' have a single, clear, commonly accepted meaning in the France of the *Belle Epoque*" (xi, 5). All these objections, however, are somewhat irrelevant to Judt's argument since for him the democratic aspects of the *Opportunistes'* program should not be mistaken for liberal ones. Judt's almost libertarian definition of liberalism as a mixture of radical individualism and extreme attachment to empirical diversity and epistemological pluralism precludes any recognition that the moderate Republicans achieved, within the framework of a long tradition of administrative centralization, at least some of the goals of the liberal program. The illiberalism of the Opportunistes had nothing to do with the content of the laws they promulgated. Rather, their republicanism was illiberal in that they conceived of rights not as guaranteed and protected ("negatively") by the vigilance of the people with the help of specific institutional mechanisms such as the balance of power, but as *given* to them by a sovereign, paternalistic power that knew in its infinite and benevolent wisdom what was best for them.

The vision of France as a moral person and of Frenchness as a morally superior national identity embodying civic virtue in its highest form implied the denial of differences within the national fabric. The messiness of the real and open-ended character of the liberal conversation described by Isaiah Berlin and Karl Popper[13] is precisely what the French republican doctrinaires could not and would not acknowledge because of the mixture of idealism and scientism they adhered to. The absolutist bent of French culture explains that the liberal space of the negotiation of difference has always been excluded from "the epistemological universe" of the progressive intellectual.

CONSTANT, ROUSSEAU, AND THE GENERAL WILL

I have quoted extensively from Judt's views because they are fairly representative of the traditional Anglo-American liberal critique of the French national idea. Liah Greenfeld argues in a similar vein that dominant conceptions of the political have subordinated the individual to the collective with remarkable consistency throughout French history. Greenfeld presents the genealogy of Frenchness as the successive reincarnations, transmutations, and displacements of a highly integrated image of national identity:

> The evolution of the French identity—from a religious-Christian to a political-royalist one with only vague religious overtones, which was in turn supplanted by national identity—implied two successive changes in the ultimate bases of legitimacy and fundamental values. The divinely appointed French king replaced the Christian Church, of which he had been the eldest son, and the state (which in France eventually became coterminous with the nation) replaced the French King. Each time, the new identity grew under the auspices of the old one and received its importance from association with it, yet, in favorable circumstances, it helped to bring about the neutralization, if not the destruction of the latter. (91)

In straightforward Tocquevillean fashion, Greenfeld sees the republican conception of the nation as a relic of the past, a survival of the absolutist state in democratic times. First, the doctrine of the divine right of kings "deified" the French polity, paradoxically facilitating the transference of the sacred from the person of the king to the authority of his state. Richelieu's policies were critical to this process of secularization and depersonalization of religiously sanctioned royal authority. Since "the state . . . was thus acquiring an existence separate from the king . . . it was not yet an independent object of loyalty, but it was a new object of loyalty nonetheless" (118). Greenfeld is quick to point out that this "emergent sphere of the sacred . . . was diametrically antithetical to the definition of 'nation' as it had evolved in England." Richelieu's reasons of state were not aimed at serving the "general good" or the "public interest" the English reformers had in mind. Absolutism, understood as a conception of the political in which "authority was to be centralized in *one* source" (my emphasis), is for Greenfeld nothing short of "an aspiring totalitarianism" (119).

During the eighteenth century, the concept of nation imported from Britain was "grafted on a body of indigenous traditions which gave it a unique twist and led the French nation away from the example on which it was initially modeled" (156). In the course of this process, the original English notion, forged in the struggle against the arbitrary power of a centralized royal authority, was eventually put to the service of an "enthronement of the nation as the origin of all values" (166). Far from representing a decisive break with earlier absolutist tendencies, the new definition of the collective being transferred to the nation the attributes of the king's state, "its unitary, abstract character, the indivisibility of sovereignty" (167). In other words, the nation became king. The French revolutionaries had therefore submitted the English idea to a fateful misappropriation, a kind of conceptual highjacking, turning it from a powerful metaphor for the association of free, rational individuals into "a super-human collective person" (167), an abstraction endowed with all the characteristics of the deity.

One of the sources of the liberal view of what is wrong with the French conception of the political is to be found in France. In his famous *The Liberty of the Ancients Compared with That of the Moderns* (1819), Benjamin Constant, while acknowledging the principle of the sovereignty of the people, called for its limitation in view of the excesses committed in its name. The leaders of the Revolution had erroneously believed that "everything should give way before collective will, and that all the restrictions on individual rights would be amply compensated by participation in social power" (320). In a well-known passage, Constant suggested that "the system of the most illustrious" of the philosophers, Jean-Jacques Rousseau, was in part responsible for the erring ways of the revolutionaries. "Transposing into our modern age an extent of social power, of collective sovereignty which belonged to other centuries," Constant remarked of Rousseau, "this sublime genius, animated by the purest love of liberty, has nevertheless furnished deadly pretexts for more than one kind of tyranny" (318).

Constant, it is true, later remarked that Mably rather than Rousseau must be held responsible for accrediting the nefarious view, borrowed from the maxims of ancient liberty, that "demands that the citizens should be entirely subjected in order for the nation to be sovereign, and that the individual should be enslaved for the people to be free" (318). Constant, being French, was condemned to live in a postrevolutionary culture permeated with the memory of the Great Revolution as founding myth, whether idealized or demonized. Perhaps caught up in the typically Gallic respect for philosophical figures, regardless of the erroneousness of their theories, he reserved his harshest criticisms for the philosophical and political disciples of Rousseau, rather than "the sublime genius" himself.

Greenfeld, writing two centuries later as a foreign scholar of French national culture, feels no need to hold back: "The revolutionary rhetoric drew on the ideas developed during several preceding decades; its idiom, specifically, was that of the *Social Contract*" (172–73). Rousseau, she goes on, "advocated nothing less than a totalitarian state with no intermediate bodies between the central power and the mass of atomized individuals" (174). The link between the citizen of Geneva's assertion that "the general will is always in the right" and the authoritarian outlook of his Jacobin interpreters is patent: "Through the idea of the indivisible and sovereign general will," the nation was "conceptualized as an autonomous entity, existing above and independently of the wills of its individual members and dominating their wills" (175).

Rousseau is for Greenfeld the key to the continuity of French cultural and political history, the vital link between the absolutist past and the monological future (the nation as republic): "Rousseau's concept of society closely corresponded to the concept of the Divine Right 'state' elaborated under Richelieu; it was its abstract and generalized descendant" (175). Furthermore, *The Social Contract* shaped the Comtean positivists' views of the superiority of the group over its individual members and of the crucial role the Platonic philosopher-savant was called to play in the elaboration of a just and rational society: "The Will of the nation was to speak through an elite of virtue—the legislator and the elective aristocracy, whom Rousseau sometimes confused with the Nation itself—thus modifying the meaning of the concept of equality as well" (176).

Greenfeld's reading of Rousseau's political treatises implies that the concept of general will, although contradictory at times, is quite transparent in its political consequences: it combines elitism and authoritarianism into a totalitarian project. Many French interpreters of Rousseau, even critics of Jacobinism such as Constant, have taken pains to dissociate the philosopher's views from their political misuses at the hands of those who claimed to draw their inspiration from him. Marx claimed he was no Marxist, and many have argued that Nietzsche was misappropriated by the ideologues of Nazism. Those who believe that the Jacobins misused *The Social Contract* contend that the notion of the general will was extremely complex and that Rousseau himself did not believe that the kind of direct democracy he was advocating in theory would ever be possible in practice.

In the context of the debate over "the return of human rights" to the forefront of French politics in the 1980s, Luc Ferry and Alain Renaut revisited the concept of general will, arguing once again that the Jacobins mistook it for "the will of all," a fateful misreading that paved the way to the dictatorship of the committees. In fact, they say, Rousseau carefully distinguished the two, as evidenced by the somewhat obscure notion of "the sum of differences" on which most of Ferry and Renaut's interpretation rests. "There is frequently a difference," Rousseau wrote, "between the will of all and the general will. The latter regards only the common interest; the former regards private interests, and is indeed but the sum of private wills: but remove from these same wills the pluses and the minuses that cancel each other, and then the general will remains as the sum of the differences" (cited in Ferry and Renaut, 52).

Ferry and Renaut start off by placing Rousseau squarely within the tradition of the philosophy of natural rights that grounds the legitimacy of political authority on the subjectivity and autonomy of human beings as rational individuals. In keeping with the *jus natural* tradition, Rousseau constitutes "the people" as subject and as sovereign. The theory of the social contract only has meaning if the people is thought of in its entirety "as an individual, an entity capable of free (voluntary) self-determination" (51).

This view of the people as a collective individual implies that the general will is not the sum total of individual wills but what Ferry and Renaut, after Alexis Philonenko,[14] call an integral, in the mathematical sense of the word, that is to say a sum of the differences among the individual wills of the members of the community. In this view, the general will is neither unanimity nor majority, since the latter is "a sum of common points among the particular wills," and not a "sum of differences":

> The general will that proclaims rights (proclaims the law) does not consist in a sum of common opinions, in a sum of identities, but rather in a harmonious integration, an attuning of viewpoints that are by definition different but in the best of cases having the same aim (the bringing into accord). We thus understand that the general will can be described as based on both the whole social body and each particular individual: based on the whole, it is the resultant or integral of all the particular viewpoints; based on the individual, it is, according to Rousseau's formula, "a pure act of the intellect, reasoning, while passions are silent, on what man can demand of his fellow man, and on what his fellow man can demand of him." (54)

The point of the whole exposition is that Rousseau's hostility to intermediary bodies, parties, and other interest groups that "fragment" the general will is not the result of a fundamental antidemocratic allergy to pluralism but on the contrary stems from a superdemocratic concern that each and every one of the individual differences be taken into account in the process of harmonization. Rousseau's social contract implies that individuals will make a reasonable use of their free will, and will never overstep their rights, resisting selfish urges and keeping their passions under sway. The unrealistic character of such an expectation did not escape the philosopher, prompting him to regret that one must have a "legislator," and even worse, a government. Rousseau readily conceded that the polity he had conceived of would only suit a race of gods and was not designed for ordinary mortals.

For Ferry and Renaut, the liberal critique of *The Social Contract* is both unfair and inaccurate, since it ascribes designs and intentions to Rousseau that a careful reading of his writings does not substantiate. He did not advocate the Terror, since the ideal deployment of the general will precludes the existence of any intermediary political body that would represent, let alone interpret and implement, the will of the sovereign. Far from facilitating totalitarianism, the doctrine of the general will can be construed in liberal fashion "as a theory of the limits of the state," for it is necessary, in Rousseau's words, "to distinguish properly between the respective rights of the citizens and the Sovereign, and between the duties which the former have to fulfill in their quality as subject, and the natural right which they ought to enjoy in their quality as men" (cited in Ferry and Renaut, 62). Rousseau was perfectly aware that the general will was a purely utopian concept, an idea of Reason rather than an applicable program of government. Therefore, it is illegitimate to link what was a purely speculative category to the politics of the Revolutionary Terror. Just as Stalin was not in Marx, or Hitler in Nietzsche, Robespierre was not in Rousseau.[15]

THE HEXAGONAL *HISTORIKERSTREIT*

This reappraisal of Rousseau's theory of the general will in relation to the Jacobin Terror, and more generally, to the whole republican tradition, took place against the backdrop of the intense controversy generated in France by the celebration of the Bicentennial of the Revolution of 1789. Dozens of books, essays, dictionaries, and monographs were published in the decade preceding the event, sparking a contentious debate among scholars and public intellectuals alike. The first salvo in what would prove to be a protracted, and bloody, interpretive war was fired in 1978 by François Furet, who claimed in his influential *Interpreting the French Revolution* that the whole thing was finally over, meaning that the French were no longer divided in any substantial way along the lines of the competing readings of the originary myth that had prevailed for the past two hundred years. What Steven Kaplan has derisively described as "the hexagonal *Historikerstreit* (-manqué)" ultimately evolved into a full-fledged historians' feud exhibiting a somewhat "triangular configuration, with the three corners represented by Furet, Pierre Chaunu and Michel Vovelle," the latter symbolizing, on each side of a "centrist," revisionist Furetian reading, the traditional rightist and leftist interpretations of the Revolution (9).

The United States, both past and present, had a prominent place in the battle of the Bicentennial: the American revolution provided the liberal revisionists (Kaplan's "Furetian galaxy") with a powerful counterexample and a striking illustration of what had gone wrong with the Jacobin experiment, while American culture became once again a foil in the hands of their neorepublican and Marxisant opponents.[16] All agreed, implicitly or not, that the two moments, the 1780s and the 1980s, were indeed intimately connected, since the diverging paths taken by both countries at the start of the democratic adventure had ultimately come full circle in the post–Cold War triumph of liberal individualism and the cultural Americanization of the planet.

The contrast between the two revolutions provided many French intellectuals with a useful distanced perspective on what had been the central questions of the revolutionary epoch, of the republican era, and of the contemporary battle of the Bicentennial: the links between the "liberal moment" and the Terror, the rival conceptions of the representation of the popular will, the place of liberalism in French life, and the tension between (negative) rights and (positive) entitlements, collective goals, and private pursuits.

There are obvious similarities between Furet's reading of the *dérapage* of the Revolution and Judt's account of the deep-seated pathology of French Jacobin republicanism, a sign of the transatlantic nature of the new theoretical realignments. Both men deplored that "the liberal moment of 89" was short-lived, both ascribed the subsequent evolution of the revolutionary movement toward despotism to a mixture of long-term structural constraints (Tocqueville's administrative centralization) and short-term conjunctural factors (Cochin's Jacobin hegemony).

In their *Critical Dictionary of the French Revolution,* Furet and Mona Ozouf urged their colleagues and readers to face squarely the "despotic potentialities" inscribed in the democratic-revolutionary project. These potentialities were particularly strong in the case of a French political culture "where the representation of the sovereign people is conceived as indivisible and all-powerful" (cited in Kaplan, 63). Tony Judt acknowledges his debt to those "recent studies" that "have paid close attention to significant changes in the meaning and use of rights-language during the Revolution . . . and have drawn our attention to the importance of the Revolution as the moment at which France both embodied and formalized a certain tradition of enlightened political thought and also began to diverge from it" (233).

Prominent among these recent studies was Marcel Gauchet's *La Révolution des droits de l'homme,* published in the year of the Bicentennial. In the book, Gauchet, a close associate of Furet and prominent member of the Institut Raymond Aron, underscored the fragility of the new regime, born of the collapse of royal authority and yet condemned to substitute a new sovereignty to the defunct power of the monarchy in order to stabilize and legitimize the new political order. The Constituants' urgent "need for authority" forced them to resolve the tension "between the concern for the protections of persons and the pressing necessity to assert the sovereignty of all" in favor of the second branch of the alternative (xi).

The comparison with the American revolution, once again, highlights the singularity of the French Constituants' historical task. The French and American revolutionaries were working at the same time on the same subject matter, but the directions for use *(le mode d'emploi)* were totally divergent. While Madison and the Federalists saw the Bill of Rights (discussed in 1789, ratified in 1791) as a means to erect barriers against power in all its forms in all parts of the government, the main concern of the French was to create a new power and to ensure its continuation (xi).

In the heat of the struggle of the summer of 1789, Gauchet contends, "the number one problem had become how to transmute individual rights into the power of the nation" (xii), even at the risk of turning, if need be, the social expression of these rights as collective power against their individual enjoyment. We are on familiar ground here: the combination of circumstances (the resistance of the court and the king's dithering, the Great Fear, the peasant unrest, the threat of a counterrevolutionary insurrection, the political divisions among the revolutionaries) and the appeal of the time-tested model of monarchical authority as the best way to solve the crisis of legitimacy and consolidate the threatened gains of the Revolution will render the sacrifice of the philosophy of natural rights on the altar of the new nationalism inevitable. The revolutionary power, engaged as it was "in a mimetic relationship of appropriation vis-à-vis the royal power," was compelled to "institute itself as chosen heir to the accumulation of public power sought after by the monarchical state" (xv).

The immediate consequence of this solicitation of legacy is to transform the Nation-as-people *(la Nation-peuple)* into the Nation-as-history *(la Nation-histoire),* which Gauchet describes as the product of a "mystical union." The self-imposed task of the writers of the Declaration, from then on, will be to draw out and manifest "the will of this transcendental person . . . over and beyond any kind of particular interests" (xv). This, however, is no simple task: the releasing of the "will of the people" will entail a political conflict of interpretations that mirrors in many ways the competing philosophical readings of Rousseau's general will.

What was the authentic expression of that ever elusive legitimate voice? The clubs and *sociétés de pensée,* the *sans-culottes* sections, and the *enragés* ("the street"), or the Assembly itself? Gauchet rightly points out that at the heart of the revolutionary process there lay an inability to conceptualize political representation, described as "the blind spot of the revolutionary political imagination . . . which will bring about its failure by hemming it within the successive versions of parliamentary usurpation" (xiv).

Here again, the appeal to the American countermodel proved both heuristically fruitful and ideologically efficient, since the American reference helped discredit the French path to political modernity. Of all the contested readings of the general will, Abbé Siéyès's conception of representation, written into the Constitution of 1791, would eventually prevail. As Ferry and Renaut rightly point out, the Abbé's definition of the nation as "a whole composed of integrating parts," which Judt and Greenfeld find so unpalatable, is in sharp contrast with Rousseau's own views on the matter, which called for an "imperative mandate" through which the representatives would depend closely on those they represented.

Such a mandate was for Rousseau a necessary evil. He would have preferred to do away with any intermediary body, since ideally the popular sovereignty, being inalienable, could not really be represented. However, the size of the French nation, the tumult of passions, and the limitations of men ruled out such a possibility: if there had to be representatives, at least they needed to be strictly accountable to their constituents, expressing as well as possible their collective "will."

The idea that the deputy must voice the particular interests of those he or she represents is common to the ancien régime definition of the parliamentarian and the American view that elected representatives are not expected to vote according to their own opinions but to reflect the agenda and wishes of their constituents in accordance with the combined imperatives of justice, democracy, and pluralism. Siéyès's doctrine of the national sovereignty, on the other hand, stipulated that once elected "the representatives named in the *départements* will not be representatives of a particular *département* but of the nation as a whole" (cited in Ferry and Renaut, 63).

Siéyès's position, contrary to Rousseau's in that it admits of the necessity of an intermediary representative body (the Assembly), is at the same time extremely faithful to another aspect of the theory of the social contract, that is, the indivisibility of the popular sovereign based on the abstract uniformity of rational judgment *("la raison est une")*. Granted, one needed representatives; but at least they should be prevented from expressing the particular interests of specific social groups or from articulating regional viewpoints. "The deputy of all the citizens of the kingdom," Siéyès argued, could not "listen to the wishes only of the residents of a bailiwick or a municipality as the will of the whole nation" (64).

Of interest here is the fact that these French commentators all consider Siéyès a "liberal," while Judt and Greenfeld reject his views as the quintessential expression of French illiberal statism. Where the latter see a fateful continuity between Rousseau and Siéyès, Ferry and Renaut consider that Siéyès's doctrine of national sovereignty is "paradoxically Rousseauan," for it stems from "a theoretical space, liberalism" that lies outside the framework of the Social Contract" and "might seem a priori hostile to it" (65). Besides, Siéyès's idea of the nation is in keeping with the tradition of Enlightenment individualism and of *jus naturale*. The national community is not thought of as a hierarchy of orders but an entity made up of a multitude of equal individuals.

In this respect, French and English civic nationalisms are closely related. Gauchet, for his part, shows that the demand for "social rights" is the logical extension of the struggle for individual rights, since a society of free and equal individuals has "the secret duty" to make sure that "its members become or remain the independent and self-sufficient beings from whom it is supposed to proceed, whether regarding the assertion of their autonomy (education), their protection against dependency (assistance) or the preservation of their capacity to subsist by their own means (work)" (xxiii).

All this points to serious differences within what could be hastily construed as a new transatlantic "neoliberal" consensus on the nature of postrevolutionary French culture and history. Indeed, most of the recent readings of the Jacobin-republican tradition I have examined so far share the
same distaste for its most authoritarian and unitarian components. Beyond
this, however, there is precious little agreement on what constitutes a liberal politics, and on the proper place and function of collective goals and
state-sponsored policies within a liberal democratic agenda, past or present.

LIBERALISM REDUX

The transformation of the French intellectual field in the last twenty-five
years or so (the eclipse of Marxism, structuralism, and the related "philosophies of revolt," and the questioning of historicism and constructivism in
the social sciences) has been widely studied and debated on both sides of
the Atlantic. In France, the proponents of the new interpretive models
have sometimes overestimated the impact of these models on their fellow
intellectuals and on the reading public. As a consequence, they have hailed
the return of theoretical references and methodologies long consigned to
the margins of the French intellectual space, dominated as it has been
since the end of the fifties by the alliance of the philosophies of suspicion
(at least in its most publicized manifestations, particularly abroad).

It is unquestionable that the return of forgotten or disqualified traditions—humanism, Kantism, pragmatism, logical positivism—to the forefront of the critical scene has been the sign of a deep and lasting shaking
up of the intellectual certainties of the golden age of existential Marxism
and (post)structuralism. The renewed interest in Anglo-American thinking, from Rawls to Rorty, was welcomed by many as a sign that French
thought was, at long last, opening up to its other, and moving away from
the endless *"débats franco-français"* about desire and difference.

Among all these returns, of the philosophical subject, of historical
agency, of individual consciousness, of social praxis or human rights, the
rebirth of "liberalism" arguably had the most profound effect on contemporary French intellectual life.[17] In 1989, Régis Debray summed up
what he perceived as a profound change in French culture and society:
"Today, 'state of law' is in, 'sovereign people' is out . . . In the name of
'socialism,' the descendants of the republican party advocate and practice
liberal democracy, and Michelet has given birth to Tocqueville" (*Contretemps,* 47, 45).

Throughout the 1980s, the French intelligentsia and its readers rediscovered the charms of "democratic individualism." The story of this revelation is well known by now, and I will only recall its most salient features.[18] Louis Dumont's anthropological studies of holism and individualism, François Furet's historical reappraisal of the French Revolution and its legacy, and Gilles Lipovetsky's sociological essays on postmodern consumerism all mark important steps in a process of revisionist interpretation of the philosophical foundations and political representations of French republican culture.[19] In fact, these converging analyses had their source in a shared Tocquevillean reading of modernity that engaged the French version of the democratic adventure.

New currents of thought call for new channels of discussion and dissemination: this could well be a structural law of intellectual fields. Founded in 1980, a doubly symbolic date, since it was both the dawn of a new decade and the year of Sartre's death, *Le Débat* gathered around historian and editor Pierre Nora a new generation of academics and writers bent on settling their accounts with the native tradition of intellectual propheticism and the sequels of what was soon to be reviled as *la pensée 68*. "What can the intellectuals do?" Nora asked in the first issue, answering that they needed to democratize the use of their own power.[20]

The notoriety soon gained by the most prominent representatives of the new currents, largely due to their strategic position at the intersection of the university, the publishing industry, and the media, as well as the label of "neoliberal" their opponents immediately attached to their names, has hidden from most observers of the new intellectual scene the deeply ambivalent character of this so-called (neo)liberalism, as well as the limits of its influence on the high intelligentsia.

What may have escaped the French chroniclers of the liberalism controversy—the clash of massively globalizing worldviews and the seduction of the new (even if, in this case, the novelty was as old as the works of Benjamin Constant or Germaine de Staël)—did not elude some Anglo-American critics, intrigued by the supposed renaissance of their own tradition in the land of Maurras and Jaurès. Tony Judt, for one, is quite skeptical about "the recent waves of enthusiasm" of the French for the works of Rawls or Popper: it may very well be just another Parisian literary fashion, since, for Judt, French culture is still profoundly hostile to liberalism: "The idea that in any compromise between private rights and public interest it is the latter that must make its case is not one with which modern French

political thought is familiar. It is thus no accident that liberal political literature in France is still largely imported and no major local figure has yet
emerged to ground liberal theory in domestic experience" (314).

Judt contends that scholars such as Furet, Rosanvallon, Gauchet,
Manent, and others who, at the Ecole des Hautes Etudes and the Institut
Raymond Aron "have perpetuated and cultivated Aron's interest for liberal
theoretical and historiographical traditions so neglected in France until
now," remain a small minority (315). Marc Lilla shares Judt's strong reservations regarding the depth of the French clerisy's conversion to liberalism:
"It would be mistaken to speak of anything like a liberal consensus in
French political thought today. Few French thinkers consider themselves
to be liberals in an unqualified sense, and fewer still in an American or British sense . . . Indeed, there is an air of strangeness, or exteriority, accom-
panying French analyses of liberal society as if they were *in* liberalism, but
not yet *of* it ("Legitimacy," 16).

A good many intellectuals from the Left have been, since 1968, or
even 1956, disappointed by Communism (the French call them *les déçus du
communisme*). The measure of humility and sobriety that comes with such
disillusionment does not however make of these men and women auto-
matic converts to liberalism. The collapse of the faith in Communism,
coupled with the disenchantment following François Mitterrand's presi-
dency, which failed to fulfill the Socialists' electoral promises, did not lead
French intellectuals to cross over in droves to a liberal camp many still
consider incompatible with the indigenous political tradition. Rather, they
were forced to compromise with their unfulfilled dreams and fall back on
a middle-ground position closer to the national memory, namely republicanism. The following chapter will examine this repositioning along
(neo)republican lines.

3
Back to la République

✑ ✑ ✑

The European left intelligentsia has no more realistic hope for state power
through left-wing parties and no more real chance to use
state power rationally to transform society in the direction indicated
by utopian ideals and correct theory than does the American left
intelligentsia. We are all basically in the same boat, at this moment
in history, and no one has a good idea of where we're going.

DUNCAN KENNEDY

What could well be dying before our very own eyes is what
politics has been since the Enlightenment: the continuation
of philosophy by other means.

RÉGIS DEBRAY

*T*o fall back on la République means
to preserve the gains of the progres-
sivist tradition while withdrawing, however reluctantly, from the more
radical positions that the demise of Stalinism and the exhaustion of social
democratic labor movements have rendered untenable today. Many left-
wing intellectuals are allergic to the postmodern ambience because of all
that still keeps them within the orbit of the critical rationalism of the Enlightenment. They simply refuse to pack up and walk over to the camp of
liberalism, radical individualism, and unadulterated free-market ideology.
They see the defense of the republican ideal as the only way to combine a
commitment to social justice with the defense of civic liberties and to reconcile the role of the state in the reduction of inequalities and redistribu-
tion of wealth with the critique of the kind of totalitarianism on which the
communist utopia ran aground.

Republicanism, as a position to fall back on, means socialism without the Gulag, Valmy minus the Terror, and the Revolution rid of Robespierre, Lénine, and Pol Pot: neither 1789 (the necessary but insufficient triumph of "bourgeois liberties") nor 1793 (the dictatorship of the committees whose legacy would prove to be so disastrous). The Republic also means *l'An II* so dear to Victor Hugo and to the generations of schoolchildren who were involved in the carefully orchestrated collective recitation of the most patriotic of his poems. In the second year of the Republic everything was possible, and everything collapsed into tyranny.

The selective memory of the Republic celebrates the beginnings of the third one, between 1871 and 1914, in the heyday of Gambetta, Ferry, and Emile Combes: the war against peasant illiteracy, the conquest of *le pays réel,* the establishment of a parliamentary democracy based on reason and social justice that remains, in the eyes of its contemporary supporters, the finest hour of French exceptionalism. Even today, after years of agonizing self-flagellation over its blanket endorsement of Stalinist totalitarianism, the French intellectual Left is not ready to swallow hook, line, and sinker the concept of a new world order peddled by Presidents Bush and Clinton. Such is the irony of history: the Bicentennial of the French Revolution coincided with the collapse of Soviet socialism, both events bringing to a close the dual cycle of the European revolutionary saga, the long cycle of the Jacobin revolution, and the shorter cycle of its younger Leninist sibling. The Bicentennial of the French Revolution, coupled with the ideological crisis brought in by the breakdown of the Communist bloc, made a revaluation of the republican tradition all the more urgent.[1]

THE NEW WORLD ORDER AS DOUBLE BIND

The return to the Republic also illustrates the impossible choice confronting many leftists who find themselves caught between the apologists of the market, consumerism, and mass culture on the one hand, and the proponents of fundamentalism, tribalism, and the mystique of blood and (Father)land on the other. "Here we are," Régis Debray laments, "secular deviants who refuse capitalism as the ultimate norm and horizon, stuck between two unacceptable rallying points, two forms of intellectual and social regression, both fatal, if unequally so, to human freedom" (181). Against liberal egoism, the "do your own thing" mentality of consumer culture, the neorepublicans wave the flag of solidarity; against ethnic or religious fanaticism, they raise the shield of *laïcité,* or secularism in educational matters. Many French authors today resort to this rhetorical figure of the impossible choice between liberalism and fundamentalism perceived as the two major ideological matrices at odds in the geopolitical space of postcommunism. Edgar Morin has described the widening gap between transnational elites, the carriers of modernity, and the peoples of the third and fourth worlds steeped in misery and tyranny as a struggle between neo-fundamentalism and neomodernism (cited in Debray, *Contretemps,* 112). In the conclusion of his impassioned indictment of the surrounding cultural barbarity, *The Defeat of the Mind,* Alain Finkielkraut describes our fin de siècle as the confrontation between consumerist infantilism and ethno-religious intolerance, "the terrible and pathetic encounter of the fanatic and the zombie" (135).

Alain Touraine also rejects the twin figures of the market and the ghetto, and the false alternative of economism and culturalism, "the system without actors and the actor without a system." On the one hand, he writes, "we have the assertion of the hegemony of a West which believes itself to be universalist and which is destroying cultures and nations along with species of animals and plants in the name of technology and technological success. On the other, we have the rise of an anti-Europeanism which quickly becomes an aggressive and potentially racist and hate-filled notion of difference" (322).

The idea of a planetary struggle between consumerism and fundamentalism is hardly original. It is arguably the most common interpretation of the tensions produced by the new world order following the Cold War. The title of a recent best-seller of American political science, Benjamin Barber's *Jihad vs. McWorld,*[2] clearly shows that this way of framing the description of current political events exceeds the narrow confines of the French debates on the Jacobin heritage. Recent acts of terrorism against the United States government, from Oklahoma City to military bases in Saudi Arabia, support the perception that the number one enemy of democracy throughout the world is no longer communism, but a deeply antimodern-ist religious and/or nationalistic radicalism based on a literal reading of sacralized texts, from the Qu'ran to the Constitution of the United States.

The specific contribution of the neo-Jacobin discourse to the current discussion on postcommunism is to provide an alternative to the impossible choice faced by intellectuals. The dissatisfaction with both liberal individualism and ethnic collectivism calls for a middle ground, a third way that would preserve freedom without sacrificing social justice and solidarity. Touraine, who can be quite critical of the most centralizing aspects of the republican tradition, frames the dilemma in the following manner:

> How can we reconcile the decay of the classical rationalist vision, which we know to be inevitable and even liberating, with the organizational principles of social life that guarantee the continued existence of justice and freedom? Is there any way of escaping both a dominating universalism and a multiculturalism that leads to segregation and racism? How can we avoid both the destruction of the Subject, which leads to the reign of self-interest and might, and the dictatorship of subjectivism, which has given birth to so many totalitarianisms? (198)

The prophecy comes with an ultimatum that lends new meaning to the notion of intellectual *engagement:* in order to escape the dilemma of postmodernity, the professionals of critical thought will have to buckle down and produce a new kind of thinking about modernity that bypasses both the logic of identity and the logic of the market. In Touraine's apocalyptic words, "if we do not succeed in defining a different conception of modernity — one which is less haughty than that of the Enlightenment but which can still resist the absolute diversity of cultures and individuals — the storms that lie ahead will be still more violent than the storms that accompanied the fall of the *anciens régimes* and industrialization" (198).

PHILOSOPHY AND THE MIDDLE WAY

Luc Ferry and Alain Renaut have attempted to provide this ambitious program (to propose a form of collective rationality compatible with the demands of contemporary individualism) with a sound philosophical foundation. Such a move is quite in keeping with the republican project itself, since for the French Republicans politics was often nothing more than the "continuation of philosophy by other means," as Régis Debray puts it (*Contretemps,* 179). Most of Ferry and Renaut's argumentation underscores the weaknesses of both the liberal and socialist conceptions of rights. Liberalism is guilty of confining itself to "freedom-rights," mostly negative liberties that limit the power of government while entrusting individual initiative and private charity ("civil society") with the task of dealing with unequal distribution of wealth and knowledge. Socialism, for its part, errs on the opposite side, consigning individual rights to the status of inadequate bourgeois freedoms that fail to challenge the asymmetrical structure of power in a capitalistic democracy. In the name of social democracy, the socialist tradition has put forward claims to an altogether different type of rights "that define not the *powers of acting* that are *opposable to the state,* but powers of *obligating the state* to a number of services, in other words, man's *entitlements* [droits de créance] on society" (*Political Philosophy III,* 16).

The inadequacy of these two conceptions of the political, the one creating injustice and the other authoritarianism, calls for the revalorization of the republican idea, which alone can safeguard *both* permissions and entitlements, *droits-créances* and *droits-libertés* by way of a third kind of rights the authors call participatory rights: "Genuine human rights are the rights of the citizen as political rights to participate in power, essentially through universal suffrage—participation rights that, on the one hand, presuppose permissions [droits-libertés], and, on the other hand, through their very exercise, guarantee the assumption of responsibility for the needs for solidarity or fraternity" (120).

Ferry and Renaut see in the notion of participatory rights "the principal source of a solution to the antinomy of permissions and entitlements, which continue to oppose the liberal and socialist traditions" (121). The notion of participation rights allows them to reconcile the rights of man with the right of the citizen to receive a civic education and to actively take part in the political process. The synthetic character of the republican project (at least in its ideal, theoretical form) is the source of its value and superiority; it exemplifies "the search for an original position that is not simply *liberal* yet without a claim to be *socialist*" (117).

In the course of the demonstration, the two competing models of negative, defensive rights and positive, proactive participatory rights are connected to specific national political traditions via the classic opposition between the French and American revolutions. The main philosophical difference between the two representations of the revolution lies for Ferry and Renaut in what is the engine of the democratic process: the state on the one hand, and history on the other. Their critique of liberalism, following Habermas's analysis of the relationship between natural rights and revolution, is based on a reading of the declarations of 1776 as assuming (wrongly) that "the *natural* function of society tends to actualize the rights of man *spontaneously*" provided the state keeps its interventions to a minimum (20, italics in the text).

On the contrary, the spirit of the French declarations implies a voluntaristic conception of the role of the state derived from Rousseau (there can only be freedom *within* the state, since true liberty is the consenting submission to the rational law, itself an expression of the general will). Similarly, the French Physiocrats' explicit critique of the "liberal conception of natural harmony" rests on the belief that the radical transformation of society can only be brought about by an act of political will orchestrated by the state as the expression of the sovereignty of the people. In the words of Habermas, "in the one place it is a matter of setting free the spontaneous forces of self-regulation in harmony with the Natural Law, while in the other, it seeks to assert for the first time a total constitution in accordance with Natural Law against a depraved society and a human nature which has been corrupted" (cited in Ferry and Renaut, 105).

This fundamental opposition between the voluntaristic moral and philosophical idealism of the French Enlightenment and the immanentist historicism that is at the core of Anglo-American liberalism crops up time and again during the early years of the Third Republic.[3] The major architects of the republican project during the Second Empire were torn between their attachment to the Enlightenment a priori conceptions of human agency (Reason predates and escapes the empirical determinations of history) and their reverence for Comtean positivism, whose main attraction, during the long winter of Napoleon III's rule, was that it asserted the historical inevitability of the triumph of democracy and social progress.[4]

There are profits to be gained today from this philosophical updating of the French republicans' historical project. Such a move opens up a way out of the dilemma of the critical intellectuals and legitimates their refusal of the twin temptations of liberalism and culturalism. Ferry and Renaut stress the eminently modern (translate: intellectually and politically still relevant) nature of the republican synthesis: it provides answers to the most pressing questions of our fin de siècle. The intellectual satisfaction derived from the philosophical coherence of the republican discourse of rights is matched only by the conviction that the return to the republican idea is a way to immerse oneself anew in the continuity of the French political tradition, to feel, once again, part of the national community, as the issue is also one of cultural identity. Hence the opposition between the French response to the rights question and the Anglo-American and German conceptions.[5] The third way stands out and compels recognition in all possible configurations. One only needs to replace the "socialism" of the 1980s with the "fundamentalism" of the 1990s to make sense of the present debates on

the new world order. In the eyes of the neorepublicans, socialism and fundamentalism are sister ideologies equally grounded in highly emotional,
organic, and unitary "totalitarian" conceptions of collective identity as
opposed to the elective, civic, and contractual nationalism of Siéyès and
Renan.

Alain Touraine also calls for a synthesis between the two founding principles of democratic modernity, popular sovereignty and human rights,
originally fused in the spirit of 1789 but unfortunately soon dissociated in
reality. He offers in passing his own version of the unfortunate divorce between Ferry and Renaut's permissions and entitlements: "The idea of popular sovereignty tended to be debased to meaning a popular power which
paid scant regard to legality as it took on revolutionary aspirations, whilst
the defense of the rights of man was all too often reduced to meaning the
defense of property" (326). The solution of the antinomy lies in keeping
together the two processes of subjectivization (individual freedom) and
rationalization (the organization of the collective) that together make up
the project of modernity. As a consequence, there is an urgent need to
"break off the debate between liberal thought and left-wing thought, as
there can be no democracy unless we can reconcile the respective ideas they
defend" (351).

One way to put together again the two faces of the democratic coin is
to rid the republican tradition of its statist and authoritarian scoria, which
is what May 68 was all about. In Régis Debray's words, the point is to in-
ject more democracy into the Republic by taking its concept to its end, to
"scrape off some of its unhealthy Napoleonic fat, the product of top-down
authoritarianism; the overload of notabilities, the monarchistic heritage,
the overweight nobility of the state" (*Contretemps*, 21). The proponents of
the republican spirit, Touraine remarks, have often forgotten the representative dimension of democracy; 1989 echoes 1789. The end of Stalinism
provides the Left with the unexpected opportunity to do away with the
centralizing drive of the Jacobin project without lapsing into the anomie
of liberalism and its purely defensive conception of rights: "To explain the
memorable events of 1989—and they were the most exhilarating to have
occurred since mid-1789—we must go beyond the dichotomy between
negative and positive conceptions of freedom, of democratic institutions
and the will to democratize. Perhaps the time has come to give the idea of
democracy a central role in our political thinking" (348).

Touraine's version of the new historical compromise of the French intellectuals mixes social-democratic principles with a pluralistic credo clearly inspired by some aspects of the liberal tradition.[6] However, it is unmistakably republican and communitarian in the sense that the nation appears as the best guarantor of democracy, since it alone can prevent pluralism from degenerating into regional and ethnic particularisms. "There can be no democracy when there is no national collectivity because it has been segmented into regions or ethnic groups or because it has been destroyed by civil war. The nation must exist if civil society is to be able to free itself from the State, and if individuals are to be able to win their personal freedom within that society" (299). The national framework offers the best protection from the two perils of despotism and anarchy, authoritarian centralization and the particularistic war of all against all.

For Touraine, "social-democratic humanism" alone can achieve the much-needed political synthesis many of the texts I have referred to so far are attempting to articulate:

> It is not easy to reconcile liberty and liberation. Many political forces and intellectuals have failed to do so, but both social-democracy— in the contemporary meaning of the term—and certain intellectuals have facilitated the existence of that combination and the creation of very democratic public spaces . . . Revolutionaries and liberals speak of these humanists with equal scorn and violence. And yet it is the humanists who are the realists. It is they who have done most to reconcile free institutions and the collective will to participate—and that is a good practical definition of democracy. (346–47)

Although Touraine does not provide the reader with an explicit definition of what he means by social-democracy, the fact that it is opposed both to liberalism and revolutionary centralism strikes a familiar chord.[7]

Touraine's reservations regarding the metaphysical heritage of the French Enlightenment come from his training as a sociologist and his belonging to an intellectual tradition (Comte, Durkheim, and positivistic social science in general) that has always distrusted the ahistorical, and at times antihistorical, thrust of eighteenth-century social philosophy. To illustrate his disagreement with Habermas, Touraine argues that in contemporary debates "the philosophical face of social thought is once more becoming a quest for the lost One, whereas sociohistorical thought is more alert to the increasingly extreme forms of the breakdown of the world order" (342). This formulation recalls the dispute between Comteans and neo-Kantians, those who claimed that "our history is not our code" (as the Jacobin Rabaud Saint-Etienne had put it) and those who believed that rights were not the product of transcendental moral principles but the results of the positive unraveling of history as a mix of tradition and contingency.

By the same token, Touraine's attraction to liberal pluralism and humanism explains his critique of the nationalistic drift of Jacobin statism: "The twentieth-century has too many reasons to associate nationalism with anti-progressivism for us to be able to understand our last Jacobins" (100). He also pokes fun at "the image of a republican, universalist and modernizing nation that is still promoted by a few intellectuals and political leaders" nobody listens to anyway and in whose national mythology nobody believes any longer. Although critical of the metaphysics and centralism of the Jacobin heritage, Touraine's reflections fit squarely within the current quest for a synthesis between the rights of the individual and the duties of the citizen. It is precisely because the republican tradition (which cannot be reduced to its Jacobin component) is quickly being forgotten that its supporters deem it urgent to produce a modified version of it, better adapted to the demands of new circumstances.

NATION IMPOSSIBLE: BOSNIA AND THE RETURN
OF THE DREYFUSARDS

The war in the former Yugoslavia provided the impetus for just such a reformulation of the national question. Bosnia was a striking example of all the evils that threatened the democratic idea of the nation in late twentieth-century Europe and it soon held a prominent place in the concerns of the French opinion makers. Indeed it was almost a textbook case of what was undermining the modernist idea of the nation-state. All the makings of the crisis of the revolutionary legacy were present in the Balkans powder keg, a harbinger of things to come in a racially polarized "postrepublican" France: the collapse of communism; the agony of a nation (the former Yugoslavia) that died of an overdose of federalism and could have used a bit of Jacobin centralization; the divisive pull of the centrifugal forces of linguistic and religious separatism; the rebirth of fascism and of its ideology of racial purity and systematic genocide, renamed "ethnic cleansing" for the occasion.

The intelligentsia's commitment to the Bosnian cause (Bernard-Henri Lévy being, as always, a paradigmatic figure) inserts itself in a long tradition of support to martyr-nations, collective victims of oppression and intolerance subjected to foreign occupation or besieged by the forces of reaction, whether dynastic or capitalistic: young American republic threatened by British imperialism and supported by the *philosophes* and the *idéologues,* occupied Greece of the leftist Romantics of 1830, quartered Poland of the 1848 democrats, Soviet "besieged citadel" of the interwar fellow travelers of communism, Algeria of the postwar generation, Cuba and Vietnam of the sixties radicals, *printemps de Prague* Czechoslovakia, Red China of the *gauchistes,* Northern Ireland, Biafra, Kampuchea, Nicaragua, and so on.

The rebirth of Serbian nationalism urged intellectuals to mobilize once again against totalitarianism. They had just buried it in its Stalinist form, and it was raising its ugly head again in fascistic guise.[8] The conflict provided the critical clerisy with new opportunities for *engagement,* either through the written and spoken word, or on the ground, via carefully orchestrated media events aimed at alerting international public opinion.

The transformations of the French intellectual field in the past twenty years have persuaded some observers of the Parisian scene to announce the demise of the prophets of Justice and Revolution. The model of the public intellectual à la Voltaire, Hugo, Zola, Sartre, and de Beauvoir did not emerge unscathed from the post-68 egalitarian wave and the overall liberalization of French society. Some see the democratization of cultural life as having relegated the producers of high culture to the margins of the collective imagination. I believe that there remains an underlying continuity between the theoretical practice of many of today's intellectuals and the native tradition of political propheticism, however reformulated. The revaluation of the republican idea plays a central role in a larger attempt to relegitimize the critical intelligentsia.[9]

Falling back on *la République* implies, first of all, a revalorization of philosophy as against the human sciences. In the present context, the latter are often blamed for the unfortunate consequences of postmodern relativism because of the untrammeled historicism they inherited from positivism and romanticism. Claude Nicolet, among many others, blames the crisis of the republican model (which, he says, postmodernists reject as "too European, and too French, to be honest") on the epistemological domination of the social sciences: "By invading the field of history, the 'human sciences' run the risk of doing away, not only with the specific, the non-repetitive, but the discursive and rational as well . . . In the great flattening-out of civilizations (read cultures), the common 'nature' of humanity may well be reduced, sadly, to mere 'codes'" (*La République en France*, 15).

Similarly, Pierre Bourdieu's work has shown the extent to which philosophy was for many decades at the center of the French school system, holding the highest position in the hierarchy of disciplines and defining the epistemological and political ethos of *la République des professeurs*. The return of the republican idea brings philosophers and philosophical questions back to the forefront. The third generation of the Annales school has been turning its attention again to political history, while numerous publications on the philosophy of law reexamine Montesquieu, Pudendorf, and the tradition of natural rights, redefining the philosophical discourse after structuralism. Discussions of the crisis of the school system and of its secular ideals get mixed up with the nostalgic celebration of *l'école communale*.

This theoretical reassessment is part of an attempt to restore the social position of the intellectuals, who once again can claim for themselves a critical and normative role even at the price of an increased isolation from the rest of society. The accusations of puritanism, archaism, and plain old-fashioned stuffiness leveled at them from all quarters are not altogether unpleasant to people who like to think of themselves as the last representatives of a long line of artists and publicists celebrated throughout French literature as beacons in the night and soaring prophets whose "giant wings prevent them from walking," as the poet would have it. Preaching in the desert often confirms the professionals of critical conscience in their conviction that Truth is on their side. Programmatic statements on the social function of the intellectual have been ubiquitous in the past decade, from the pen of writers and thinkers of diverse backgrounds yet united in a common resistance to the abdication of thinking they equate with the complacent hedonism of our times.

For Alain Touraine, the healthy questioning of professorial arrogance and the much-needed democratization of intellectual authority does not imply that the critical voice, the hallmark of the professionals of thought, is to be silenced: "The main task of the intellectuals is to build the alliance between the Subject, reason, freedom and justice . . . The lower intelligentsia which speaks in the name of the individual and human rights must take the place of an upper intelligentsia which speaks of nothing but the meaning of History" (365). Here, Touraine echoes Finkielkraut, for whom the defenders of culture-as-task have a duty to battle the proponents of culture-as-origin.

Pierre Bourdieu, usually quite critical of the social and political power the high intelligentsia derives from its cultural capital, has nonetheless taken an active part in recent efforts to redefine the *engagement* of public intellectuals. In a postscript to his study of the mechanisms of the French literary field and of the sociological implications of Flaubert's novels, Bourdieu turned to contemporary issues and offered "a realistic program for a collective action of the intellectuals" (461). This program owes a lot to the epistemology of republicanism and to the memory of the Dreyfusards as the model "of an intellectual collective capable of proffering a discourse of freedom" (462). Intellectuals worthy of the name are called to engage in a resistance against all forms of power (whether economic, political, or journalistic) beyond the differences of their respective national histories.

Bourdieu invites those who make up what he calls *"une internationale des intellectuels"* to support a genuine and unabashed "corporatism of the universal" that also refuses to choose between liberalism and totalitarianism. The point is to avoid both the ivory tower of the practitioners of art for art's sake (the marginalization induced by the liberal order) and the submission to external political and ideological interests advocated by the recipients of state patronage, the *doxosophes* and other "heteronomous clerics" open to any compromise in order to become counsel to the Prince (the Gramscian model of the organic intellectual, whether of the bourgeoisie or the proletariat).

Intellectuals are urged to get involved in political struggles, but their action needs to benefit their own interests as a corporate group rather than further the agenda of a party, a bureaucracy, or a class. To be defended at all costs, Bourdieu writes, are "the economic and social conditions of the autonomy of the privileged social worlds where the material and intellectual instruments of what we call Reason are produced and reproduced" (472). By arguing unequivocally for a (relative) autonomy of Reason, Bourdieu clearly parts company with Foucauldian theorists of the knowledge-power syndrome, for whom the positivistic concept of a separate site of epistemologically grounded scientific truth wrested away from the illusions of "ideology" or ordinary doxa smacks of metaphysical idealism.

It is easy to see why such a call to arms hails the Dreyfusard struggle as an example of successful resolution of the tension between withdrawal and involvement via a "politics of purity that is the antithesis of the Reason of State" (465). This type of collective action, carried out by what Bourdieu considers to be genuine autonomous intellectuals, not mere cultural pro-

ducers turned politicians like Guizot or Lamartine, implies a belief in what
Benda called an *idéal de clerc,* a set of values free of historical contingency
and pragmatic concerns. Although his work aims at embedding values in
a determined social field, Bourdieu nonetheless maintains that they somehow transcend the immediate demands of political power games and economic calculation. He remains quite faithful to the classical French republican view of reason as breaking away from the realm of the empirical.
The ground-breaking interventions of the Dreyfusards in the public sphere
carried with them "the assertion of a right to transgress the most sacred values of the community . . . in the name of values transcending those of the
city, or, if you prefer, in the name of a particular form of ethical and scientific universalism that can serve as a basis not only for a kind of moral
magisterium but also for a collective mobilization aimed at struggling for
the promotion of these values" (465).

Alain Finkielkraut was probably overly pessimistic when he wrote that
there were no longer any Dreyfusards, while François Furet erred on the
side of optimism (at least from his own point of view) when he argued that
the French Revolution and the debates surrounding it were finally over.
The values and behaviors that have shaped the invention of political
modernity by the French revolutionaries, which have left a long-lasting imprint on the life of the political and cultural history of their country, are
alive and well in the writings of a good many native intellectuals today.
Benda's clercs are doing well indeed, never so loquacious as when the *Zeitgeist* deplores their silence or celebrates their disappearance.

THE NATIONALITY OF THE REPUBLIC

The strategy I have briefly sketched in the preceding pages can be described
as a somewhat Hegelian attempt to go beyond the historical sedimentations of French republicanism in order to reconcile opposites such as rights
and duties, or rationalism and historicism, while at the same time saving
the best of the Enlightenment heritage. Such a strategy cannot avoid the
moment of critical negativity and shirk the necessary confrontation with
its others, meaning those doctrines that stand in clear opposition to its
fundamental project. The will to go beyond the dichotomy between negative and positive conceptions of freedom (Ferry and Renaut) and to reconcile liberty and liberation (Touraine), to recapture the lost unity of modernity by bringing together Rousseau and Montesquieu or Michelet and

Tocqueville, implies freeing liberty itself from a liberalism that offers only a defensive, narrowly individualistic version of freedom. It also means rescuing the notion of civic duty from the intolerant nationalism it became entangled with in the past.

The republican discourse is so intimately linked to the French national idea that it often accentuates the foreign origins of its ideological rivals. At the same time, the *aggiornamento* of the republican program helps reassert the place of the native political and philosophical tradition in a world of ideas gone transcultural. The French difference reasserts itself via the critique of individualism and ethnic communitarianism and both ideologies are rejected as exogenous bodies. Rather than taking to task those elements within the national political discourse that have resisted republicanism, the neorepublican rhetoric is often directed at the foreign versions of these countertraditions. The rise of individualism in post-68 France is blamed on the Americanization of the country, while the rise of ethnic and religious particularisms induced by post–World War II labor migrations is said to signal a revival of German romantic nationalism.

The return of the republican idea is thus wedded to a discourse of nationalness based on the close historical association between the nation and the republic. It is also a reaction to the threat that European integration and immigration from Africa and Asia pose to the national identity. The nationalization of discourse in the media and political parties stresses French exceptionalism, meaning in this case the specific nature of the French national idea. The return to the Republic becomes a national, at times nationalistic, movement, mindful of the specificities of the Gallic past. "Since 1789, and mostly since 1793," Régis Debray argues, "a time when insane individuals were bold enough to wrest from God, for the first time, the government of men in one corner of the planet, the concern for the universal, our own particularism, makes us a marginal people, forever standing against the current" (*Contretemps,* 18). In 1889, there were only two republics in Europe: France and Switzerland. In a hundred years, Debray says, things have not changed much. Alain Finkielkraut writes for his part that "in the century when nationalism reigned, France—to its credit and originality—refused to accept the idea that the spirit had ethnic roots" (102).

It should not come as a surprise, then, that Ferry and Renaut's relegitimation of the republican tradition goes hand in hand with an impassioned indictment of the Germanization of postwar French philosophical thinking.[10] The main thrust of their argument in *French Philosophy of the Sixties* as well as in *Heidegger and the Moderns* is that the theoretical radicalism of the sixties is nothing but a grafting of German antihumanism onto the otherwise healthy organism of the French tradition. The transplant was eventually rejected by the antibodies of a humanism championed by the greatest heroes of the native tradition, from Rousseau to Sartre:[11]

> Far from being a purely indigenous product, '68 philosophy is in fact the use of themes and theses borrowed, in more or less complex combinations, from German philosophers, for example, Marx, Nietzsche, Freud, and Heidegger, to mention the fundamental ones . . . By taking what it had inherited from German philosophy, French philosophy came to the point of denouncing any form of thought where man in his essence (or the essence of man) was the basis of the subject of reality (historic, psychic, or cultural) . . . French philosophy has basically been not so much an original and creative moment in intellectual history as simply a secondary growth. (*French Philosophy*, 19, 25)

This kind of nationalization of philosophical differences is nothing new, and one could write a history of French intellectual life from the point of view of its tumultuous relationship with German culture.[12] In the 1880s, following the humiliation of his country at the hands of Bismarck's Prussia, Renan opposed Teutonic organicism with his own definition of the nation as a daily plebiscite (itself a reconceptualization of the revolutionary concept of civic nationalism). Forty years later, Julien Benda placed German historicism at the core of "the treason of the (French) intellectuals":

> It must be admitted that the German clerks led the way in this adhesion of the modern clerk to patriotic fanaticism. The French clerks were, and long remained, animated with the most perfect spirit of justice towards foreign cultures (think of the cosmopolitanism of the Romantics!), when already Lessing, Schlegel, Fichte, Goerres were organizing in their hearts a violent adoration for "everything German," and a scorn for everything not German. The nationalist clerk is essentially a German invention. (*Treason*, 57–58)[13]

In the final pages of *The Rebel*, Albert Camus opposed classical Hellenism, with its cult of measure and beauty, to the German ideologies of history, "where action is no longer a process of perfection but pure conquest . . . an expression of tyranny" (300). Camus read late modern European history as the struggle between the authoritarian conceptions of northern European historicism and the libertarian tradition of the French, Spaniards, and Italians, informed by what he called *la pensée de midi*, a solar mode of thinking that had its source in classical antiquity. "The profound conflict of this century," he wrote, "is perhaps . . . between German dreams and Mediterranean traditions, between the violence of eternal adolescence and virile strength, between nostalgia, rendered more acute by knowledge and by books and courage reinforced and enlightened by the experience of life—in other words, between history and nature" (299). More recently, Marc Fumaroli, responding to critics of his controversial book *L'Etat culturel,* a spirited defense of *l'esprit français* against the debasement of arts and letters by the cultural politics of the socialist government, remarked that "'culture' today is this sociology of recreation that lends itself so easily to the manipulation of collective thinking by commercial advertising and political propaganda. It is a modern and even relatively recent notion, which recapitulates German 'Kultur' and Anglo-Saxon 'culture,' to embrace the mass phenomena of consumption" (*The State*, 133).[14]

The deliberate comparison between German and American conceptions of culture is symptomatic of the way current debates about liberalism, multiculturalism, and postmodernism are framed in France today. The trouble with German and American cultures, the argument goes, is that they share a common origin in the romantic movements that rebelled against the French Enlightenment and the French Revolution. The Romantic legacy was of course a key ingredient of German nationalism. But it also had a lasting influence on anthropological thinking in the United States.

Alain Finkielkraut, for example, traces American multiculturalism back to German romanticism, and argues against grounding interethnic harmony on the glorification of differences: "We create an impossible contradiction in seeking to establish rules for welcoming diverse ethnic groups based on principles affirming the primacy of cultural roots" (93).[15] The romantic worldview has migrated from central Europe to North America and has contributed to the historicist thrust of the social sciences in the United States. Finkielkraut links contemporary forms of multiculturalism with the American Anthropological Association's 1947 rewriting of the Declaration of the Rights of Man (at the request of the United Nations) in a way that "would cure the great humanitarian principles of their tendency toward formalism and abstraction, and of their ineffectuality" (75).[16]

In the writings of many contemporary French authors, the traditional critique of German romantic irrationalism informs the resistance to "Anglo-Saxon" multiculturalism, mainly because cultural pluralism is perceived as the cool, soft-core liberal version of an ethnic-religious separatism always about to harden into fascism or fundamentalism. This amalgamation between multiculturalism and chaos leads to a picture of America as a society threatened by the imminent apocalypse of total racial war. This common representation of the United States as a divided nation on the verge of ethnic war in turn comforts the partisans of diversity in their belief that the French will never learn, blinded as they are by the Jacobin legacy.

For the French neorepublicans, liberalism is complicitous with ethnic nationalism, if only because it tolerates it. Today, the most modern elements of European culture contribute in their view to the return of the most archaic ones, which is why the Yugoslavian tragedy, because it combined the new postcommunist market liberalism with precommunist ethnic Balkanization, was central to the revival of the national-republican idea. Liberalism must be resisted because it is devoid of any moral project and of any transcendental principle: it only has mobility and consumption to offer against the seduction of archaic regressions of all sorts. In the absence of a liberal collective imaginary (a contradiction in terms), the void created by the collapse of the communist utopia can only be filled by another mythology, whether national or religious. Stalinism was a little bit of both, granted, but it did still partake, via Marxist universalism, in the rational emancipatory program of the Enlightenment.

Metaphorically, the fall of the Berlin Wall means that the last bulwark against the tidal wave of liberal consumerism and ethnic-religious fascism has been removed. Régis Debray contends that "with the barbaric rerouting and high-jacking of communism, a major opportunity of civilization was wasted away. We can once again, far to the East and the West, even in France—but is it really new?—back away from the universal idea to the local one, from nation to *ethnie,* from humanity to native heath. The *Vendéens* are chasing the Jacobins away, and law gives way to custom" (178). Finkielkraut shares similar views: in the 1980s "communism was experiencing an irreversible decline, but what died along with it was not totalitarian thinking but the idea of a world common to all people" (74).

Along with Marx, it is Rousseau and the whole French Enlightenment tradition that yield to the combined pressure of Locke's children and Herder's
disciples.

The supporters of the Republic argue that the relation between liberalism and the global rise of intolerance is not one of opposition (as in the
politics of difference as the last hope against the hardening of the politics
of identity), but one of complicity, a causal relationship. Not only is liberal
democracy not a (civic) religion in the root sense of the word, not only
does it not form any bonds, but on the contrary it dissolves all social ties,
which are left to reconstitute themselves outside the social in the form of
a threatening differentialism. For many French intellectuals, the sides have
been heard: identity politics is the direct consequence of the failure of the
modernist project, the collapse of the notion of a common good and the
disappearance of a shared culture of universal improvement. "As society
comes increasingly to resemble a market in which there are no more ideological or even political issues at stake," Touraine writes, "all that remains
is the struggle for money or the quest for self-identity" (181). Unemployment and marginalization are central to the social double bind: those who
are excluded from the banquet of consumption are left to put together for
themselves, as a result of a sort of ideological *bricolage,* a makeshift sense of
belonging made up of the bits and pieces of past communal memories.
"Anyone who is no longer defined by their activity soon constructs or re-
constructs an identity based upon their origins" (183).

Nowhere does the radical dissonance between these two conceptions of
the social appear more clearly than in an essay Régis Debray devoted to the
French republican exception a few years ago. Originally published in *Le
Nouvel Observateur,* it was reprinted in a collection of ironical and bitter-
sweet essays on the celebration of the bicentennial of the French Revolution. The subtitle of the volume, *Eloge des idéaux perdus* (In praise of lost
ideals), conveys the mood of Debray's book. The author laments, in a series of acerbic, disenchanted, and often humorous comments on the Bicentennial, the passing of the great Jacobin tradition, taking up one last
time, for the record, the lost cause of the republican project.

Debray's critique of the new world order rests on a binary opposition
between "republic" and "democracy," the latter meaning, despite a few examples drawn from northern and Protestant Europe, American society,
and some of Debray's critics were quick to dismiss his views as the latest
version of the traditional anti-Americanism of French intellectuals. In a

lecture given at New York University (reprinted in *Contretemps* as "Confessions of an anti-American"), Debray complained that it was increasingly difficult to criticize the American way of life in a new France where most people have traded the native political tradition for the delights of imported liberal democracy.

An essay entitled "Are You Democrat or Republican?" (which plays on what are also American political categories, albeit with almost completely opposite meanings) skillfully transfers Debray's quasi-ontological opposition from one domain of the social to the next. He suggests thereby that republic and democracy are separate and largely incompatible worlds that recent history has finally made to coexist in contemporary French society. The republic/democracy split is applied in turn to education, the media, the justice system, political philosophy, the relationship between church and state, and, of course, the construction of the national community. The main thrust of Debray's argument is that the crisis of the educational and political institutions has a lot to do with the fact that politicians and educators persist in acting as Republicans while the students and the voters live and feel like Democrats. In other words, to quote from Finkielkraut, the school system may still be modern, but the pupils are already hopelessly postmodern (*Defeat of the Mind*, 126).

One could take a systematic tally of the many differences between the French and North Atlantic versions of the democratic experiment according to Debray: the Republic, born in a catholic, absolutist environment, is unabashedly secular, while democracy, the offspring of Protestantism and dissent, has remained deeply religious (it even retained the ruling dynasties in northern Europe). The Republic protects the state from the church and democracy protects the churches from the government. The former sees man as a reasonable creature and privileges the political forum; for the latter, the individual is primarily a producer, and economics rules supreme, shaping the content of the educational project. "The Republic," Debray says, "does not like children. Democracy does not respect adults" (29). Here the state and the public good, there civil society and private interests carry the day. "Here men are brothers because they share the same rights, there because they have the same ancestors" (22).

Abstract universalism versus concrete particularisms, nation versus community, idea/image, written/oral, *Le Monde* versus *Libération*, the Sorbonne versus l'Ecole des Hautes Etudes, the people and the masses, equity/equality, justice/charity, memory/amnesia, professor/lawyer, patriotism/nationalism, civism versus moralism (the latter confusing the public and the private, and blaming public men and women for their private shortcomings)—there is a long list of incompatibility between the two worlds. The Republic is an example, Debray says, that should inspire; democracy is a model, and wants to be exported.

Beyond the rhetorical brilliance of a seductive demonstration that caused quite a stir at the time,[17] the most interesting part of Debray's argument is the celebration of the philosophical project of the historical Republicans. In the preface to an edited volume published in honor of Jacques Muglioni, his former philosophy teacher at the selective Parisian lycée Jeanson-de-Sailly, Debray explicitly links the Republicans' pedagogical program with the formation of the nation:

> It is one and the same thing to proceed by definition, postulates and axioms, and to place the unity of the human species above populations and folklores. Republican universalism does not add up local peculiarities, no more than the rule of right results from the summation of its specific cases . . . It is the only way [the analytical mind] can think the historical unity of humanity, which does not vary in any essential way according to latitude, instead of fragmenting humanity in space according to the kind of "transcendental exoticism" anthropology and sociology sometimes offer under the name of cultural relativism. (67)

Nation building starts in the classroom, because the unity of the cognitive processes of human reason applies equally to mathematics and to the study of human culture. One clearly sees here how the neo-Kantism of the philosophy professors of the Third Republic naturally leads to a questioning of the various components of contemporary "cultural relativism." Ideological politics is nothing but the continuation of philosophy by other means, today as it was a hundred years ago. As for the philosophical debate, its terms are surprisingly unchanged, replicating almost to the letter the disputes of the 1790s, 1880s, or 1930s, opposing once again Rousseau and Herder, Renan and Barrès, Zola and Brunetière, or Maurras and Benda, via the simultaneous invention and reproduction, or production and reinvention, of homologous transhistorical positions ("traditions"). It is a truism to say that the republican project was not only a political program: it aimed at creating a brand new symbolic community, a rational polity based on positivistic principles codified in the academic discipline of philosophy, the cornerstone of the whole pedagogical enterprise. That is why the struggle of the intellectuals today is concerned with symbolic forms and provides a critique of contemporary *culture* as the unfortunate revival of ethnic romanticism in the name of multiculturalism.[18]

Unsurprisingly, the French critique of liberalism as the philosophical basis of contemporary decadence focuses on individualism. In fact, postmodern liberalism is often equated with the most virulent, radicalized forms of the process of individualization Tocqueville described as the engine of modernity. The question of the consequences of individualism is the one thread stitching together the successive French revolts against liberalism, right and left, from de Maistre and Maurras to the recent debates over postmodernism, consumerism, and the liberal-democratic recentering of French political culture. It also provides the argument with highly moral implications, since individualism is equated with egoism, self-centeredness, and the sacrifice of solidarity to the pursuit of personal happiness.

Regarding the rise of free markets and the dislocation of the various communities of the ancien régime by capitalism (from the Republic of letters to the rural parish), many French intellectuals continue to endorse Tocqueville's aristocratic moralism. The French aristocrat's depiction of the sorry state of the denizens of American democratic bliss illustrates how highly ambiguous his assessment of the consequences of the crowning of the individual was. "The vices which despotism produces," Tocqueville noted, "are precisely those which equality fosters. These two things perniciously complete and assist each other. Equality places men side by side, unconnected by any common tie; despotism raises barriers to keep them asunder; the former predisposes them not to consider their fellow creatures, the latter makes general indifference a sort of public virtue" (102). In the eyes of modern-day Tocquevilles, liberal individualism is twice guilty. To its own internal weaknesses it adds the responsibility of fostering intolerance and fanaticism, for want of the political will to oppose them and of the moral standards to discredit them. Pluralism and tribalism are "objectively" complicitous: the one prepares the ground for the flowering of the other.[19]

The discourse on contemporary decadence lumps together German thought and the Anglo-American tradition, the two foreign cultures with which the French intelligentsia has most consistently confronted itself for the past two hundred years. Since the enemy has two faces, the battle must be fought on two fronts. On the one hand, we have countless descriptions of the way the liberal solvent has eaten away at the moral fiber of republican humanism; on the other, discussions of extreme cultural pluralism as striking a decisive blow at the integrity of the nation, understood in the tradition of Michelet and Renan as a voluntary association of free and equal individuals. No wonder that an event such as the so-called "affair of the veil" played such a crucial role in redefining ideological positions within the intellectual field. It represented in an almost paradigmatic way the connection between the crisis of the public school system and that of the national consciousness.

4

Cultural Studies, Postcolonialism, and the French National Idea

◦◦◦ ◦◦◦ ◦◦◦

Our special quality (sometimes our ridicule, but often our finest claim)
is to believe and to feel we are universal—by which I mean,
men of universality . . . Notice the paradox: to specialize in the sense
of the universal.

PAUL VALÉRY

France is an indivisible, secular, democratic and social Republic.
It ensures equality before the law to all citizens without distinction
of origin, race and religion. It respects all beliefs.

FRENCH CONSTITUTION (1958), ARTICLE 2

*T*he preceding chapter described how the rearticulation of the republican idea was wedded to the critique of liberalism in contemporary France. To shift the focus of the discussion from the Republic to the nation is to encounter issues of postcolonialism and multiculturalism. The national question is as central to the discussion of contemporary French culture as the issue of the republican legacy. In France, the rise of two political forces informed by rival culturalist ideologies, the National Front and radical Islamism,[1] in combination with the inability of the state to ensure the peaceful inclusion of immigrant communities, has led to a reassessment of the national idea. In America, interpretive models derived from the new paradigms of postcolonial discourse analysis and cultural studies have been transferred to the discipline of French studies, opening up new ways of looking at French culture and society. These new paradigms are themselves a response to the national question in the United States as it relates to the new structure of immigration, the evolution of race relations, and the debates between supporters of the melting-pot ideal and promoters of multiculturalism.

One of the most widespread notions on both sides of the Atlantic is that nation building and immigration policy in the two countries are totally at odds with each other. In my view this notion rests on an overly reductive and simplistic opposition between a liberal-pluralist American model of ethnic relations and a monolithic and centralized French conception of the national community. A comparative approach to what has become of late another transatlantic controversy may help to dispel some of the most enduring misperceptions surrounding the relation of national cultures to the theory and practice of multiculturalism.

THE BATTLE OF THE VEILS

As a starting point for my discussion, I will revisit briefly a series of events that greatly contributed to turning the issue of multiculturalism in France into a full-fledged national debate, namely the so-called *affaire du foulard.* In the fall of 1989 (ironically a few months after the celebration of the Bicentennial of the French Revolution), three female Muslim students were expelled from a middle school north of Paris for having gone to class wearing a *hidjab* or *khiemar,* a religious veil/scarf/headdress. To the Muslim community, the veil has social-religious significance; the school principal saw it as a symbol of Islamic terrorism. The principal (himself a "postcolonial" subject, since he was from the French West Indies), justified his decision by appealing to the law of the land, which has required for almost a century the strict separation of church and state, and which has at times been interpreted as calling for the banishment of distinctive religious and political signs, emblems, or dress from public schools.

The orthodox, traditionalist members of the local Muslim community took up the cause of the teenagers in the name of antiracism and religious freedom, and when the national media jumped on the bandwagon, what might have remained a local incident quickly became a cause célèbre. Five years earlier, both Jean-Marie Le Pen's National Front and the mainstream right-wing parties had come to the defense of Catholic schools threatened by a Socialist plan to integrate them into the state system. All of a sudden, the same political forces had become the self-appointed champions of *laïcité,* or secularism in educational matters, claiming that Islamic fundamentalism was about to take over the country and destroy French national identity.

The controversy split the ruling Socialist party, which was torn between its respect for tolerance and its historical association with secularism. Some favored appeasement while others demanded the strict application of the law. Minister of Education Lionel Jospin, aware of the powerful ideological time bomb he was left to deal with, at first tried to minimize the problem, arguing that only three individuals out of five hundred Muslim students in the school were involved. He noted that wearing the scarf in school was nothing new, although it had never caused such a stir before: the incident, he argued, was both minor and isolated. Surely the conflict could be resolved locally, through a dialogue between the Muslim community and educational authorities. This, however, did not come to pass. In the United States, the issue would most likely have been framed in terms of individual freedom and constitutional rights and might eventually have been settled in court. But in France it became literally an affair of state, *une affaire d'Etat,* carrying in its wake a public debate on the foundations of the Republic and uncovering deep collective anxieties regarding national identity and the future of a multicultural society.

The intellectuals, predictably, soon entered the fray, raising the debate to the somewhat abstract level of the universal principles of a timeless civic republican tradition. The academic Left's traditional forum, *Le Nouvel Observateur,* published an open letter to Lionel Jospin written by five "philosophers," all of them leading figures of the Parisian intellectual scene.[2] The five blasted the government's handling of the affair, arguing that concessions to religious and political fanaticism undermined the legal and constitutional protections the French had secured during two hundred years of struggles against reactionary forces. How ironic, if the Socialists were the ones to undo democracy! "The French version of democracy," they wrote, "is called Republic. It is not a mosaic of ghettoes where the rule of the strongest can be dressed up as freedom for all. Dedicated to free inquiry, committed to the growth of knowledge, and confident in the sole natural light of men, the Republic has its foundation in the schools. That is why the destruction of the school system would hasten that of the Republic."

Many disagreed, arguing that academic sanctions would only push the Muslim youth into the arms of the *intégristes,* as religious traditionalists are called in France, and lambasting the abstract nature of the five philosophers' own brand of (republican) fundamentalism. Historians of immigration and specialists in French law reminded everyone that the country had changed since the heroic days of Michelet and Ferry, and that fin de siècle Islam did not pose the same threat to the republican state as the Catholic Church had a century ago. Besides, they argued, in a postmodern society most students wear distinctive cultural markers, from creatively colored hairdos to pins, buttons, and badges of all kinds. Why not allow Muslim youth to display their difference in a similar, quite harmless way? Surely, they asked, the champions of the République did not suggest going back to the days when all schoolchildren wore the same gray coat, as on the yellowed postcards of la Belle Epoque?

Beyond the excesses of those who appealed to political principles frozen in time, the debate involved genuine philosophical questions and revealed how seriously discrete ethnic, racial, and religious communities challenged a secularized democratic society based on the rule of law. The division within the Left and beyond, within French public opinion, was a sign of a real tension between the demand for tolerance and the universalism of rights, between the respect for diversity and the juridical egalitarianism that form the basis of democratic justice and demands that the law be applied to all equally, without exception.[3]

The controversy also pointed to the crisis of the emancipatory grand narratives that have accompanied, and often justified, the rise of the nation-state. French society seems less and less capable of providing its citizenry with shared collective meanings powerful enough to mobilize large fragments of the population (meanings conveyed by words such as "the people" or the "working class and its allies") around unifying political and cultural goals. The increased visibility of Muslim communities cemented by common values, memories, and rituals is all the more threatening to "native" French people as they themselves feel deprived of shared values and are often left with a nostalgic yearning for the bygone days of ideological and moral national cohesion, variously defined.

The issue of the veil also divided the Muslim community as liberal, secularized Arab intellectuals equated the affair of the veil with the Rushdie affair and warned French public opinion against confusing genuine Islamic religious beliefs and Muslim *intégrisme* as a political ideology. "What passes in the eyes of a French democrat as a gesture of understanding toward teenagers under psychological stress," historian Mohammed Harbi wrote in

Le Nouvel Observateur, "takes on a different meaning for us. By accepting, in the name of tolerance, the exhibition of signs that *purport to be religious,* one plays into the hands of those who, in Muslim countries, oppose gender equality and democracy. If the French validate an obscurantist interpretation of the religious tradition, how can we defend the laicist ideal in a Muslim environment?"[4] Habib Boularès, a Tunisian writer and politician, argued for his part that the veil was the product of social use rather than Koranic dogma. "What these young women are wearing is a political uniform . . . The [fundamentalist] movements decree and pretend to impose a dress code to all the Muslims in the world!"[5]

Muslim intellectuals also argued over the interpretation of the very few passages of the Qu'ran mentioning the veil. Hamadi Essid, a representative of the Arab League, declared that the veil belonged to "a pagan tradition," while Haytham Manna, a Syrian anthropologist living in France, claimed that the word *hidjab* appears only seven times in the Qu'ran, and only once concerning women as a way to disguise their identity so as not to be importuned, presumably by men.[6]

These exegetic debates and the multiplicity of terms, both in French and Arabic, used to refer to the garment the young students wore in order to signify their difference, are symptomatic of the ideological complexity of the *affaire du foulard.* Press reports and political commentaries sometimes used the term *foulard* (scarf) and sometimes *voile* (veil), the latter describing not only a headdress (*khiemar* or *hidjab*), but also the long robe covering the totality of the body (*chador* in Farsi) worn by women in theocratic Islamic societies such as Iran and Afghanistan.[7] This semantic slippage opened the way to a political interpretation of the veil as opposed to a religious-cultural one. Wearing the scarf was now associated with open support of Islamist militancy both in France and abroad, an association with little basis in reality. This was especially true in 1994, when the issue again came to the fore following a decision by the minister of education (no longer a Socialist) to ban the veil from public schools. Pictures of veiled Muslim women appeared once again on the covers of French newsmagazines, this time with captions such as "the Islamist octopus" and "Scarf: The Plot. How the Islamists Are Infiltrating Us."

In fact the social uses of the veil are as varied as its meanings. Older migrant women wear it as an unquestioned, integral part of their traditional culture's definition of womanhood; some girls wear it because they have no choice, others as a useful form of compromise with parental expectations;

finally, some high school and university students and working youths elect to wear the veil as a marker of their divided self and of their dual allegiance to French and Islamic cultures (an equivalent of the hyphenation of identities in the American context). The veil becomes the sign of a valorized difference, a claim to personal dignity, and/or the symbol of a religious conversion to their parents' or ancestors' beliefs.

Both the adoption of the veil by otherwise perfectly acculturated young Muslim women and the hostility of a non-Muslim population increasingly deprived of shared collective moral norms and clear cultural landmarks are symptoms of the disintegration of the collective utopias based on the nation, democracy, and working-class consciousness.[8] The women who wear the veil (with varying degrees of freedom of choice) and the neorepublican intellectuals who criticize them for it both capture in their own way the anxiety of homogenization generated by an increasingly atomistic society. Many acculturated daughters of immigrants are looking for a personalized form of identity, while the intellectual elite continues to denounce the uniformization of the market-oriented society.

A RACIST CONSENSUS?

Events such as the affair of the veil can only comfort Anglo-American critics of the French integrationist model in their belief that there is very little room indeed for cultural and ethnic diversity in the land of Jean-Marie Le Pen.[9] In *Fast Cars, Clean Bodies: Decolonization and the Reordering of French Culture,* Kristin Ross argues for the existence of an overwhelming "neoracist consensus" in French society today (196), presumably evidenced by the electoral gains of the National Front and the toughening of immigration policies. For Ross, ethnicity has superseded class in French society, both as an interpretive category and as a source of conflicts. Ross claims that "class conflict, after all, implies some degree of negotiability; once modernization has run its course, then one is quite simply, either French or not, modern or not: exclusion becomes racial or national in nature" (12).

The most unexpected consequence of such a view is a striking disappearance of the old stock working and lower-middle classes *(les Français de souche)* from the postmodern social landscape now made up, it seems, only of white bourgeois cities and nonwhite ethnic suburbs: "In today's Paris, that frozen temporal lag appears as a spatial configuration: the white, upper-class city *intra muros,* surrounded by islands of immigrant communities a long RER ride away" (12). Not only is the working class finished as a social and political force, it has even vanished from the greater Paris area! But then, who votes for the National Front in those faraway *banlieues?*[10]

In fact, the French "native" population is profoundly divided on the question of ethnic pluralism, and recurrent demonstrations against the National Front and the government's immigration policies show that the notion of a neoracist consensus holding the entire country in its grip is highly questionable. There is no consensus either regarding the legality and constitutionality of the sanctions against Islamic students wearing a veil in class. A 1992 order of the Conseil d'Etat, the highest court in the land, stipulates that the republican "principle of *laïcité*" requires both the "neutrality" of teachings and curricula and the respect of the students' freedom of conscience. Students are allowed to express their religious beliefs in school provided they respect "pluralism and the freedom of others." The Conseil also stated that "wearing signs by which [students] intend to manifest their belonging to a religion is not in itself incompatible with laicist principles" (cited in Gaspard and Khosrokhavar, 189).

Recent data on exogamy also disprove the notion that France is currently experiencing an unprecedented wave of racism and xenophobia. A 1992 study by a researcher from INED (National Demographic Institute) showed that among Algerian men who had arrived in France after age fifteen, 20 percent had a French spouse or partner (excluding daughters of parents born in Algeria). Twenty-two percent of those who had settled in France before turning fifteen were in a similar situation. Although these numbers are smaller for women who immigrated after the age of fifteen (9 percent of them had a spouse or partner born in France of parents born in France), figures are comparable for those women who came to France as children: in 1992, 20 percent of them had chosen a mate outside the Algerian immigrant community.[11] The proportion of children of Algerian women born of an unwed mother or whose father was not Algerian rose from 6.2 percent in 1975 to 27.5 percent in 1990, a clear indication of the rapid breakup of the traditional immigrant family.[12] These figures are significant when compared to the low rates of racial intermarriage in colonial Algeria. During the year 1880, .3 percent of European males and .3 percent of European females married Muslims in French Algeria. The segregation rate had not improved at all by the eve of decolonization. In 1955, a year after the start of Algerian war, .5 percent of European men and 1 percent of European women had married outside the colonist group.[13]

These figures are not meant to suggest that there is no racism in France today, but simply that the racially motivated taboo against intermarriage so prevalent in colonial Algeria is slowly eroding in postcolonial France.[14] The strong hostility of the French toward the communitarian, patrilinear, and endogamous system of the North African family, which played such a role in the battle of the veils, does not imply a kind of essentialized, a priori rejection of intermarriage, provided the immigrants subscribe to the dominant sexual mores of the host country. The same is true in the United States as well, as periodic legal battles involving polygamous Muslim immigrants make patently clear.[15]

Opinion polls taken since the rise of the National Front put issues of immigration and national integration at the forefront of the French public discourse suggest that a strong minority of respondents harbor what commentators describe as a "racist" ideology. A recent poll (November–December 1997) conducted on behalf of the French government's Commission nationale consultative des droits de l'homme (from a "representative" sample of 1,040 people) reveals that 18 percent of the respondents describe themselves as "rather racist."[16] The description of the contents of the self-described racists' ideology by the director of the polling institute, political scientist Roland Cayrol, shows a hodgepodge of complaints that do not so much articulate a clear notion of the essential superiority of the French "race" over Third World people as they express the anxieties and misgivings of the "native" populations of all Western industrialized nations regarding the rate and size of immigration in times of rampant unemployment at home and nationalist revivals all over the globe.

Both the groups labeled by Cayrol as "racist" or "tempted by racism" (40 percent of the sample) argue that "in France one does not feel at home any longer," that there are too many blacks and Arabs in the country, that the latter will never be able to become French, that immigration is linked to crime and unemployment, and that immigrants abuse welfare benefits. A transnational survey of public opinion in countries of the European Union (spring 1997) shows that the French do not significantly differ from their neighbors on these issues: 51 percent of Italians think that legal immigrants who are unemployed should be sent back to their country of origin, half of the Germans feel that things would be better at home without foreigners, and 40 percent of the British argue that there are too many minorities in their country. Figures available for the United States are strikingly similar: a 1986 CBS News/*New York Times* poll found that 52 percent of the respondents favored cutting immigration levels, and the same poll in 1994 found that 59 percent of responses were anti-immigration.[17]

The fact that more French people (38 percent) than Germans or Italians (23 and 21 percent) openly acknowledge being racist may have more to do with the memory of fascism in Germany and Italy and the self-censorship it encourages than with some French specificity in the matter. What most of these polls reveal is how little "race," if equated, as is often the case in discussions of multiculturalism, with skin color, has to do with the French scale of xenophobia. A 1992 survey established that while 19 percent of the respondents harbored some antipathy toward Asians, and 21 percent toward black Africans, the figure was doubled (41 percent) regarding immigrants from the Maghreb.[18] The significant hostility toward Arabs is clearly more correlated with political (the legacy of the Algerian war), religious (Islamic radicalism), and cultural (family structure, status of women) factors than with racial characteristics. This is confirmed by the 1997 survey: while 73 percent of the respondents feel that "there are not too many" Jews and 64 percent not too many blacks in France (up from 47 percent in 1990), 56 percent of those polled still argue that there are too many Arabs (down from 76 percent in 1990).

On the other hand, the fact that the vast majority of individuals declared in 1997 that a democracy must be judged according to its capacity to integrate foreigners (67 percent), that immigrant workers need to be accepted since they contribute to the national economy (68 percent), or even that the presence of immigrants is a source of cultural enrichment (54 percent) shows that French society today is not hopelessly xenophobic. Other responses confirm long-term trends in the way French culture has dealt with difference. While only 20 percent of the respondents believe in the inequality of races, 88 percent disapprove of students wearing *hidjab*s in school. French nationalism is still overwhelmingly of the civic, not ethnic, kind, and the principles that regulate acceptance in the national community are political, not racial.

At the level of principles, the French tend to favor the strict application of republican law: 67 percent of those polled in 1997 support the repatriation of most illegal immigrants and favor granting legal status only to a small number of *sans-papiers*. However, when confronted with individual cases and "concrete situations," the majority of respondents support the "regularization" of undocumented aliens, and this across the political spectrum (with the exception of Front National sympathizers). Similarly, while

73 percent of respondents blamed many immigrants for coming to their country only to benefit from Sécurité sociale, thus showing their unwillingness to "become French," 61 percent of the French people surveyed in the European poll said that they had "friends" in minority groups (as opposed to 38 percent of the German sample).

These figures illustrate a specific feature of the culture, the universalist nature of French individualism. The French are likely to be hostile to immigrant groups (taken as a whole) if they are perceived as "unassimilable" in terms of cultural behavior, but they will be quite indifferent to ethnic differences in individuals as long as those newcomers are willing to belong to French society. The issue today in France is not between assimilation and exclusion (according to polls, ethnic nationalists remain a minority) but between assimilation and "integration." What is at stake is how much of their "culture" (language, kinship system, religious and inheritance practices, political beliefs, etc.) individual members of immigrant groups have to give up in order to become part of the French imagined community.

PLURALISM VERSUS ASSIMILATION

Despite its oversimplification of racial and cultural-religious issues in contemporary France, the narrative of the crisis of French multiculturalism is gaining ground on both sides of the Atlantic, reflecting recent developments in the English-speaking academic world and in the American media. In many ways, to paraphrase Marx, the ideas of the dominant nation (in this case differentialist ideologies made in America) are becoming the dominant ideas in the periphery of the empire. In the imperial center, on the other hand, the transfer of interpretive models based on the trilogy of race, class, and gender to the study of literature, culture, and society has already profoundly transformed the discipline of French studies, not only in terms of methods, but also in the choice of the objects of research.

The new models, mostly constructivist and historicist in outlook and centered on the notion of difference, lead to a radical questioning of all the national mythologies elaborated by former colonial powers that also happen to be the preferred destination for immigrants. The various postcolonial discourses available on the academic market today are very critical of these national ideologies, and apply new methods to objects long ignored, or repressed, by traditional French historiography: immigration movements, the treatment of minorities by the state, racism, anti-

Semitism, colonial representations and practices, theories of race and the nation, and so on.

Until quite recently, French historians, reflecting and reinforcing trends in public opinion, have tended to overshadow those elements of the national past that did not fit in squarely with the harmonious vision of a community unified around the ideal of fraternity. Gérard Noiriel has remarked that Fernand Braudel's *The Identity of France* is informed by "a philosophy of rootedness" previously shared by the French positivist school: "Everything seems to indicate that immigrants did not belong to the history of France for him . . . Braudel considers that the history of France is over when industrialization begins" (*The French Melting-Pot,* 30, 40). This erasure of immigration from the national memory helped fashion what Paul Yonnet has called *le roman national,* the French narrative of the nation. In *Qu'est-ce qu'une nation?,* Ernest Renan argued that forgetting the past, or at least a certain past, was a necessary condition of the manufacturing of collective memory. National histories have their blind spots, where that which cannot be thought and represented is foregrounded by its very exclusion: France has the German Occupation and the Algerian War, America has Hiroshima and the Vietnam War, Germany the Holocaust, Russia its Stalinist past.

Anglo-American historiography must be credited with throwing some new light on events and periods that had been neglected—even suppressed—by professional historians, politicians, and the public at large. Paxton and Marrus's books on Vichy and the Jews, Eugen Weber's work on l'Action Française, and the many studies of the Dreyfus affair by North American scholars have forced the French readership to confront the darkest periods of its national past. As a matter of fact, a good part of the historiography on late modern and contemporary France written in English today focuses on the three moments of acute crisis of the republican model of national integration: the Dreyfus affair, the interwar and Vichy, and the contemporary situation. The comparative analysis of these three moments, and of the immigration policies that define them, has many critics today claiming that a racist, anti-Semitic, and xenophobic thread runs through most of French history. Many of these critics are quick to denounce the republican discourse of human rights and of France as *terre d'asile,* a land of refuge for the oppressed, as a pack of lies and hypocrisy.

On the contrary, they describe French integration policies as a double movement of forced assimilation of immigrants in the name of the universalistic principles of the Jacobin ideology and of exclusion of those foreigners deemed unassimilable in the name of patriotism and of the maintenance of national cohesion. Far from being incompatible, the two processes are seen as complementary, even complicitous, since they derive from the same "monological cultural imagination," [19] an all-or-nothing logic that knows only citizens *or* foreigners and that draws a sharp line between those who are welcomed into the sacred circle of the national community and those who are excluded from it. In its most radical versions, the suspicion toward the republican model of national community leads to the erasure of the differences between conservatives and progressivists, monarchists and *radicaux,* who are now seen as sharing the same unitary conception of the nation in spite of the many differences in their ideological definitions of it.

While the optimistic version of the national contract (from the Left) aims at the assimilation of newcomers via their acculturation to the symbols and practices of the majority, the pessimistic version (from the Right) demands the rejection of all those unassimilable elements that threaten to corrupt common values.[20] In either case, this French model of nation building is said to prevent the advent of a pluralistic, multicultural society in which respect for differences and a willingness to give full recognition to immigrant communities are central values.

One encounters this type of interpretation in France as well. In an issue of the daily *Libération* devoted to the hunger strike of dozens of illegal African immigrants in a Parisian church in the summer of 1996, Algerian writer Benjamin Stora deplored that "the idea of the nation in France has not been identified with 'melting-pot' values but on the contrary with the acceptation and the imposition of leveling principles enacted by the republican state. The purity of the republican culture is maintained through the negation of cultural or religious differences." Stora acknowledged that what he called "postmodern racism" involved an exacerbation of differences; he insisted, however, that "the negation of all differences" was not an adequate "antidote" to the current radicalization of difference.

Explicitly or not, this French model is often contrasted with an Anglo-American, "liberal" model of national identity, which is said to be thriving despite tangible obstacles and temporary setbacks in the former settler colonies of the British empire, Australia, Canada, and the United States. It is precisely in those countries where individualism and pluralism have combined in a specific form of liberalism that has remained relatively uncontaminated by either Jacobinism or ethnic-linguistic nationalism that the new multicultural paradigms have been the most successful, especially among minorities and postcolonial populations who struggle for the recognition of their rights. It is not by chance that many of the leading theoreticians of colonial discourse analysis are from former British colonies (Bhabha, Spivak) or else were trained in the British intellectual tradition (Said). In many ways, the current critique of the French national idea derives from an earlier but still resilient liberal hostility toward the centralizing tendencies of the Jacobin, and later socialist, traditions.[21]

FRENCH CULTURAL STUDIES?

Sandy Petrey has aptly described the extent to which the new analytical grids of cultural studies radically subvert the French conception of literature as a sacred symbol of the historical continuity of the nation, a conception that has had a long-lasting influence on the teaching of French in the United States:

> One of the foundational lessons of Cultural Studies is that every modern nation consists of multiple identities, that any attempt to impose a single identity is a brutal assault on justice and reality at once . . . Cultural Studies is in part an insurgency against the idea that "France" is capable of holding itself together, much less all that we American teachers of French place within its conceptual boundaries. To argue that French studies can be "restored" and "resurrected" by Cultural Studies is rather like saying dirty oil paintings can be restored by a bath of sulfuric acid. (389–90)

The point here is that the Republicans' ideological investment in the artistic and literary tradition of their country was so strong that it even shaped the teaching of French literature and civilization abroad. The universalistic mythology that French cultural products were supposed to embody came, as it were, with the package. In other words, one could not separate the cultural material, texts, paintings, and monuments from the ideological work the discourse on the *mission civilisatrice* had performed upon them. To teach French culture was at the same time to celebrate its universal nature, since, as Ernst Curtius, one of the most perceptive foreign students of French "civilization" remarked half a century ago, "all the claims made by the universal idea are imported into the national idea. It is precisely because France fulfills her national ideal that she believes that she can realize a universal value" (19).[22]

The institutional control of the literary canon by the French school system and the major publishing houses in France is now perceived by many teachers and scholars of French in the United States as the imposition of a colonial form of cultural marginality. Witness the following comments, prefacing a collection of critical essays on French and Francophone literatures:

> To judge from recent conferences and publications, the lists of works vital to the current thinking about French literature on this side of the Atlantic is becoming more and more different from the curriculum promoted by the formidable French educational establishment. This continental drift creates no insurmountable obstacles for us in our scholarly lives, since we have already developed our independent publication channels. However, in our pedagogical lives we still live as colonials, dependent on the mother country for essential resources: the reading lists for courses on French taught in America are determined in large part by the selection of works available in the collections—from Classiques Larousse to Garnier-Flammarion— edited for French schoolchildren.[23]

American educators, like colonized people, are said to suffer from the cultural schizophrenia Frantz Fanon diagnosed a few decades ago in his writings on the colonial psyche. Consequently, critics of French cultural politics call upon their colleagues to mobilize for independence and self-assertion in a manner reminiscent of anticolonial struggles: "If we do not work to create new options, then we will be forced to live with those created by and for teachers of French in France, to continue to live in cultural marginality, influenced by our native critical tradition but dependent on a foreign cultural patrimony" (DeJean and Miller, 9).

This statement is particularly striking in view of the extensive power it grants to the French educational establishment, described as a kind of cultural Leviathan impervious to change or even criticism because of its direct implication in the state apparatus to a degree unparalleled in liberal societies. Salvation can only be found in the establishment of a counter-canon in the United States, since it seems unlikely that the French university system, and by extension French society as a whole, will ever question the "official version" of the national literature. Recent reactions in France to what is perceived as the destruction of the French and European classical literary traditions on American campuses only reinforce in many scholars of France in the United States the feeling of being faced with an unreformed cultural hegemony.

It is precisely because the link between the legitimate corpus of *belles-lettres* and the national-republican idea is so strong that any questioning of the latter (the critique of French colonialism or immigration policies) implies a rejection of the former (the critique of the Eurocentrism of Enlightenment metaphysical rationalism). In other words, the charge against the imperial, assimilationist past of the French Republic goes hand in hand with the deconstruction of its literary canon as the agent of cultural imposition for the nation-state. As a consequence, the critique of the French model of nation formation often resorts to the colonial trope, even when dealing with cultures and peoples inside *l'hexagone*.

Take for example the conclusion of *Peasants into Frenchmen*, Eugen Weber's classic study of the nationalization of peasant communities by the government of the Third Republic. In the final pages of the book, Weber offers a colonial reading of the political and pedagogical work of republican national construction referring explicitly to Fanon's views: "Fanon's account of the colonial experience is an apt description of what happened in the Landes or Corrèze. In France as in Algeria, the destruction of what Fanon called national culture, and what I would call local or regional culture, was systematically pursued" (491).[24] Here, as in numerous instances of more recent postcolonial criticism, the denunciation of French imperialism is intricately woven with the critique of republicanism.

Yet Weber does not entirely subscribe to Fanon's views in the matter, mainly because he feels Fanon underestimates the choices available to, and the autonomy exercised by, the colonized.[25] In France, Weber argues, traditional cultures were not nationalized entirely against their own will: "New ways that had once seemed objectionable were now deliberately pursued and assimilated—not by a fawning 'bourgeoisie' or self-indulgent 'intellectuals,' as in Fanon's account—but by people of all sorts who had been exposed to such ways and acquired a taste for them" (492).

Weber's reservations regarding an absolutist kind of Fanonism, guilty of negating the relative freedom and autonomy of the subaltern, anticipates some of the most debated issues in colonial and postcolonial studies today. A reductive view of cultural domination that describes both modernization in the metropolis and colonialism overseas as a process of deculturation of premodern societies ends up denying any possibility of resistance to the subjects of foreign hegemony. Terms such as "deculturation" or "cultural genocide" are often problematic because they imply that the void left by the destruction of traditional cultures can only be filled with absolute submission. A Manichean interpretation of this kind can only conclude with a complete dispossession of the conquered communities. Moreover, it lays itself open to attacks from those who see situations of contact between cultures as complex processes whereby dominant and dominated groups interact, struggle against, and influence one another, in a postmodernist version of the Hegelian dialectics of master and slave.

The promoters of *métissage* are taken to task by the advocates of the assimilationist paradigm, who accuse them of underestimating the impact of structures of domination. In an influential article, Henry Louis Gates Jr. has described the critical double bind produced by the two rival positions: "You can empower discursively the native, and open yourself to charges of downplaying the epistemic (and literal) violence of colonialism; or play up the absolute nature of colonial domination, and be open to charges of negating the subjectivity and agency of the colonized, thus textually replicating the repressive operations of colonialism" (426).

One way out of the predicament is to acknowledge that situations of domination rarely destroy cultures and societies entirely (except in extreme cases of systematic genocide). Instead, they transform them, making those practices that are incompatible with the new configuration of power obsolete without annihilating the human capacity to survive. In any case, the debates over colonialism have a direct impact on the assessment of the French republican ideology, if only because of the close historical ties between the republican project and colonization.[26]

Herman Lebovics's study of the intersection between French identity and imperialism starts off by examining "the paradigm of an exclusive French identity" that holds that "there can be only one way to participate in the culture of a country and only one natural political organization that fits the society" (xiii).[27] The dominance of such a model of identity assumes hegemonic proportions since it is equally shared by the Right and the Left, thus covering almost the totality of the ideological spectrum. Although Lebovics's study is limited to the period between the Dreyfus affair and the end of World War II, the assumption here is that the monolithic conception of national consciousness that prevailed at the time is rooted in previous developments in French culture and still continues today to hold sway over the minds of all those French men and women who support or tolerate the National Front.

In Lebovics's view, the discourse on "True France," while particularly acute in the writings of right-wing nationalists, is the offspring of a widely shared French cultural universalism derived from "Gallican Catholicism, absolutism, the Enlightenment and Jacobinism, and finally conservative republicanism" and driven by "an often contested but never-defeated logic of convergence and conformism" (xiii). The enduring power of such a legacy, made up of long-standing discursive habits that constitute "the peculiarity of the French," explains the ideological consensus surrounding the definition of national identity, "the zero-sum combats between left and right for the right to speak on behalf of True France in anthropological discourse, in colonial ideology, in folklore theory, in the 1920's, during the Popular Front, under Vichy rule, and even today" (xiii).

The republican model of integration is still so prevalent today that the Muslim population is faced with an impossible choice, since "to reconcile the republican contract [of citizenship] with the claims of place and kind requires immigrants, colonials, even provincials either to abandon their first identities (few can easily see themselves as "Afro-French or "Arab-French") or to be wrapped in the straitjacket of a state-approved identity that since the Third Republic has excluded the religious dimensions of people's lives" (196). In the French context, the hyphenation of identity so characteristic of the description and self-definition of ethnic groups in the United States is impossible.

In this view, the struggles among the various forms of ontological nationalisms are not contentions over the definition of what constitutes *francité*, but rather over which camp can legitimately articulate the essential features of nationhood in the most appropriate way. Even the Communists are not immune from the power of the dominant model, since "the PCF's ambivalence about anticolonial struggles—and domestic cultural ones—stemmed from an acceptance of the validity of the European essentialist high cultural paradigm" (99), while "important spokesmen of the left, even in statements assailing the inheritors of France, continued to think within the Maurrassian paradigm" (159). Didn't Louis Aragon himself write at the time of the Popular Front that "our French novel is French because it expresses the profound spirit of the French people . . . It is the arm of the true French against the two hundred families who run the banks, the gambling houses and the brothels"? (159).

To Aragon, the foreignness of the bourgeoisie (to him it is not *truly* French) accounts for its moral deficiency and political bankruptcy. This kind of proletarian patriotism echoes the Jacobins' claims that the Frank-ish (i.e., not native, not Gallo-Roman) origins of the aristocracy explained their penchant for treachery. All of this seems to suggest that there was very little room indeed for any resistance to the overwhelming force of such a widely shared definition of national belonging. Only the Surrealists and other dissident groups of the Ultra-Left were apparently immune to the interwar epidemics of nativistic essentialism. Breton and his cohorts successfully staged a counter-Exhibition aimed at discrediting the assimilationist views of "Greater France" propagated by the 1931 Exposition coloniale internationale in Paris.

In fact, as the subtitle of the book, *The Wars over Cultural Identity*, suggests, there is in Herman Lebovics's argument a tension between statements that seem to support the view of French cultural discourse as a monolithic "metaphysic of national identity" and passages where the supposed consensus becomes the contested site of competing expressions of national consciousness. The preface urges the reader to approach national cultures "not as simple repositories of shared symbols to which the entire population stands in identical relation," but rather "as sites of contestation in which competition over definitions takes place" (xii). Presumably, this applies to French conceptions of the national community as well and is enough to render the notion of a monolithic discourse in these matters somewhat problematic.

Lebovics eventually qualifies his earlier assertion that both Right and Left contributed in similar and complicitous fashion to the imposition of the metaphysics of True France. "In France," he concedes, "the traditional impulse came from the politically conservative side, and the cosmopolitan one was the position of the left—at least some of the left in the 1930s" (7). More importantly, the compelling analysis Lebovics makes of the ideology of Greater France embodied in the Colonial Exhibition underscores the tensions and contradictions within the dominant narratives of empire between assimilationist and associationist views of the colonial enterprise. The rhetoric of the Exposition does not support the view that French cultural imperialism aimed unequivocally at the complete eradication of colonial cultures described as premodern and consequently prerational. On the contrary, the vision of the colonial empire as La Grande France implied the preservation of traditional ways of life among the colonized peoples. The official guide to the Exhibition hopes that "our Africa, tightly bound to us now for both its defense and its prosperity, will become a magnificent and direct extension of French humanity" (79).

The expanded, renewed definition of what constitutes Frenchness in the imperial era combines integration and association (or pluralism): the inclusion of colonized peoples and cultures is congruent with the celebration of native ways, the very object of the exhibition itself. Higher education in the colonies, for the culturalist reformers of the imperial idea, ought to be adapted to "the mentalités and the habitat of each of the great colonies, to their resources, needs, and special conditions," as a resolution at the 1931 Congress of the Société Générale de Géographie commerciale stated. According to Lebovics, "the line between here and there, between metropolitan France and the colonies, is erased; it is a pictorial representation of an ethnically diverse but politically unified and centralized French empire" (69).

Of course, the preservation of pre-imperial ways of life and thought in the colonies is not born of a disinterested respect for difference per se. As Lebovics is quick to point out, the apology of traditional peasant societies in France as well as abroad was part and parcel of the ideological struggle of the conservative establishment against the forces that threatened to undermine the political order, that is, the forces of industrial modernity: the working class, the unions, progressivist ideas, the Communists at home and in the colonies, and so on. Which shows, once again, that culturalism can be put to the same reactionary uses as regionalism, and that the celebration of difference, yesterday as today, can serve the most regressive and repressive agendas.[28]

The reformers aimed at reviving traditional cultures as a bulwark against modernization. Lebovics is at his best when he shows that the ideology of Greater France, the result of close collaboration between "scientific" anthropologists and forward-looking, reform-minded soldiers and administrators, such as Lyautey, marked "an important new departure in French thinking about the place of indigenous culture under colonial rule" (101). In the same way that Barresian and Maurrassian regionalisms aimed at undoing modernity by turning Frenchmen into peasants, the new policies strove to reroot the Vietnamese into their villages to insulate them from the pernicious influence of modern times. The point was "to persuade the French to accept an imperial sense of Frenchness and to persuade colonial people to return to French-nurtured roots so that by becoming more native they could be more French" (189).

The problem of course is that you can't—in the name of the civilizing mission—have your traditional cake and eat it too. The conquest as contact had set in motion forces that no amount of effort to reinvent tradition and reroot the uprooted would ever reverse. The new cultural policy of enlightened ethnography involved, as Lebovics puts it, "the French invention of a new native cultural tradition for the people of Indochina to don" (101). But it was of course not possible to keep all the peasants in the village, to exclude all promising indigenous students from studying in the metropolis. The needs of the colonial administration, that is, the valuation of native traditional cultures for political purposes, and the ideology of human rights that stood at the heart of republicanism demanded the formation of a colonial elite.[29] Although they expressed different viewpoints and crystallized the demands and concerns of competing constituencies, administrators, politicians, educators, and savants, various forces converged to apply pressure to the system.[30] What *émigré* students and immigrant workers acquired in the metropolis, as the biographies of Césaire, Senghor, or Ho Chi Minh amply demonstrate, is both a renewed sense of the value of their own culture *and* tools for revolt and resistance borrowed from Western philosophical modernity, from Rousseau to Marx.

The interpenetration of cultures is a two-way street, even if the various participants in the process do not wield equal amounts of power, and empire and colony are not two ontologically distinct entities. Lebovics ends up rejecting Fanon's use of the Sartrean model of oppressor and oppressed since it "fits badly into most contemporary discussions of resistance struggles" (124). On the one side, we see "colonial administrators who admired the civilizations of Indochina and tried to revive them," albeit in the name of repressive tolerance, and on the other, "Westernized native radical intellectuals seeking European knowledge" (124). Fittingly enough, the ideas of the French Revolution once again figure prominently at the core of this "European knowledge." In their struggle against empire, the students from the colonies "invoked the values of the French Revolution and of republicanism in their combats with the French Republic" (124).

Lebovics's argument, it seems, has come full circle: the republican ideal is turned against the reality of an imperfect Republic. His conclusion somehow reverses his previous considerations on the all-encompassing reach of "French cultural universalism" and its attendant monolithic conception of identity as essence. We are told at the close of the book that French culture alone may hold the key to the cultural and racial crises of our fin de siècle:

> France can point us in the direction toward which we should move the emancipatory project [of the Enlightenment] that recognized diversity, toward a non-repressive unity of mankind. Because of both

its ideology and often, its history of being the second home of humankind, the heartland of cosmopolitanism, as it were, France today
is in a position to lead the world by example in the creation of a culture of modernity which combines tolerance, non exclusivity, open-
ness, and the ethics of humanity. (200)

Lebovics's position resembles the quest for a third way between ethnic
nationalism and liberal differentialism that can be found in the writings of
contemporary French authors discussed in the previous chapter. Lebovics
claims that the pluralistic universalism that has set France "off from other
nations and yet has marked it as the special seat for the hopes of humankind" renders French culture more apt than its American counterpart to
ward off some of the worst consequences of the liberal politics of difference, and to create "a new world that transcends variety without suppressing it, that achieves new unities and syntheses of cultural life" (200). The
value of French universalism lies in that it "will never yield to any ideology
of incremental pluralism such as the United States proclaims with each
newly recognized ethnic group being taken into the polity after overcom-
ing the bigotry and poverty that held it back" (200).

The rehabilitation of universalism as pluralism is supported by a reading of French history as a struggle between *two* Frances, one tolerant and
pluralistic, the other xenophobic and essentialist. Lebovics cites as defining
moments in the French narrative of tolerance Henri IV's Edict of Nantes
(as political compromise and solution to religious strife), Candide and the
Enlightenment, the French Revolution, 1848 and the Commune, the victory of the Dreyfusards, the "magnificent and noble pluralism" of the Surrealists, decolonization, and the recent "acceptance of the idea of Europe."
Lebovics champions in the end the view of a progressivist, enlightened
France popularized by the very same republican and leftist traditions that
could be seen as complicitous in the elaboration of the interwar ideology
of True France at the beginning of his book.

Lebovics's account of colonial policies in the thirties calls into question
the view that the French model of national identity is destructive of diversity and advocates a more contrasted view of the various strands that make
up the fabric of French cultural politics. His conclusion regarding the contested character of the country's political history, as well as the explicit link
he makes between regionalism at home and culturalism abroad, calls for a
reexamination of the way recent historiography describes the mechanisms
of nation formation in the French context.

THE REGIONAL REPUBLIC

The jaundiced view of the republican synthesis shared by many British and American critics of the French national idea does not go unchallenged on this side of the Atlantic. Brett C. Bowles notes that Eugen Weber's theses were paradoxically very well received in France at the time, since they answered a collective need to be reassured of the continuity of a national identity threatened by European integration, Americanization, and immigration.[31] Yet Bowles argues against Weber, insisting that to instill a durable feeling of nationalness in the French villages could only be achieved through the acceptance of local and provincial attachments. Central to Bowles's reassessment of the early years of the nationalization of French culture and politics is what he calls "the regional Republic," a necessary compromise on the road to national loyalty, an intermediary stage between the concrete village community and the abstract universalism shared by the republican ideologists.

In fact, as Maurice Agulhon has shown, the establishment of the republic in the village rested on the fusion of imported urban ideologies and traditional rural practices, which explains "the coexistence, throughout a long period in nineteenth-century France, of folk life and left-wing ideas" (*La République au village*, 265). Historically, the national consciousness had to be rooted in local communities if it was ever to gain the support of the peasantry. The schoolteachers themselves, the so-called apostles of the Republic, came from these same rural communities and grew up speaking the very dialects they are blamed by some for having forcefully eradicated in the name of the metanarratives of Reason and Progress.

Herman Lebovics, whose work, as we saw, is at times quite critical of French cultural universalism in the name of a Foucauldian dissolution of identity, acknowledges the limits of linguistic and cultural centralization in early republican France. He cites the work of French historian Jean-François Chanet, who, "basing his conclusions on the preliminary results of an extensive survey of what in fact were the attitudes and practices of teachers toward the local patois, found little of that infamous crushing of the local language or of the children who spoke it." Lebovics goes on to say that "in surprising numbers of cases the teachers spoke the regional patois and used it in class as they needed it or as they found pedagogically useful . . . What republicans were trying to get at was less the local language than the clerical and conservative things said in it" (144). Lebovics concludes that "already a powerful myth before World War I, the charge that the secular republic tried to destroy regional peculiarities with its cultural centralization, carried out primarily by the village schoolmasters, has recently come seriously into question" (144).

This myth has also been questioned by Caroline Ford's illuminating study of the rise of Catholic republicanism in Brittany during the Third Republic.[32] Ford refutes the thesis that the Republican government succeeded in imposing cultural and political uniformity from the top down, arguing that "the introduction of the social Catholic movement [in Brittany] . . . provided the electorate with the means to reconcile the democratic claims of a larger republican nation with religious and regional loyalties" (134).

Ford concurs with Chanet's findings and Lebovics's comments. Despite the traditional association in leftist discourse between regional languages and federalism, clericalism, religious fanaticism, and counterrevolution,[33] Ford argues that "the founders of the Third Republic did not . . . make linguistic or cultural unity essential to republican efforts to integrate the country's diverse social groups. Republicans who included Jules Ferry and Léon Gambetta openly acknowledged the vitality of regional differences" (18). In the early years of the new regime, educators "with impeccable republican credentials" tolerated the use of regional languages in schools. The ministry of education, although strongly supportive of the popular diffusion of the French language in the village classroom by primary schoolteachers (the "black hussars of the Republic"), nonetheless often recommended "gentle means of persuasion and tolerated bilingual methods of language instruction" (19). It is only after the replacement of the Opportunistes by the Radical republicans that regional languages and cultures became the target of government policies aimed at eradicating what the Jacobin Left ritually denounced as the Trojan horse of reactionary fanaticism.

Ford's central thesis is that local culture was not simply the reactionary site of resistance to the Paris-led political liberalization and economic modernization of backward areas, but served as a mediator between the village community and the nation. "The history of the lower Breton department of Finistère shows that political change and national awareness were effected not through the wholesale importation of urban values, Parisian political movements, and the assimilation of the periphery into the center, but through an indigenous movement that emerged in the countryside and ultimately came to represent the periphery at the center" (9).

This religious, cultural, and political movement eventually blossomed into the establishment of a full-fledged Christian-democratic party in lower Brittany. It shared elements of right-wing and left-wing ideology, and at the same time refused to align itself unconditionally with either the republican or the royalist camp. "The introduction of the social Catholic movement in the department, which rejected the hierarchical, antirepublican politics by birthright while simultaneously voicing the legitimacy of the religious identity of the region, provided the electorate with the means to reconcile the democratic claims of a larger republican nation with religious and regional loyalties" (134). In short, it contributed to the establishment of Bowles's regional republic.

The example of Brittany is particularly telling, since it was one of the last feudal estates to be incorporated as a province in the royal domain in 1532. The combination of poverty and archaic agricultural practices, pre-Roman language and culture, and unusual devotion to the most traditional forms of Catholicism helped create an image of Brittany as an antimodernist, backward-looking land of pagan mysteries, crass ignorance, irrational barbarity, and unenlightened fanaticism, in other words, the perfect antithesis of the "civilization" the Republicans had taken as their mission to propagate into the remotest corners of the nation. The notion that Brittany, Vendée, and most of northwestern France were counterrevolutionary strongholds makes the dissemination of republican sensibilities among the peasantry all the more striking.

Ford's conclusions indicate that neither the progressivists nor the traditionalists succeeded in imposing their competing though complicitous versions of an essentialized True France. The success of the clerical republicans, an oxymoron for both the advocates of the secular Republic and the supporters of the Catholic Right, shows that there was indeed a space within the supposedly intractable iron maiden of French centralism for practices that escaped the dominant politics of national identity. For the Breton peasants who rallied the republican camp and the priests who led and represented them, the defense of local and regional interests was not perceived as antithetic to a national-republican consciousness, even when the anticlerical policies of the *radicaux* led to open rebellion against the government, as in 1902.

That year, the recently elected radical republican government of Emile Combes, a former seminarist turned fiercely anticlerical, had started to implement the Law on Associations devised a few months earlier by his more moderate predecessor, René Waldeck-Rousseau. The bill, directed at religious orders such as the Assomptionists who had actively opposed the republicans during the Dreyfus affair, required teaching congregations to be authorized by the Conseil d'Etat and to accept the jurisdictional authority of the bishop. The implementation of the law by the *radicaux* met with indifference in widely dechristianized southern France and with mere reprobation in the north. In Finistère it caused an uprising. The Breton insurrection, reminiscent of the Vendée uprisings of 1792–94, fueled the republicans' paranoia and comforted them in their belief that rural Brittany had hopelessly remained a bastion of counterrevolution. "The government and to a large extent historians who have adopted its language," Ford writes, "took the incidents of 1902 in Finistère to be a revolt of a superstitious and barbarous population completely cowed by châtelain and priest. This merely reinforced the government's belief in the legitimacy of the state's mission civilisatrice" (169).

In fact, the main consequence of the implementation of the law, that is, the closing of many confessional schools in villages and small towns, had social consequences that went far beyond the results of a purely ideological war, since religious institutions played an important role in the lives of rural Bretons by providing education (notably to women) and social and economic assistance (the traditional function of the church in poor areas). The peasants and fishermen "could only view the government legislation as a policy whose result would be the financial ruin of communes and families and the collapse of local institutions and networks of public assistance" (169). The fact that republican towns and fishing villages also joined the struggle is a clear indication that the revolt was motivated not only by royalist, reactionary sentiment.

The supporters of Combes and Waldeck-Rousseau admitted of no third party between their views and the factious antirepublicanism of the reactionaries. Republican politics were driven by a dualistic conception of a clear-cut struggle between "them and us," where them meant a monolithic, extremist catholic Right that manipulated the backward rural masses and brainwashed them into clinging to their irrational beliefs in order to keep them from embracing the emancipatory narratives of reason and progress. The radical republicans failed to appreciate the extent to which, as Ford puts it, the "Bretons framed their petitions and protests in the language of the Republic and in the terms of the revolutionary Declaration of the Rights of Man and Citizen, a framework indicating the degree to which these admittedly devout communities had assimilated and transformed the discourse of the Republic into a public defense of local institutions" (169).

The successful articulation of Breton and French identities, and, more generally, of local and national concerns described by Ford and other historians of nation building in France, is another instance of transculturation, which is almost always a two-way process.[34] In fact, this is what cultural work is all about: the interpenetration of cultures, the constant refashioning and updating of time-honored beliefs and practices in the face of social and economic change, cultural contact, and outside political influences or domination. The nation the Breton republican peasants associated and identified with was not that of their secular rulers in Paris: the successful challenge they mounted against the latter at the grassroots level in local elections showed that they were determined to articulate their own version of what the Republic should be, and find their own place, and their own voice, within the national framework.

This brief review of some recent scholarship on the dynamics of the republicanization of provincial France reveals how phantasmic it is to represent French culture as a ruthless totalizing juggernaut bent on eradicating all traces of ethnic, religious, or linguistic difference. As Mona Ozouf has remarked, the struggle between the Jacobin spirit and local attachments was never as hard and dramatic as republican ideologues and radical regionalists wished it to be, for obvious political reasons. Belonging to the larger nation did not always require renouncing the smaller homeland. "People were not in any way betraying their own region in pledging allegiance to France," Ozouf writes, "since France was less an empirical and natural nation than a rational one" (273). This explains in turn why separatism has remained rather weak in France and why, as in Brittany, "republican loyalism has constantly reasserted itself, in spite of the less than gentle repression of minority languages . . . No doubt French politics continues to ward off centrifugal temptations in advance and to invent federalist enemies for itself. But that is precisely the point: it invents them. Since the Revolution, they have been paper tigers" (273).

The same might be true of multiculturalist enemies, whether they are purported to favor ethnic minorities or the "native" majority. After all, for all the anti-Semitism that plagued both the patriotic Left and the nationalistic Right during the Dreyfus affair, the defenders of the Jewish captain, not their powerful opponents in the government, the church, and the army, are the ones who carried the day.[35]

5

Multiculturalism
and Its Discontents

◦ᴗ· ◦ᴗ· ◦ᴗ·

*P*ostmodernist critics of the French
national idea do not hold a mo-
nopoly on generalization and oversimplification. Some of the most vocal
guardians of the republican faith in France today are guilty of the same,
even though they paint a strictly inverted picture of the relationship between cultural pluralism and national identity. The notion of a radical incompatibility between a liberal-pluralist and a rationalist-universalist project of nation building, historically carried out in Britain and the United
States on the one hand and in France on the other is not limited to Anglo-
American scholarly literature and printed media. This view is shared by
many French intellectuals as well, the difference being, not surprisingly,
that they see *their* national tradition as superior and most likely to ensure
the interethnic harmony of postcolonial societies.

The same is true of politicians and journalists, not to mention individuals who voice their hostility to *le différentialisme anglo-saxon* in letters to the editors of leading French newspapers. The coverage by the French media of the debates on political correctness in America is often limited to a flat-out rejection of multiculturalism, construed as the excessive radicalization of minority claims that will lead inevitably to the tearing of the national fabric.[1] Once again, the United States stands out as the pathological future of Europe, as the harbinger of the interethnic cataclysms that would threaten France itself if it were to espouse the radical liberalism, epistemological relativism, and cultural pluralism of the American postmodernists. Jean-François Fourny rightly talks of "the specter of Anglo-Saxon multiculturalism" that haunts the French imagination (50).

A few examples drawn from recent publications show how the rejection of the American model of national integration (or rather, in this case, disintegration) is rooted in the present reactivation of civic nationalism as the ultimate line of defense against racial and religious wars. Régis Debray, for example, contrasts the neo-Kantian humanism of the philosophers of the Third Republic with the various strands of contemporary antihumanism undermining civic values. At this point, the argument links up with current debates on the culture wars and on epistemological skepticism (the so-called "science wars"), since one of the consequences of the triumph of what Debray calls democracy (i.e., Anglo-American "liberalism") over republican principles is an irrationalist return to ethnic communitarianism.

Alain Finkielkraut's critique of multiculturalism in *The Defeat of the Mind* shows why the debates of the 1790s can profitably be imported into those of the 1990s, since the book explicitly links contemporary cultural relativism with late eighteenth-century Herderian romanticism. Finkielkraut quite correctly reminds his readers that German cultural nationalism unfolded historically as a response to the abstract universalism of the French Enlightenment (as in Herder's critique of Voltaire). The German ideology later served to legitimize Prussian expansionism and the annexation of Alsace-Lorraine in 1871. The German historicist conception of the national community as all-encompassing totality was at odds with the French idea of the nation, defined by Renan and Fustel de Coulanges as a free and voluntary association of consenting individuals: nation as genius (or genus) versus nation as contract. The French Right's paradoxical appropriation of the German conception of *l'être ensemble* after the Franco-Prussian war of 1870–71 would place the contest between the two competing definitions of the national at the very heart of the politics of the new republic, all the way to the philosophical civil war that was the Dreyfus affair and beyond, to contemporary struggles over the national idea.

Régis Debray, for example, takes up again the opposition between nation as genius and nation as contract:

"Nationalism" is a huge misunderstanding. For the word has two meanings: one, reactionary or medieval, based on race and heredity: the ethnic nation. The other, progressive and born of the French Revolution, based on the willful adherence to a common project: the elective nation. Those who confuse the first meaning with the second take Déroulède's France for that of Valmy, and mix up Pétain with de Gaulle . . . What if tomorrow's choice was not "federalism or nationalism," but the nation according to de Gaulle or the tribe according to Le Pen? (*Contretemps*, 160)

This distinction between two kinds of national community is constitutive of most histories of European nationalisms, and reappears under different guises. Eric Hobsbawm opposes an "objective" definition of the national community based on collective, inherited characteristics and a "subjective" one, predicated on voluntary choice. Hobsbawm also speaks of "revolutionary-democratic" and "nationalist" concepts of the nations: "The equation state = nation = people applied to both, but for nationalists the creation of political entities which would contain it derived from the prior existence of some community distinguishing itself from foreigners, while from the revolutionary-democratic point of view the central concept was the sovereign citizen-people = state which, in relation to the remainder of the human race, constituted a 'nation'" (22).

Liah Greenfeld's typology opposes civic and ethnic types of nationalisms, based on rival interpretations of popular sovereignty. The first category (civic) is itself broken down into two groups: individualistic-libertarian (the source of sovereignty and legitimacy lies in the individual) and collectivist-authoritarian (the source of sovereignty and legitimacy lies in the incorporation of individuals into a higher, transcendent totality). Greenfeld's own interpretation of the genealogy of nationalism clearly identifies the first type (civic-individualistic) with Anglo-American conceptions of the national, while the French discourse of the nation belongs to the second category (civic-collectivist). German romantic nationalism obviously fits the third category (ethnic and collectivist). The contested terrain of national ideologies is almost always framed within a triangle whose apices are occupied by English, French, and German cultures as archetypes of Western national sentiment.

The second half of Finkielkraut's argument consists of making nineteenth-century romantic nationalism the matrix of contemporary culturalist ideologies, thereby uncovering a profound continuity in the history of ideas, including the affinities and complicity between structuralism and the various kinds of postmodernism. Finkielkraut reinscribes these discourses in the long history of the critique of metaphysics that began with Herder and his disciples, arguing that the French traditionalists (from de Maistre to Maurras) have replaced Pascal's God with that of the German Deists, moving away from Christian universalism and doing away with transcendence. "Behind the appearance of a simple return to the past, the counterrevolution abolished all transcendental values, divine as well as human. The abstract individual and the superterrestrial God were subsumed at the same time into the soul of the nation, as culture . . . Paradoxically, *this return to religion required the destruction of metaphysics*" (italics in the text, 18–19).

Finkielkraut's critical genealogy of nationalistic romanticism incorporates the postwar philosophies of suspicion within the legacy of counterrevolutionary historicism. From Lévi-Strauss's critique of Western universalism and evolutionism to the Foucauldian theory of the death of Man, what Finkielkraut calls the "philosophy of decolonization" opposed the Subject (or Man) and Difference, just as German romanticism had done:

> Denouncing the basic inhumanity of humanism and looking for the particular, the historic, the regional behind everything that might be mistaken for universal, they found themselves staging an old play, changing the characters and scenery only slightly . . . The drama remained essentially the same: the conflict between those who saw man in the singular and those who saw him in the plural. Thus the philosophy of decolonization fought ethnocentrism with the arguments and concepts molded by the German romantics in their struggle against the Enlightenment. (64–65)

The common thread linking romanticism to poststructuralism is antihumanism. The Heideggerian sacralization of language (the theme of the philosopher-poet as the shepherd of Being) and the notion of collective unconscious so germane to the linguistic turn of postwar French philosophy are for Finkielkraut a direct legacy of the romantic outlook. The historicist side of romanticism, which implies the basic heteronomy of human beings vis-à-vis nature, language, or society, resurfaces in the Althusserian view of history as a process without a subject.[2]

Finkielkraut is quite close to both Touraine and Debray in these matters. With Touraine, he shares the conviction that there is no third party between those who see man in the singular and those who see him in the plural, between ethnic and civic conceptions of the national: "There is no place for the individual in the logic of identity politics" (69). The critique of the contractual and consensual space of liberal-democratic politics, even in the name of a generous concern for minorities and diversity, can only lead to a differentialism that inevitably ends up sanctioning separatism, racism, and the war of all against all. With Debray and with the whole French republican tradition, Finkielkraut shares a deep-seated belief in the necessity to maintain the transcendence of ethical categories, to resist historicism, to make transhistorical reason the ultimate judge of history.

MULTICULTURALISM, THERE IS THE ENEMY

At first sight, the philosophy of decolonization and the contemporary forms of relativism and skepticism seem to inhabit incompatible worlds. The former implies, as in Fanon's case, the rejection of Western universalism as a particularly hypocritical form of cultural imperialism. It also implies a celebration of indigenous cultures common to many anticolonialist nationalisms. The cult of difference and the antiracism shared by many multiculturalists, on the contrary, rests on the pluralization of identity and the foregrounding of *métissage* and hybridity. On the one hand, we have the focused, intense struggle for national liberation anchored in the modern imaginary of revolutionary violence, and on the other, the cool, relaxed ethos of postmodernism, all open-mindedness and tolerance.

While acknowledging that both programs are in many ways "rigorously antinomic," since the postmodern sensitivity substitutes eclecticism for exclusiveness, fluidity for rootedness, and "everyone's right to the specificity of the other" for an older, more militant right to be different, Finkielkraut nonetheless insists on their similarities: a staunch antimodernism, the rejection of universalism, and repeated claims for the absolute equivalency and equality of cultures. Ethnic separatism and cultural *métissage* are ultimately characterized as two versions, one hard, the other soft, of what

Renan stigmatized in his days as "the ethnographic and archeological politics" of the Prussian annexionnists. Apparently incompatible, the two discourses work together in opposing the unitary, civic, and voluntaristic conception of national belonging of the neo-Kantian Republicans.

Finkielkraut clearly wishes to position himself within a prestigious line of prophetic voices who, from Renan to Benda, have made it their duty to safeguard what they take to be the *French* idea of the nation. They did so in moments of deep crisis of the philosophical consensus that supports the national idea: in the 1870s, 1920s, and 1980s—each time the counterrevolutionary cult of the local raised its ugly head and threatened an always fragile national unity. In a glowing review of *The Defeat of the Mind,* Roger Kimball stresses the continuity between "the young French philosopher and cultural critic" and his illustrious predecessors. Finkielkraut "took up where Benda left off, producing a brief but searching inventory of our contemporary cataclysms . . . The book is a *trahison des clercs* for the post-Communist world, a world dominated as much by the leveling imperatives of pop culture as by resurgent nationalism and ethnic separatisms" (12).

Finkielkraut's numerous references to Condorcet, Renan, and Benda, as well as Kimball's endorsement of this legacy, again show that the intertextuality of the French Enlightenment contributes to the upkeep of a particular version of the French national character. Kimball highlights the philosophical filiation between Finkielkraut and Renouvier, one of the founding fathers of French philosophical republicanism, a filiation that leads back to Greek rationalism: "Julien Benda took his epigraph for *La Trahison des clercs* from the nineteenth-century French philosopher Charles Renouvier: *Le monde souffre du manque de foi en une vérité transcendante:* 'The world suffers from lack of faith in a transcendent truth.' Without some such faith, we are powerless against the depredations of intellectuals who have embraced the nihilism of Callicles as their truth."[3]

Meanwhile, Kimball's enthusiastic support of Finkielkraut's project enlists the Frenchman in domestic struggles within the American intellectual field itself, pointing once again to real homologies between the structures of the debates on both sides of the Atlantic.[4] At one point, Kimball lifts off from his close reading of *La Défaite de la pensée* to embark upon a spirited diatribe against "the stunning array of anti-Enlightenment phantasmagoria congregated under the banner of 'anti-positivism,'" all considerations that are not part of Finkielkraut's argument (13). The assessment of Finkielkraut's achievements becomes the occasion of a settling of accounts with specific fractions of the *American* intellectual community, namely the adepts of critical science studies who never were the target of Finkielkraut's attacks.

In addition to American supporters of the traditionalists' literary canon, many French thinkers share Kimball's belief that the politics of identity and difference are nothing but a left-wing version of romantic antihumanism. Because they promote the same logic of identity and the same cultural relativism as romanticism, they, too, are powerful corrosive solvents of citizenship. The amalgam between multiculturalism as "a fetishism of difference" and "fascism" (often a generic term applying to all the historical variants of fundamentalist and authoritarian nationalisms) is quite prevalent among proponents of the republican idea. This denotes a profound skepticism as to the possibility of building a viable community on the basis of cultural specificities. The celebration of otherness is bound to fail and will ultimately turn into its xenophobic alter ego.

Régis Debray sees the "return of Maurras via the left" in neoregionalist movements (the *vivre au pays* agenda) and related claims to cultural and local particularity as a direct consequence of the replacement of the republican credo by the politics of difference. Alain Touraine argues for his part that the appeal to identity "produces dangerous moral majorities and still more dangerous national fronts. It is also producing a new leftist theory of difference which recognizes no general truths and which demands histories written from the point of view of Indians, women or homosexuals, as opposed to what it denounces as written by and for white men" (320). Characteristically, right-wing national front discourses, on the one hand, and leftist theories of difference, on the other, are rhetorically juxtaposed as results of the same ideological position. They are simply two closely related by-products of equally perverse species of the anti-Enlightenment vulgate.

Once again, it is in the most liberal of societies that the return on the Left of ethnic nationalism is the most troubling and the most paradoxical for all these critics. Touraine deplores that "the best American universities have seen the development of a broad movement which is paradoxically defined as 'politically correct' when it is actually based upon fundamentalist tendencies that have nothing to do with democracy" (321). In France, the rise of rival particularisms is seen as a direct consequence of the weakening of the Left, and, by implication, of the retreat of the republican culture: "A combination of intolerant minorities and a truly reactionary loyalty to a universalism . . . rapidly results in a narrow particularism that is deaf and blind to different or new social and cultural demands" (321).

For Finkielkraut, multiculturalism, although full of good intentions, is doomed to failure, if only because it is illusory to pretend to hold together in a national community groups and individuals previously valorized by their differences: "We must make a choice; we cannot celebrate universal communication at the same time we insist on the existence of non-transferable differences . . . We create an impossible contradiction in seeking to establish rules for welcoming diverse ethnic groups based on principles affirming the primacy of cultural roots" (93). The only viable pluralism, he argues, is that of the republican tradition, which maintains a strict separation by way of the notion of *laïcité* between the political arena (the public sphere) and the sphere of religion and culture (the private realm), and expects all the groups that make up the national body to respect the law of the Republic. The alternative to separatism does not reside in forced homogenization but in applying to civil society the principles that govern the political sphere: "The spirit of modern Europe accommodates itself very well to the existence of ethnic or religious minorities, on condition that they conform to the model of a nation comprised of free and equal individuals" (108).

This interpretation of multiculturalism as the latest version of the ethnic nationalism of the German romantics or of the Barresian nationalists is problematic because it insists on reading the ethnic and cultural pluralism of contemporary social formations in the light of the nationalistic tensions that bloodied the European continent during the century and a half following the Treaty of Vienna of 1815. Contemporary France, however, is not the Austrian-Hungarian empire, nor is the United States the nation of immigrants it was at the turn of the century, when isolated, unassimilated, foreign-speaking enclaves were perceived as a threat to Americanism. Today the children of immigrants in France, Britain, and the United States are not linguistically or culturally distinct from the population of the receiving countries to the extent that turn-of-the-century immigrants were. In France, interracial tensions today arise from the fact that second-generation so-called *immigrés (les Beurs)*, although perfectly acculturated to French society (they share, for example, many of the dress codes, speech mannerisms, and musical tastes of other French youths), are in large numbers not integrated into the economy and the social structure or fully included in the fabric of French life.

As a consequence, the ethnic problem in France is not cultural, linguistic, or political, but mostly socioeconomic. It is no longer a question of socializing potentially separatist foreign elements through civic and language education, but of dealing with the consequences of poor education, unemployment, and discrimination against French citizens of recent foreign origin. In many ways, as Finkielkraut's attempt to replace multiculturalist claims within the genealogy of romantic nationalism clearly shows, the discussion is still framed within notions of immigration that were predominant at the turn of the century and that were responses to developments in neighboring countries. In 1911, Jacques Berthillon, the "founding father" of French demography, predicted that France would soon have to face a *Fremdenfrage* (a foreign question) like Russia or Austria-Hungary: "Foreigners of the same nationality will group themselves in certain corners of the country: Italians along the Mediterranean, Spaniards along their borders, Belgians in the North, Germans in the East."[5] The prediction, obviously, never came to pass. Indeed, the widespread French aversion to national and cultural separatisms made sure it would never happen.

This fear of the multinational mosaic has its source in historical developments that clearly precede the xenophobic eruptions of the late 1800s or of the interwar period. The anxiety of national fragmentation goes back at least to the French Revolution. The collective trauma of the civil war and of revolutionary Terror was such that it colored most of French social philosophy with an organicist tinge. The obsessive concern for the cohesion of the social fabric is a constant feature of a lot of French postrevolutionary thought, from Saint-Simon and Comte to Durkheim, and universalism figures prominently as the ultimate line of defense against regionalisms and provincialisms of all kinds.

The unitary, centralizing thrust of the revolutionaries, and later of their republican followers, was as much a response to the particularistic agenda of their right-wing opponents as it was the expression of a blind faith in the unity of metaphysical Reason. The long-term memory of civil war explains in turn the present hostility of French public intellectuals to American-style cultural pluralism understood as the proliferation of separate but equal communities competing for economic resources, social benefits, historical reparations, or specific rights granted by the federal government and state and local authorities.

Although the anxiety generated by the rise of separatisms, in their hard-core militarized version (as in the former Yugoslavia) or in their soft, cool, and pluralistic versions (as in Western democracies), is not limited to French intellectuals, it is particularly salient in France because of the dominance of universalistic models in the national culture, and because the schools have played a crucial role in the dissemination of these models. For many, the choice is clear: either one succeeds in preserving the republican model of integration based on Renan's conception of the nation as a contract and a daily plebiscite or one ends up importing the dreaded "Anglo-Saxon model of communities." In the latter case, one creates unassimilable minorities, from radical Islamists to Corsican nationalists, who will not rest until they have destroyed the Republic.

THE ANGLO-SAXON MODEL OF COMMUNITIES

In what will undoubtedly appear to partisans of multiculturalism as an undue amalgamation of pluralism and fragmentation, Alain Touraine denounces in the same sentence "the absolute separatisms and the unrestricted multiculturalism that we can observe in vast regions of the world and which, in the best American universities, sometimes take the form of ideological pressure to declare and enforce an absolute multiculturalism that bears the seeds of racism and wars of religion" (193). To equate multiculturalism with separatism in such a manner often means comparing the United States to the Austrian-Hungarian and Ottoman empires of the late nineteenth century. Hence the use in discussions of multiculturalism of terms such as "Balkanization" or "Lebanonization," which clearly refer to historical precedents in southeastern Europe and southwestern Asia. Hence also the symbolic role played in the debates by the war in Bosnia, conceived as the archetype of multiethnic anarchy.

For the critics of American pluralism, hyperliberal tolerance threatens the American republic with the same self-destructive tendencies that beset the multinational dynastic empires of central and eastern Europe a century ago. History repeats itself: the neo-Jacobins feel justified in resorting to nineteenth-century categories to interpret the contemporary situation precisely because in their eyes current events simply replicate turn-of-the-century politics. This is what political scientists and journalists mean when they say that communist rule had only "frozen" ethnic rivalries in central and eastern Europe. Ethnic conflicts were simply waiting for the thaw so they could sprout up again as if nothing had changed.

Just like national romanticism, the specter of ethnic strife has migrated from central Europe to the New World. In all the texts I have examined, American society appears as fertile ground for what the French call *le différentialisme*. The term itself has become ubiquitous and is found in scholarly essays, newspaper articles, and political speeches. As yet another "ism," it connotes a kind of systematic dogmatism. Given its wide currency, we should not be surprised to find the term cropping up in an interview Lionel Jospin gave to the journal *Le Débat* in the aftermath of the affair of the Islamic veil. Significantly, Jospin used the term in connection with what he called (in order to better reject it) the "Anglo-Saxon model of the communities." The education minister again denounced the hypocrisy of the Right and extreme Right, whom he accused of concealing racism behind the flag of secularism. He also criticized the uncompromising stance of the neorepublican intelligentsia, who had displayed, he said, the worst qualities of the native intellectual tradition: its arrogance, its rigidity, its scorn for experimentation, its propensity to "teach the world a lesson when we have so much to learn from the world." "We will not face the twenty-first century," Jospin added, "by closing in on the French model in its most narrow and most inflexible version" (18).

Although he admitted that the French national idea was in need of some flexibility, Jospin argued that it should not be altogether disposed of, and certainly not replaced with American views of interethnic relations: "As far as I am concerned, I don't see any reason whatsoever to change the French model. I am not in favor of substituting the Anglo-Saxon model of the communities for the integrationist, individualistic French model. In a word, I am opposed to differentialism, but I am also against assimilation" (16–17).

Jospin's framing of the issue calls for several comments. The reference to American immigration policies and ethnic diversity is hardly surprising, since they are part of almost every discussion of multiculturalism and racism in France. There are many reasons for this, the most obvious one being that what is happening on the other side of the Atlantic has become, more than ever, a major concern of the French media, from tropical storms, landslides, tornadoes, and forest fires to other, more cultural, disasters such as the new trends in film, music, lifestyles, or consumer behavior. The second reason for the almost obligatory reference to America in the discussion of multiculturalism is that France and the United States have the highest proportion of immigrants in the North Atlantic region. Both societies are faced with similar challenges and have tried to meet them by drawing on their respective political and cultural national histories, which are different but not altogether incomparable.

More importantly, the reference to the American experience, euphemized as the Anglo-Saxon model, is part of a rhetorical strategy that refuses to choose between assimilation and differentialism. In this triangular configuration, the United States (and to a certain extent Great Britain) occupies the pole of differentialism while assimilation refers to discredited practices of the French state that construed immigrant communities as a threat to the country's unity. The so-called Anglo-Saxon paradigm functions as a countermodel and as a pretext for suggesting a superior form of collective integration clearly identified with French exceptionalism.

The quest for a third way between assimilation and differentialism is shared by many French people today, undoubtedly because it is seen as the only way to satisfy the demands of democracy and respect to human rights, to combine tolerance and universalism, pluralism and national unity. The key word here is *intégration,* defined by Jospin as "the respect of differences with a concern for what brings us all together" (17). François Mitterrand himself placed the imperative of integration at the center of his cultural project for the New France. "We have a . . . universalist view of culture, and we thus take everything into consideration; and, in this whole, there are real differences in expression which are internal to France, the political entity: minority languages, 'languages,' traditions, art forms. We integrate them: why reject them?"[6] Integration is a key component of the Left's discourse on immigration and citizenship as it is distinguished both from old-style republican "assimilation" and from Le Pen's xenophobic *préférence nationale.* It is predicated on a decoupling of the notions of citizenship and cultural identity, which are no longer seen as equivalent or coterminous: French citizens of all races and ethnic origins can presumably engage in a variety of religious-cultural practices provided they accept the political requirements of the Republic.

The weight of a national past of civil war now open, now latent, accounts for the fact that even those contemporary French intellectuals and politicians who are looking for a third, middle way between the centralizing, assimilationist program of the Jacobin Left and the racism of the radical Right cannot bring themselves to look for it outside their own national tradition. In *Nations without Nationalism,* a volume written for an English-speaking readership, Julia Kristeva also raises the specter of differentialism and dismisses the British and American models of nationhood, both deemed incapable of insuring national cohesion in the face of growing minority claims:

> The United States suffers in its immigration, which, from within, challenges not only the idea of a national "organism" but also the very notion of confederacy (particularly through the establishment of new immigrant islands whose autistic withdrawal into their originary values is not easy to deal with) . . . Does not the manifest tolerance of the ethnicities and differences that are included in the notion of British subject, which does not invite them to share an *esprit général* but claims to respect their particularities, end up in *immobilizing* the latter and perpetuating the racial or religious wars that are shaking up the Commonwealth as well as the United Kingdom?" (11–12)

BACK TO MONTESQUIEU

The notion of *esprit général,* seen as sorely lacking in the excessively particularistic British idiom of nationhood, clearly refers to Montesquieu and plays a central role in Kristeva's view of a French response to "tribalism." In a letter to Harlem Désir, founder of S.O.S.-Racisme, an association devoted to the struggle against racism and discrimination in France, Kristeva argued that Montesquieu's thought needs to be at the core of any updated redescription of the national idea for the following reasons: (1) the author of *The Spirit of Laws* conceived of the nation as a historical entity, that is, comprising both continuity (tradition) and change; (2) Montesquieu's thought has a "transitional" character, that is, it views the national community as the articulation of the various levels of social life (individual, familial, ethnic) into a structured and hierarchized whole while at the same time respecting differences; and (3) this line of thought opens up the possibility of going beyond the various groups that make up the general spirit to embrace larger entities, such as Europe and the world.

The national idea Kristeva draws from her reading of Montesquieu allows her to reconcile the individual with the whole and to preserve the sexual, religious, linguistic, and cultural specificities of the various groups that make up society while ultimately absorbing them into "the secular aggregate of the nation where such differences, although duly acknowledged, leave some space for the general interest." This conception of the national space as "a texture of many singularities" makes it possible to combine the cosmopolitan and the national without erasing national barriers, since the latter remain, according to Kristeva, a historical necessity at least for the next century.

Kristeva acknowledges that Montesquieu's federate vision, based as it is on a precarious balance between the general and the particular and on the articulation of individual and group rights, is a challenging ideal. However, it is the only answer to the question she asks at the beginning of her letter to Désir: "Is there a way of thinking politically about the 'national' that does not degenerate into an exclusory, murderous racism, without at the same time dissolving into an all-encompassing feeling of 'S.O.S. Absolute Brotherhood' and providing . . . all who represent groups . . . (that have been respectively persecuted and persecuting) with the delight of being on a boundless ocean?" (51).

Montesquieu's model of *vivre ensemble* avoids the twin pitfalls of racist violence and cultural relativism, the latter being the cardinal sin of the intelligentsia: "I am grieved to have heard on many occasions left-wing intellectuals, for the sake of a misunderstood cosmopolitanism, sell off French national values, including and often mainly the values of the Enlightenment, considered once more—and wrongly so—to be too French or too unaware of the particularities of others" (37). Here, Kristeva neatly reinscribes French national characteristics within the universal claims of the Enlightenment.

There are several reasons for the centrality of Montesquieu's thought in recent French writings on cultural difference. Long before postmodernism, the philosopher celebrated what we call today heterogeneity and hybridity, and he can be used as a profitable alternative to the Jacobin tradition. In his study of French reflections on human diversity, Tzvetan Todorov remarks that Montesquieu's epistemological moderation, his aversion to absolutist modes of understanding, led many of his contemporaries to reject his vision of society. Republicans and royalists alike never forgave Montesquieu for his penchant for the positivity of social and cultural variations, his refusal to condemn what is in the name of what ought to be. On the contrary, rationalists and absolutists of all kinds relied on indivisible principles: unity of the Reason for Condorcet, unity of the divine creation for Bonald.[7]

The return to Montesquieu highlights the weakening of the absolutist ideologies that have occupied the field of French politics almost exclusively since the Revolution. By falling back on the "general spirit," a cool, pluralistic substitute for Rousseau's discredited general will, one retains some of the unifying legacy of republicanism while both abandoning the more radical positions deemed untenable now that Communism is *passé* and resisting the relativism of the mistaken cosmopolitans Kristeva is taking to task.

The choice of Montesquieu as the main representative of the French Enlightenment (rather than say Rousseau or even Voltaire, too close to the English model perhaps) is a response to the double threat of ethnocentrism, whether in its universalistic, conquering mode or in its nationalistic, defensive version. In Kristeva's writings, Montesquieu serves as a foil to two of his major contemporaries, Rousseau and Herder. All three thinkers gave considerable weight to culture as a product of both tradition and change in the genesis of the political. But the use by the revolutionaries of Rousseau's concept of the sovereign as the expression of the general will (as distinct from the will of the majority) led to the assimilationist statism of the Jacobins and to the 1793 xenophobic decrees of the Committee of Public Safety that excluded all foreigners from civil service and deprived them of their civil rights.

Rousseau himself obviously viewed minority rights as a major obstacle to the general will, particularly when minorities were allowed to organize into pressure groups. In a well-known passage of *The Social Contract* the philosopher warned his readers against what de Gaulle, two hundred years later, would denounce as *le régime des partis:* "But when the social bond begins to loosen and the state to grow weak, when particular interests begin to make themselves felt and lesser associations to influence the whole, then the common interest deteriorates and encounters opposition; unanimity no longer prevails, the general will ceases to be the will of all; contradictions and debates arise; and the best opinion does not go by any means undisputed" (114).

Montesquieu's pluralistic vision helps steer the integrationist imperative away from the centralism of the Jacobins' appropriation of Rousseau. At the same time, it functions as a useful corrective to the cultural romanticism of Herder's disciples, which paved the way to the German model of nationality, a reaction to French universalism leading directly to Nazi barbarity (which Kristeva, in straightforward rationalist manner, views as "mystical").[8] The appeal to Montesquieu serves a third purpose: it prevents excessive cultural tolerance from dissolving the social bond, as in the case of Britain and the United States, where diversity becomes an absolute leading to "the establishment of new immigrant islands" and "their autistic withdrawal into originary values." Kristeva's own wish to find in the French national tradition itself an adequate response to the crisis of French identity echoes the views of Debray, Touraine, and Finkielkraut in that it points to the intimate complicity between the radicalized, atomistic form of pluralism associated with Anglo-Saxon liberalism and the rise of ethnic separatism (the German legacy).[9]

Many French responses to the challenge of multiculturalism acknowledge that the quest for a third way between Jacobin assimilationism and intolerant nationalism calls for a critical redefinition of universalism.[10] Such a critique, however, has to be limited and circumstantial because of the dangers inherent in the complete rejection of any "horizon of universality" and its consequence, the double threat of ethnic nationalism and relativism.[11] In this view, what needs to be corrected is a "false universalism" that claims to naturalize the historical culture of a specific nation. For Tzvetan Todorov, the *moraliste* tradition is basically flawed since it consists in "the unwarranted establishing of the specific values of one's own society as universal values" (1).

Todorov describes the French tradition as a transhistorical alliance between classicism and Enlightenment rationalism. His critique of ethnocentrism and scientism as perversions of universalism does not imply that one is to give up all references to a transcendent principle when evaluating cultural diversity. If the cure were the relativism of a Montaigne (inclusive) or a Barrès (intolerant), it would be worse than the disease. The move Todorov advocates is a complex and perilous one, for it implies the refusal of ethnic homogeneity and of Anglo-American differentialism. The recourse to Montesquieu is again crucial in this matter, since his "federalism" makes it possible to refute both authoritarian uniformization (the Rousseauan temptation) and cultural Balkanization (the Herderian paradigm).

The space for what Todorov calls a critical humanism that makes of universalism "an analytical tool, a regulatory principle allowing the fruitful confrontation of differences" (391) can be cleared only if one rejects the classical opposition between unity and diversity, the universal and the particular, that is so central to the traditional history of ideas. Kristeva makes a similar gesture when defending the cosmopolitan humanism of the Western tradition:

It would seem to me that to uphold a universal, transnational principle of Humanity that is distinct from the historical realities of nation and citizenship constitutes, on the one hand, a continuation of the Stoic and Augustinian legacy, of that ancient and Christian cosmopolitanism that finds its place among the most valuable assets of our civilization and that we henceforth must go back to and bring up to date. But above all and on the other hand, such upholding of a universality, of a symbolic dignity for the whole of humankind, appears as a rampart against a nationalist, regionalist, and religious fragmentation whose integrative contractions are only visible today. (27)

Both Todorov and Kristeva borrow from Montesquieu the sense that universality (as the basis for tolerance) must operate at the level of civil society and not of the state.[12]

UNIVERSALISM AND THE SYMBOLIC ORDER

Redescriptions of universalism have been central to recent French political philosophy, especially in the works of former disciples of the Marxist philosopher Louis Althusser such as Jacques Rancière and Etienne Balibar.[13] Post-Marxist political philosophy in France today illustrates the vitality of the republican tradition within the intellectual Left, while suggesting that French universalism may have less to do with the imposition of home-grown political categories on the entire planet than with the conviction that language is at the core of democratic politics. In this view, the truly universal category is that of the symbolic: what all human cultures have in common is the capacity to use language and to regulate social interactions through a set of narratives (constitutions, programs, declarations, manifestos, myths and legends of the communal past, etc.).

In his own genealogy of the democratic process, Rancière argues that "the initial claim for universality is that of the universal belonging of speaking beings to the community of language" (86). Democratic politics is predicated upon the idea that human beings are equal because they all have access to the symbolic order, because they share a common capacity to speak. Equality, which Rancière calls the "only universal" (64), forms the basis of republican-democratic claims to participation in the political process throughout European history, from the secession of the Roman plebs and the Law of the Twelve Tables to the Declaration of the Rights of Man. What the plebeians and the members of the Third Estate were asking for was a place in the symbolic order of the community of speaking beings, a place that did not exist in the dominant social arrangement. The idea that human beings are equal through their common ability to speak is both an unreasonable idea according to the ways in which societies have traditionally structured themselves, from ancient sacred monarchies to contemporary expert societies, and a dangerous one, since it lays bare the contingent character of historical formations of power.

Rancière's critique of contemporary "post-politics" focuses on the disappearance of politics as the sphere of the symbolic, the site of the struggle for voice and political agency. Globalization-with-particularization is the opposite of universalization because the management of consensus and tension between nations and groups within the overarching consensual framework of the new liberal world order (in which individuals are reinscribed in a multiplicity of ideally peacefully coexisting cultures) aims to erase the antagonism inherent in the political process, that is, the struggle of the disenfranchised to find a voice in the community of language users. The demand for equality, Rancière's only universal, is always suppressed by the reigning power structure and always in need of reassertion, with those who are denied a voice in the community of speakers reduced to articulating their claims in the idiom of the universal, that is, in the name of the whole community (the people, the nation, or humankind).

Rancière's emphasis on the symbolic dimension of democratic politics is consistent with neorepublican claims that *mondialisation* under American leadership carries with it the triumph of the imaginary (film, video, computer graphics, hyperreality, the manufacturing of political "reality" through electronic technology, as in the movie *Wag the Dog*, etc.) over the symbolic universe of logos, the written word, universal law, the sovereign nation-state, rational argumentation, truth as correspondence to reality, and so on, historically embodied in the French public school system now under siege.

By way of the symbolic/imaginary split, the multiculturalism debate lends itself to psychoanalytic interpretations, especially of the Lacanian kind. The collapse of the symbolic order, at both the individual and social levels, induced by the erosion of paternal authority (as the locus of Lacan's symbolic Law) in the new liberal world order clears a path for the return of formerly repressed archaic images, especially fantasies of the bad Other threatening the collective enjoyment ("jouissance") of the group. The collapse of the symbolic fuels the spread of proto-Fascist ethnic nationalism all over the globe, whether it is the nationalism of the majority or the nationalism of the minorities. Slavoj Žižek, one of the leading contemporary exponents of Lacanian theory, shares with the French critics of image-driven consumerism the conviction that multiculturalism is "the ideal form of the ideology of global capitalism." [14] Relying on Balibar's latest work, Žižek wishes to salvage a good kind of universalism from the post-Enlightenment critique of subjectivity. In his attempt to rescue the progressivist side of Eurocentrism and to "imagine a leftist appropriation of the European political tradition" (207), Žižek identifies three varieties of universalism, each one corresponding to an element of the Lacanian triad of real, imaginary, and symbolic: the "real" universality of global capitalism, the universal fiction of imagined communities, and, last but not least, universalism as symbolic Ideal, "as exemplified by the demand for [Balibar's] *égaliberté*... setting in motion a permanent insurrection against the existing order" (213).

In the French context, one could say that republican universalism, as a never achieved Idea of Reason, a utopian horizon of political mobilization, time and again opposes and subverts the various sedimentations of the republican ideal in "actually existing" unequal regimes of power. These insufficiently democratic republican regimes betray the radical character of *égaliberté* by privileging an imaginary identification with the nation that sets limits to the inclusion of all speaking beings in the political community. The engine of politics is then the gap between the universal ideal and its imperfect realization in institutions that always fall short of the demands for democracy, in part because they reinscribe the excess of the symbolic within the confines of organic collectivities (the nation as "them against us," with the double polarities of assimilation as the incorporation/erasure of difference and ethnocentrism as the exclusion of difference).

MULTICULTURALISM AND THE LIBERAL-COMMUNITARIAN DEBATE

This reevaluation of universalism in the aftermath of its poststructuralist critique points to yet another way in which one can look at the limitations of the multicultural debate on both sides of the Atlantic. In many respects, the resistance to multiculturalism looks like the latest version of the traditional antiliberalism of the French intelligentsia. This rejection of liberalism is rooted in what may be the most widely shared set of philosophical convictions in French intellectual life, namely anti-individualism. Arguably the strongest, most durable ideological current in modern French intellectual culture, anti-individualism has brought together political theorists and political figures who disagreed on just about anything else, from Rousseau to Maistre and Sorel, and from Tocqueville to Maurras and Durkheim.

In this view, it is precisely because liberal societies do not provide their members, as Charles Taylor puts it, with "some commonly recognized definition of the good life" that individuals eventually turn to ethnically defined identities and particularistic ideologies in order to lend meaning to their lives. Multiculturalism, then, is the wrong response to individualism, because it eventually leads to the same erosion of the national community. America is equally blamed for being too individualistic and too eager to promote the "model of the communities."

The issue of individualism is another strand connecting French and American intellectual debates today. The reflection on the respective role of holism and individualism in the nation's history has been central to the tremendous ideological changes France has undergone in the past two decades. Louis Dumont and François Furet, among many others, have examined the place of individualism in the theory and practice of democracy, and have been instrumental to the replacement of Marx, Sartre, and Foucault by such liberal icons as Tocqueville, Constant, and Rawls in the French pantheon of master-thinkers, at least in some intellectual circles.

At about the same time, the liberal-communitarian dispute, which also centered around the issue of the nature and consequences of individualism, figured prominently in academic journals and the op-ed pages of mainstream weeklies on this side of the Atlantic. In an essay stressing the need to go beyond the sterile oppositions entrenched in the liberal-communitarian debate, Charles Taylor espoused many of the views shared by the French neorepublicans.[15] In opposition to the purely juridical, "procedural" conception of the social compact put forward by proponents of individual rights-liberalism such as Dworkin or Rawls, Taylor advocates a "republican," "civic humanist" definition of the common good, based on patriotic identification with the national community and the active participation of citizens in public affairs.

In Taylor's view, full participation in citizen self-rule is the only way to reverse the noxious consequences of radical individualism, since "pure enlightened self-interest will never move enough people strongly enough to constitute a threat to potential despots and putschists" (175), and, one might add, ethnic and religious separatist leaders as well. It will not come as a surprise that Montesquieu is one of Taylor's main references in his attempt to stake out a viable position against liberal individualism. Montesquieu's virtue alone can transcend egoism "in the sense that people are really attached to the common good, to general liberty." Virtue leads to a kind of patriotism that is "a continual preference of public interest over one's own" (165).

Of particular interest to my own discussion of the transatlantic traffic in ideas is the fact that Taylor nationalizes the tradition of liberal individualism, limiting its relevance to the English-speaking world. The dominance of procedural conceptions of society in the United States is, according to Taylor, a consequence of the fact that "the unexamined views on these matters in Anglo-Saxon philosophical culture tend to be heavily infected with atomist prejudices" (164). In the thrall of "commonsense atomist-infected notions of the instrumental model of society," American society has unfortunately moved away from its civic republican roots. The ethnocentric nature of procedural liberalism implies for Taylor that it cannot be successfully imported into other national cultures, such as his native Quebec. "There are also modern democratic societies," he writes, "where patriotism centers on a national culture, which in many cases has come (sometimes late and painfully) to incorporate free institutions, but which is also defined in terms of some language or history . . . A society like Quebec cannot but be dedicated to the defense and promotion of French culture and language, even if this involves some restriction of individual freedoms" (182).

The example of Quebec is particularly striking since the defense and promotion of French culture in the context of a multicultural *Canada* justifies for Taylor the restriction not only of specific individual freedoms, but of some of the collective rights of non-French-speaking minorities in the context of a multicultural *Quebec*. The paradox here is that in order for the French language to survive in a mostly English-speaking federal polity like Canada, the immigrant communities and linguistic minorities in Quebec would have to be denied the freedom of choice between schooling in French and English, since most of the newcomers would opt for the majority language outside Quebec, that is, English, thereby threatening the survival of Francophone culture.

CONTRADICTIONS OF THE MODERNIST PROJECT

Taylor's position reveals some of the most enduring contradictions of the Enlightenment project. While advocating liberal ideas and embracing the *philosophes'* ideal of a common good transcending individual and group self-interest, Taylor is also willing to accept the restriction of individual freedoms in order to protect the threatened collective identity of the French-speaking Quebeckers. The tension between the universal equality, and interchangeability, of rational individuals and the recognition of the unique quality of discrete cultural formations is constitutive of the dual legacy of the Enlightenment, in its romantic and rationalist components. The conflicts surrounding the issue of multiculturalism are themselves an illustration of the uneasy coexistence, in our contemporary imagination, of what François Furet has called "the two figures of the democratic idea, the national and the universal," noting that the tension between the universal and the particular was at the heart of the French Revolution itself (*Le Passé d'une illusion,* 36).

Taylor himself is quite aware of this, and he has reflected on many occasions on the tension between a politics of the universal based on the equal dignity of all citizens and a politics of recognition that wishes to take into account the authenticity of multiple cultural traditions. The two claims are ultimately incompatible, in Taylor's view, because the politics of recognition "asks that we give acknowledgment and status to something that is not universally shared" (*Multiculturalism,* 39). In other words, "we give due acknowledgment only to what is universally present—everyone has an identity—through recognizing what is peculiar to each. The universal demand powers an acknowledgment of specificity" (39).

Furet, for his part, has remarked that the same people today seem to demand the right to equality and the right to difference. Following Tocqueville, he noted that democratic societies are driven by a need for distinction that results from the egalitarian pressure itself, as though people feared above all the risk of being undifferentiated. "Difference," Furet wrote, "is no more easily compatible with equality than cultural relativism is with a pedagogy of the universal. The tension between the two poles is part and parcel of democracy itself, of a social imagination that is both individualistic and egalitarian" (*La République du centre,* 63).

Economists speak of the perversity of some behaviors or phenomena that generate unintended consequences, sometimes totally at odds with their original purpose. In the same way, the ambiguities of the politics of recognition have something to do with the perversity of differential claims. If a little bit of difference brings more freedom and more civility, too much of it may achieve opposite results. As the proponents of deconstruction have ceaselessly reminded us, difference is what circulates and disseminates between polarities; once difference itself becomes a polarity, once it is hardened, congealed, "essentialized" as differential *identity,* it reinscribes itself within unequal hierarchies of meaning, and the asymmetry of power and violence is, once again, let loose in the world. The elusiveness of difference not only wreaks havoc in postmodernist theory, opening each and every theorist in turn to the damning charge of essentialism, whether strategic or not, but also points to the ambiguities of the current struggles over the politics of diversity.

The critique of the ethnocentrism of Western cultural categories is itself a contested discourse, conflating a variety of ideological currents. One of the historical sources of multiculturalism is Finkielkraut's philosophy of decolonization, a discourse that legitimized the struggle of Third World peoples against the metropolis by asserting the equal, if not superior, symbolic and spiritual value of non-Western civilizations. This critique of European ethnocentrism did not lead to the rejection of all ethnocentric positions, however: on the contrary, it described cultures as distinct entities with clearly marked boundaries that enabled their carriers to free themselves from Western influence by going back to their roots.

This type of culturalism is presently challenged by a more recent component of the politics of diversity that argues on the other hand that there are no such things as national cultures, or rather, that they cannot be described in essentialist or nativistic terms. The postmodern and postcolonial versions of cultural dynamics have replaced the old philosophical couple of difference and identity by the now familiar notion of hybridity or *métissage*. The meaning and operation of difference change dramatically from one position to the next: for the cultural nationalists, difference goes *between* cultures, separating them from one another; for the postmodernists, it works *within* cultures, dividing each one from itself. Difference is no longer difference *from,* but difference *in,* self-difference. While culturalists are bent on preserving their identity, postmodernists are busy dissolving it.

Each of these positions poses a different threat to the supporters of the republican model of integration on both sides of the Atlantic. The cult of difference threatens the Republic because it leads to ethnic and racial feuding; the dissemination of difference is a menace to democracy because it dissolves shared ethical and political values. French integrationists, heirs to a long history of civil wars, first religious then political, have a tendency to focus on the first threat; American liberals, children of the British Enlightenment, carriers of a pluralistic culture informed by the ideal of religious tolerance and the discourse of individual rights, are more inclined to fear the second.

TWO NATIONS OF IMMIGRANTS

Anxieties born of the rise of particularistic ideologies are obviously not limited to French or even European intellectuals. In *The Disuniting of America,* Arthur Schlesinger comes quite close to the neo-Jacobin line of argumentation I have discussed at length in this book. "The cult of ethnicity," the historian writes, "threatens to become a counterrevolution against the original theory of America as 'one people,' a common culture, a single nation" (43). Schlesinger, whose liberal credentials are impeccable, concludes his essay with a plea against the dangers of the same differentialism to which Alain Touraine alerted his French readers. "The future of immigration policy," he warns, "depends on the capacity of the assimilation process to continue to do what it has done so well in the past: to lead newcomers to an acceptance of the language, the institutions, and the political ideals that hold the nation together" (121).

Amitai Etzioni, a prominent figure of the communitarian movement in the United States, strikes a similar chord when he calls for limits to be set on multiculturalism in order to safeguard what he calls the community of communities. "Without a firm sense of one supra-community," Etzioni argues, "there is considerable danger that the constituent communities will turn on one another. Indeed, the more one favors strengthening communities, a core of the Communitarian agenda, the more one must concern oneself with ensuring that they see themselves as parts of a more encompassing whole, rather than as fully independent and antagonistic" (155). The concept of a community of communities defined as "a more encompassing whole" comes close to Kristeva's *esprit général* and to Montesquieu's attempt to open up a political space more inclusive than that of the civic nation-state or the ethnic nation.

The similarity between the arguments advanced on both sides of the continental divide in favor of keeping the political (the public sphere) and the ethno-religious (the private sphere) separate should provide enough evidence that the notion of an absolute incompatibility between French and American views on immigration and multiculturalism is an ideological construct. In the same way that calls to maintain some kind of national integration in the political and juridical sphere can be found on both sides of the Atlantic, Kristeva's reading of Montesquieu recalls Horace Kallen's view of America as "a federation or commonwealth of national cultures . . . a democracy of nationalities, cooperating voluntarily and autonomously through common institutions . . . a multiplicity in a unity, an orchestration of mankind" (122).[16]

Lines between monologic and pluralistic versions of communal identity cut across national traditions. Herder, the godfather of German ethnic nationalism, was the compatriot of Goethe and Kant, who both remained true to the spirit of the French Enlightenment. In the same way, liberal societies such as Britain and the United States have produced xenophobic ideologies every bit as extreme in their rhetoric as those of the Continent, even though they did not lead to the extreme forms of fascism and state racism that have plagued European history in this century.

A careful examination of the respective histories of immigration in France and the United States reveals striking similarities between the two countries. At first glance, they seem to offer contrasting examples of the role of immigration in shaping the national consciousness. Transatlantic migratory processes are constitutive of the America nation in its formative stage; modern mass immigration in France, however, took place at a time when France had long been a nation-state, deeply marked by centuries of political and administrative centralization. While the American mythology tends to overestimate the role of immigration in the weaving of the national fabric (the "nation of immigrants" topos), the French preferred pushing immigration to the margins of the national memory, stripping it of any significant role in the formation of the country. This being said, France has been, and remains, one of the nations with the largest immigrant population in Europe.

If one moves from national myths to the sociology of migration, the similarity between demographic processes in the two countries is even more striking. In 1930, France had the largest proportion of foreign-born people in the world: 515 per 100,000 versus 492 in the United States. In the 1970s, the relative size of the second generation in the total population was comparable in both countries. In the 1980s, France still was, together with America, the favorite destination of displaced people; there was 1 refugee per 1,000 French people, in contrast to only .05 in Germany and .03 in Britain and Sweden.[17] Gérard Noiriel, among others, argues that the acculturation of the second generation proceeded as steadily in France as in the United States and that the resistance of immigrant cultures to the "integrating machine" of the French and American melting pots is largely a myth created by third-generation ethnic intellectuals in search of roots and group identity.[18]

All of this supports a questioning of the absolute opposition between French and American national idioms I have reviewed so far. This type of rhetoric may well work wonders in the media and in debates among public intellectuals, but it reduces the historical complexity of migrations to the ideological responses they generate. Ideologies are not to be taken at face value, and one should not mistake the model of reality for the reality of the model. French universalism was more a political program than an all-encompassing social and cultural reality, and there was much wishful thinking on the part of those who carried its banner.

In at least one respect, the Republicans, whether as modernizers or as colonizers, made the same mistake: they overrated the extent of their impact on the peoples they took upon themselves to "civilize," whether in Brest or Brazzaville. Their assimilationist ideology was the expression of a renewed attempt on the part of urban, French-speaking elites to hold together within the framework of the monarchical and later republican state a territory that was ethnically and linguistically diverse in the extreme.

In *L'Invention de la France,* a book that made quite a stir when it was published because it called into question the national myth of cultural homogeneity, Hervé le Bras and Emmanuel Todd argued that the different anthropological structures inherited from the Celtic, Germanic, and Romanic pasts of "France" reproduced themselves through time in regional peasant communities, producing a great variety of kinship systems, forms of sociability, political opinions, matrimonial and reproductive strategies, and rules of inheritance or attitudes in the face of death, at least until World War II. For centuries, France was a plural nation, closer in this respect to the United States than to such ethnically homogeneous nations as Germany, Japan, or Ireland: Le Bras and Todd write that "most nations, large or small, in Europe and in the world—England, Germany, China, Japan, Sweden, Ireland, Poland, for example—are little more, in a way, than primeval and homogeneous systems, tiny ancient tribes that have swelled disproportionately through a thousand years to reach their current size as nations . . . The United States alone can be considered a cousin of France, in terms of anthropological diversity as well as national unity" (77).

The family resemblance applies to political systems as well. American federalism has a lot in common with French republicanism in that both are based on civic definitions of the national community. American federalism is essentially political, based on the sovereign rights of the various states of the Union and not on territorialized ethnic or linguistic differences as in truly multicultural nations such as Spain, India, or Canada. The obsession with the breakup of the Union along linguistic, ethnic, or political lines (Franklin and the German minorities, the Civil War, today's English Only movement) produced in the United States the same integrationist discourse that the fear of regionalist separatisms (from the Vendée uprising in 1793 to recent independentist movements in Brittany, Corsica, and the Basque Country) produced in France. In both cases, the seeds of division contained in the ethnic diversity of the population rendered an integrative concept of the nation both necessary and extremely challenging.

Neither the liberal nor the Jacobin versions of democracy have managed to wipe out racial tensions and nationalistic claims. Today, the need to respect cultural diversity in a postcolonial world defined by the extreme mobility of individuals and groups creates parallel challenges in France and the United States. Although both cultures approach the challenges of multiculturalism in different ways as a consequence of their distinct national political and intellectual histories, the various positions that structure the field of the debate are found on both sides of the Atlantic. Ideological lines are drawn not only between national cultures but within each national culture as well. There is a definite homology between the structure of positions in the debates on liberalism, individualism, and multiculturalism in France and the United States, if only because the embattled traditions of civic republicanism draw from common sources, from Montesquieu and Condorcet to Jefferson.

There is another reason why the clear-cut opposition between French and American ideas of the nation is unsatisfactory, and it has to do more with practices than with ideologies. French culture was never as centralized and as homogeneous as some of its critics today would have us believe. Both the French keepers of the republican memory and their Anglo-American multiculturalist critics share the same view of the French national ideology as incompatible with cultural pluralism. There is ample historical and sociological evidence, however, to suggest that this view of nation building in France is, if not totally erroneous, at least greatly reductive, more myth than reality. The danger here is to interpret historical developments only from the point of view of the actors who took part in those events. The image of a homogeneous France (on both sides of the Atlantic) was from the beginning nothing but a fantasy, a powerful form of wishful thinking on the part of people obsessed by the fear of irreconcilable differences.

Conclusion

❧ ❧ ❧

Le racisme réduit le principe d'identité à la relation d'appartenance,
liens pour lesquels la logique et les mathématiques écrivent
deux signes différents. De là fondent sur le monde tant de malheurs
qu'il vaut mieux redresser cette erreur.

MICHEL SERRES

*O*f all the French critics of American differentialism, Emmanuel Todd is arguably the most radical, in the etymological sense of the word, since he roots what he calls the American obsession with difference in long-lasting anthropological structures going back to the traditional familial system of the English peasantry.[1] For Todd, the ideologies of cultural diversity, ethnic nationalism, and universalistic individualism that make up the current debate on multiculturalism are the product of unconscious "mental matrices that define a priori the perception of ethnic differences." These cultural matrices are themselves rooted in transhistorical structured practices like kinship systems and rules of inheritance that displaced populations carry with them when they leave the motherland.

Todd's typology distinguishes the egalitarian family dominant in northern France, Spain, and Italy from the inegalitarian systems (Le Play's famous *famille souche*) that prevail in Germany, Japan, or the Basque country. The first system, based on an egalitarian partition of the inheritance among the children, "tells the unconscious that, if the brothers are equal, men in general are equal, and that people are equal" too (24). Political cultures born of such anthropological matrices will tend to minimize difference and encourage universalistic views of humankind. Hence, the universalism of Jacobin republicanism (prevalent in northern France, the cradle of the French Revolution) and of Roman imperial ideology, or the assimilationist character of Spanish and Portuguese colonialism.

On the other hand, the *famille souche* rewards its children unequally in terms of inheritance and predisposes its members to see individuals and peoples as *essentially* different. Todd ascribes the rise of authoritarian, hierarchized racist ideologies in interwar Germany and Japan to the persistence through time of these deep-seated, a priori, "metaphysical" notions of human difference. The American nuclear family represents a third type of kinship pattern inherited from England, a system that defines children as different from one another, but not unequal, as in the German, Japanese, or Basque family structures (28).[2] American culture, by insisting that ethnic groups should remain "separate but equal," precludes both the universalistic assimilationism of symmetrical egalitarian systems and the intolerance of authoritarian anthropological structures.

The explanation of "conscious" ideologies by "unconscious" structural determinations has a dual advantage: it accounts for the remarkable continuity of national and local definitions of cultural community through time, and also contributes to our understanding of why the universal-rationalist principles of the Enlightenment and of Marxist internationalism have encountered, and are still encountering, so much resistance all over the world. The resistance to modernity leads to passionate rhetoric and violent uprisings as far as it is in part the expression of deep structures of feeling rooted in the social uses of the body (especially in terms of biological reproduction and gender relations) and in psychosexual dynamics learned and reinforced throughout childhood. The anthropological roots of the competing ideologies of unity and difference lend their distinctive emotional tone to identity politics, whether in early nineteenth-century Germany, postwar liberationist struggles in Asia and Africa, or in Iran and Serbia today. What unites all of these otherwise specific historical struggles is a common enemy: a modernist, Western-centered discourse that sets the demands of political unification and economic rationalization above the psychosocial rewards of the *Gemeinschaft*.

In Todd's view, however, the principles of political and social equality (whether defined in universalistic or differentialist terms) put forward by liberal-democratic advocates of "civic" definitions of nationhood are equally grounded in prereflexive categories of perception and action. That is why the French are so indifferent to ethnic identity[3] and the Americans so sensitive to diversity, while the American way of life is denounced by its opponents worldwide as the main engine of cultural homogenization on economic, political, and/or ethnic-religious grounds.

The tension between consciously articulated ideologies of the self and the other on the one hand, and unexamined *mentalités* rooted in the body and the psyche and produced by the naturalization of forgotten social processes on the other, contributes to the irritating aura of unreality that often surrounds the multiculturalist controversy. Not only do French and American participants in the contest often gloss over the ideological heterogeneity of each national debate (as when American critics assert that Le Pen's views are taking over all of France or when French writers claim that the United States is on the verge of ethnic war à la Bosnia), but they seldom acknowledge the extent to which each culture holds contradictory representations of the other.

While American critics tend to blame the French for refusing to integrate newcomers perceived as too different *and* for demanding that they assimilate (different kinds of French people are likely to advance each of these conflicting claims), French anti-Americanism has always had a dual nature, finding supporters on both the Right and the Left, but for opposite reasons: for some, there is not enough equality in America, while for others there is too much freedom. As Todd rightly point out, while some French people criticize America "in the name of equality, underscoring disparities in wealth or the situation of black people," others "are irritated by American anarchy in the name of an ideal of law and order" (216).

The resilience of patterns of (self)segregation, residential or otherwise, among blacks and whites in America flies in the face of the liberal-egalitarian discourse on toleration and indifference to difference (the "color-blind society") constantly reaffirmed by the cultural and political elites. Inversely, in France the official discourse of republican unity often masks the vitality of localist, regionalist, and culturalist ideologies that appeal to a broader constituency than the electorate of the National Front, including within the Left (the autonomist program of the Ligue Savoisienne is but a recent example of these centrifugal tendencies inherent in French political life).[4]

On both sides of the Atlantic, discourses of the nation set up inverted mirror images of one another while harboring illusions about the processes at work in their respective countries. Americans insist on maintaining the distinctiveness of ethnic groups in the midst of an economic system that disrupts rural communities, celebrates urban cosmopolitan values, and commodifies ethnic subcultures, ancient folkways, and foreign artifacts, turning them into ever new grist for the consumption mill. The claim of French homogeneity is equally phantasmagoric, more myth than reality, as I hope to have shown throughout this book.

Ever since the Dreyfus affair, part of the acrimony surrounding the debate on the assimilationist nature of French society has been fueled by the insistence on the part of all parties concerned on equating "France" with a republican ideology itself reduced to its most absolute universalistic component. Once "France" has been essentialized as the "country of human rights," any violation of those rights is perceived as treason, the rejection by "the French" of the essential core of their collective identity. But France is no more a unified, homogeneous cultural and political entity than any other "nation": Zola's France is not the France of Maurras, Barrès, or Le Pen, de Gaulle's France is not Pétain's. Like other Western democracies, the country was, and still is, the site of bitter struggles between competing visions of the national community.[5] In a sense, critics of France's cultural centralization wish to have their cake and eat it too: one cannot both resent French culture for rejecting others as too different and fault it for ruthlessly assimilating them, that is, for forcefully eradicating the slightest trace of their difference.

Current discussions of cultural pluralism often fail to recognize that ethnic diversity is largely symbolic in contemporary immigrant societies such as France and the United States. This is not only because most immigrant groups have been deterritorialized and are speaking the language of the host country, thereby losing two of the markers of identity most central to cultural essentialism, the land and the language, but also because the second and third generations tend to intermarry in ever increasing numbers, rendering the core component of ethnic nationalism, mainly biological identity ("the pure blood and the pure race") even more mythical a notion than it was in the old country. Immigrants will become part of the social fabric of their new homelands as long as the democratic process remains operative. The question is how painful and contentious the laws of the host countries, the behavior of their "native" populations, and the rhetoric of political representatives will make this inevitable process.

There is a positive side to the symbolic nature of ethnicity in contemporary industrial societies today, that is, the fact that ethnicity is not predicated upon political claims of territorial sovereignty and on biological claims of essentialized identity. This makes diversity less threatening to the democratic process than the critics of multiculturalism would have us believe. Developments associated with postmodernity such as the erosion of the disciplinary, authoritarian culture of modernism and the weakening of identification with the nation-state among youth makes it quite unlikely that strong identity claims along ethnic or religious lines will ever coalesce in outright tribal wars in industrialized Western nations. Democracies such as Germany and Japan, immersed in the recent past in extreme forms of ethnic nationalism, are making significant moves toward adopting civic definitions of national membership, replacing *jus sanguinis* by *jus solis* as the basis for citizenship.

On the other hand, the new politics of difference are by no stretch of the imagination as unambiguously progressive and inclusive as some of its advocates would have us believe, and the fact that the French Nouvelle Droite or American white supremacists celebrate differentialism in their own way (claiming that different races cannot peacefully share the same territorial space, let alone intermarry) should at least give advocates of difference pause to think. The truth is, difference cuts both ways. It can be as liberating as it is limiting, for the recognition of minority status may ensure its recipients that they will never be part of the majority. The drawing of the line identifies and protects even as it defines and excludes, and those who claim difference for themselves do not necessarily like it in others.

African American or Asian American community activists, writers, artists, or actors often bemoan the fact that their newly acquired fame as "minority" authors, leaders, or movie stars means that their influence is limited to a particular segment of the population when it comes to readership, community support, or character casting. The institutionalization and commodification of difference by "the system" often implies that black actors can only star in black sitcoms and a Latina novelist can only write for Hispanics. Unsurprisingly, these individuals often resort to refashioned notions of aesthetic universalism, strategic or not, and common humanity to justify their legitimate claims to reach a wider audience than their own ethnic segment of the market, however defined.

Barbara Christian, for example, argues against the marginalization of the marginals that often passes for empowerment through difference and points to the inferiorization of minority writing even as it is given recognition: "It is called 'political,' 'social protest,' or 'minority' literature, which in this ironic country has a pejorative sound, meaning it lacks craft and has not transcended the limitations of racial, sex, or class boundaries—that it supposedly does not do what 'good' literature does: express our universal humanity."[6] Similar processes of disqualification by exclusion from the canon of legitimate aesthetic creation were at work for regionalist, working-class, or folk literature in nineteenth-century Europe and "native" art and literature in colonial settings.

Discussions of identity politics in contemporary societies need to avoid the dogmatic reassertion of values and beliefs uncritically borrowed from the past. This is not because of some modernist attraction to the new for novelty's sake, but because the ways in which people tried to come to grips with these kinds of issues fifty, one hundred, or two hundred years ago, although they may help us orient ourselves in the present and throw some useful light on our current predicaments, cannot offer us blueprints for the present and ready-made recipes for dealing with the challenges of the age. The mantra-like recitations of what have become the dogmas of American eighteenth-century liberalism, French nineteenth-century republicanism, or postwar cultural nationalism are not going to take us very far down the road to democratic pluralism.

There is a sense today that another road, this one leading back to Enlightenment conceptions of the polis and the national community, has been cut off by the various developments commonly associated with postmodernity or postindustrialism. That is why, among those who wish to salvage from the floundering of the modernist project some of its most valuable possessions, there is so much talk today about "reinventing universalism" and "refashioning republican civic culture." When it comes to facing the challenges of an increasingly individualistic, libertarian contemporary culture that transcends national boundaries, old conceptions of the civic contract, embedded as they were in metaphysical, moralistic, and ethnocentric notions of the Universal, will not do without a measure of refashioning. But their historical rivals, the myths of blood and soil, will not do either in a world increasingly marked by spatial mobility and the dissemination of multiple, subject-centered, personalized social identities.

The challenge is to acknowledge what has changed and how much has changed while discerning at the same time what is worth rescuing. In France as in the United States, as indeed in most other Western industrialized nations, the most astute participants in the nationalism debate have recognized both the ambiguous nature of difference and the impossibility of not giving difference its due. That is, I believe, the paradox Jacques Derrida meant to address when he spoke of the double duty confronting those who want to make sure that the politics of recognition do not end up threatening the democratic rights of the citizenry: "The *same duty*," he wrote, "dictates welcoming foreigners in order not only to integrate them but to recognize and accept their alterity. . . . The *same duty* dictates respecting differences, idioms, minorities, singularities, but also the universality of formal law, the desire for translation, agreement and univocity, the law of the majority, opposition to racism, nationalism, and xenophobia" (*The Other Heading*, 78).

As I have argued, Derrida's insistence that the duty to integrate is also a duty to recognize alterity, as well as Jospin's definition of *intégration* as "the respect of differences with a concern for what brings us all together," point to the current refashioning of the national idea in contemporary France. One way to read the repeated call for integration on the part of a wide array of French theorists and political figures in the wake of the renewed interethnic tensions in the country is to see it as a desire to move civic nationalism away from cultural content to political form, from a definition of civic membership based on language, beliefs, or mores toward a sense of belonging based on the commitment to democratic institutions. Inasmuch as the French increasingly live their lives, willy-nilly, within liberalism (without necessarily all yet being converted to liberalism, as many of the texts I have examined in this study clearly demonstrate), some of them (say, those who are neither neorepublicans nor neonationalists) may well be coming to share a more liberal view of the polis, a view best exemplified by Kwame Anthony Appiah when he argues against the need for a "centering common culture" in contemporary democracies. "What I think we really need," Appiah writes, "is not citizens centered on a common culture, but citizens committed to common institutions, to the conditions necessary for a common life."[7] Whether this view will prevail in "postnational" France as well, and in what form, remains to be seen. The notion of *intégration*, however ambiguous it may remain, and ubiquitous appeals to *la France multicolore* are certainly gestures in that direction.

In the concluding pages of *Democracy in America*, Tocqueville moved from a descriptive to a prescriptive mode of exposition. After hundreds of pages of what he meant to be a carefully documented account of the American laboratory experiment in modern individualism, he finally took to task those of his contemporaries who failed to acknowledge the inevitability of the democratic process. Tocqueville's greatness lies in his capacity to overcome the limitations of his own socially and culturally situated self in order to see the unstoppable march of democratic individualism from what he called "the point of view of God." His uncanny ability to transcend the boundaries of his own aristocratic distaste for the spread of the "universal uniformity" of the democratic age, which he readily confessed "saddened and chilled" him profoundly, afforded him with the bird's-eye view of a genuine transcultural perspective from which he could try, however imperfectly, to see the whole picture and "view and judge the concerns of men" (333).

No wonder Tocqueville disagreed with the great number of his contemporaries who undertook to "make a selection from among the institutions, the opinions, and the ideas that originated in the aristocratic constitution of society as it was; a portion of these elements they would willingly relinquish, but they would keep the remainder and transplant them into their new world." But all this was in vain: the sweep of history will not allow us to pick and choose among the relics of the past. For Tocqueville, those who wish to do so "are wasting their time and their strengths in virtuous but unprofitable efforts." The point, he told them, and many of those who nostalgically clung to the old ways were members of his own family and social circles, was not to "retain the peculiar advantages which the inequality of conditions bestows upon mankind, but to secure the new benefits which equality bestows upon us" (333).

Today many of those who answer the challenges of pluralism with ideas borrowed wholesale from the days of Abbé Siéyès or Israel Zangwill would do well to heed Tocqueville's advice. The hypnotic recitation of past dogmas threatens to lead us to a form of intellectual short-sightedness, a methodological error that fails to apprehend the incommensurability of cultural practices across time and place. "Care must be taken," Tocqueville warned, "not to judge the state of society that is now coming into existence by notions derived from a state of society that no longer exists; for as these states of society are exceedingly different in their structure, they cannot be submitted to a just or fair comparison" (333). As Paul Veyne, following Michel Foucault, has argued, historically situated clusters of practices are *rare,* for they arise from social and cultural conditions that can never be duplicated by some ideological fiat, no matter how generous and high-minded its motivations.[8]

Those among the contemporary interpreters of nation and culture that persuade me follow Tocqueville's methodological principle: they avoid opposing French and American concepts of the national as if they were stable, homogeneous, and irreconcilable entities. Too few among the participants in the multiculturalism controversy acknowledge with *Esprit*'s editor-in-chief Olivier Mongin that there are not two sides to the issue, but at least three, and perhaps more.[9] In France, those who are not content with reproducing ad nauseam the sterile polemics of the culture wars are careful not to equate American multiculturalism with the ethnic feuds that are spreading like wildfire all over the world. Between a universalistic individualism that wrests individuals from all their communitarian moorings and an ethnic nationalism that aims at annihilating the Other, the idea of multiculturalism opens up for Mongin "a space in which to ponder the question: what makes a communication of cultures possible?" In this respect, the lesson of American multiculturalism would be "to examine the conditions of a political space suited to welcoming the diversity of cultures" (86).

In the same issue of *Esprit,* Joël Roman concurs, sketching out what might be a French response to the multicultural challenge. Rightly reminding us that the practice of the Republic was never as intolerant of differences as its official discourse might have implied, Roman, echoing Tocqueville's call to secure the new benefits that equality bestows upon us, pleads for a cross-fertilization of the "two great universalistic rival cultures," the French and the American. "It may be possible," he writes, "to somehow correct the centripetal tendencies of French society by injecting in it a dose of multiculturalism, while American society, suffering from a reverse centrifugal tropism, might benefit from our own republican tradition" (151).

The point is not to call for an ideal reconciliation of opposites based on the fear of confrontation, but to acknowledge that both cultures are grounded in democratic soil. While the cult of ethnicity has proven time and again how quickly it can squelch democratic achievements, democracy alone can, in the words of Benjamin Barber, "create a form of ethnicity that knows how to limit itself" (144). To put democracy first is not to negate ethnic and religious affiliations, but to recognize that while the communitarian impulse does not by itself imply the respect of democratic principles, the democratic framework is the only sure guarantor of the cohabitation of differences.

Part of the transatlantic misunderstanding stems from a confusion between political citizenship and cultural identity. Granted, the most centralist conceptions of the French Republic have often collapsed the two notions, requiring cultural assimilation as the prerequisite for political integration. To the extent that those requirements were fulfilled in the past, and it was far from being always the case, the equation between political unity and cultural uniformity is clearly not workable today. This being said, a plurality of social and cultural identities does not necessarily entail the implosion of the political community, as neorepublicans fear. Conversely, the fact that people agree on the principles governing a given political community does not imply that they have to share the same values, behaviors, or practices, as multiculturalist critics of the French national idea would have it.

Pierre-André Taguieff, speaking from within the French republican tradition, also argues for setting priorities straight and putting democracy first. Like Barber, he calls for a limitation of the right to difference in the name of a Levinasian "infinite obligation" to the individual other. "The right to difference," Taguieff writes, "cannot be understood as a collective right, a right of communities, but 'as a subject's right to communitarian integration: each subject has a right to his culture, no culture has any right on the subject,' as Robert Lafont excellently put it" (*Sur la Nouvelle droite,* 104). At this point, American and French theorists find a meeting ground. In the cacophony of cross-cultural accusations hurled across the transatlantic divide, their voices contribute to reversing the continental drift.

Notes

❦ ❦ ❦

INTRODUCTION

1. See my *Extrême-Occident: French Intellectuals and America* (Chicago: University of Chicago Press, 1993), 257–72. Chapter 1 of the present study takes up again, while widening their scope, some of the issues I raised at the end of *Extrême-Occident*.

2. Richard Rorty, *Consequences of Pragmatism* (Minneapolis: University of Minnesota Press, 1982).

3. Jonathan Yardley, cited in Richard Rorty, "Trotsky and the Wild Orchids," *Common Knowledge* 1, no. 3 (1992): 141.

4. One of the most extensively argued of these attacks was E. P. Thompson's critique of Althusserian (post)structuralism in *The Poverty of Theory and Other Essays* (New York: Monthly Review Press, 1978). "I commence my argument at a manifest disadvantage," Thompson ironically conceded at the beginning of the book. "Few spectacles would be more ludicrous than that of an English historian—and, moreover, one manifestly self-incriminated of empirical practices—attempting to offer epistemological correction to a rigorous Parisian philosopher."

5. Alan Sokal, "Transgressing the Boundaries. Toward a Transformative Hermeneutics of Quantum Gravity," *Social Text* 46–47 (spring/summer 1996), and "A Physicist Experiments with Cultural Studies," *Lingua Franca* (May/June 1996): 62–64. See also Sokal's reply to Robbins and Ross in *Lingua Franca* (July/August 1996): 57.

6. Andrew Ross, "Reflections on the Sokal Affair," *Social Text* 50 (spring 1997): 150.

7. Alan Sokal and Jean Bricmont, *Impostures intellectuelles* (Paris: Odile Jacob, 1997). Reviewing the book in its customary tongue-in-cheek manner, the French satirical weekly *Le Canard Enchaîné* feigned outrage at the fact that, of all people, an American and a Belgian (Belgians, like the Swiss, are the butt of French ethnic jokes) "dare mess up with our philosophers!"

8. David Simpson, *Nationalism, Romanticism and the Revolt Against Theory* (Chicago: University of Chicago Press, 1993).

9. Joan DeJean, *Ancients against Moderns: Culture Wars and the Making of a Fin de Siècle* (Chicago: University of Chicago Press, 1997), x.

10. Liah Greenfeld, *Nationalism: Five Roads to Modernity* (Cambridge: Harvard University Press, 1992).

11. Camille Paglia, "Ninnies, Tyrants, Pedants and Other Academics," *New York Times Book Review* (5 May 1991): 29, 33.

12. Cited in Tony Judt, *Past Imperfect: French Intellectuals 1944–1956* (Berkeley: University of California Press, 1993), 348.

13. Lévy's concept of *l'idéologie française* (patterned after Marx's *German Ideology*) puts French culture in the same position in which German culture has found itself since World War II at least, that of a matrix of unredeemed evil. The controversy surrounding the publication of Daniel J. Goldhagen's book *Hitler's Willing Executioners* is just one recent example of the ideological stakes involved in the reevaluation of what happened during the 1940s.

14. For a recent example, see Jonathan Fenby, *On the Brink: The Trouble with France* (New York: Little, Brown, 1998).

15. Roger Cohen, "France's Allegiance: To Things French, Like Hypocrisy," *The New York Times* (24 August 1997).

16. The metaphor of French theory as a dead star still shining in faraway academic galaxies long after its original energy source on the Left Bank has become extinct is common among critics of poststructuralism. See, for example, Judt, *Past Imperfect,* 299.

17. See Richard F. Kuisel, *Seducing the French: The Dilemma of Americanization* (Berkeley: University of California Press, 1993).

18. Throughout this book, I use the term "liberalism" (perhaps one should only speak of multiple liberalisms) quite loosely, sometimes in its classical, Old World sense, which emphasizes the protection of individual rights and of a free-market ideology, and sometimes in its American egalitarian inflection, which stresses pluralism and the tolerance of differences, especially in its recent multiculturalist versions. Both traditions often end up on opposite sides of the Anglo-American political spectrum: conservative Republicans or Thatcherian Tories who advocate small government, tax reduction, and deregulation are called "liberals" on the continent. However, the insistence on individual rights and tolerance of diversity in most brands of "liberalism" makes classical Whiggish liberals and contemporary multiculturalists alike strong critics of the Jacobin tradition.

19. On French views regarding "political correctness" and multiculturalism, see Marie-Christine Granjon, "Le regard en biais. Attitudes françaises du multiculturalisme américain (1990–1993)" and Eric Fassin, "*Political Correctness* en version originale et en version française. Un malentendu révélateur." Both articles appeared in *Vingtième siècle. Revue d'histoire* 43 (July–September 1994): 18–29 and 30–42, respectively. See also the special issue of *Esprit,* "Les défis du multiculturalisme," *Esprit* 187 (December 1992): 58–133.

20. Alain Touraine, *Critique of Modernity* (Oxford: Blackwell, 1995); Alain Finkielkraut, *The Defeat of the Mind,* trans. Judith Friedlander (New York: Columbia University Press, 1995); Julia Kristeva, *Nations without Nationalism* (New York: Columbia University Press, 1993); Régis Debray, *A demain De Gaulle* (Paris: Gallimard, 1990) and *Contretemps: Eloge des idéaux perdus* (Paris: Gallimard, 1992). One finds in *A demain De Gaulle* the following prediction, which echoes so many contemporary meditations on the return of the Dark Ages: "Will the year 2000 bring about the second feudalization of Europe? . . . Probably. The new lords of money, . . . Italian-style *condotierre,* are making off with the means of communication, production and exchange. Clerical powers are attempting to divide among themselves the spoils of our public schools, just as ethnic and religious communities share out by lots what is left of the public space" (168).

21. John Rawls, *A Theory of Justice* (Cambridge: Harvard University Press, 1971); Ronald Dworkin, *Taking Rights Seriously* (London: Duckworth, 1977); Charles Taylor, "Cross-Purposes: The Liberal-Communitarian Debate," in *Liberalism and the Moral Life* (Cambridge: Harvard University Press, 1989); and Michael Sandel, "The Procedural Republic and the Unencumbered Self," *Political Theory* 12 (1984): 81–96.

22. Judt, *Past Imperfect,* 313.

23. The victory of *les bleus* in the World Cup Final in July 1998 and the central role played by black and Maghrebin members of the national team in the outcome briefly reversed the usual representations of French ethnic relations in the American media. Headlines celebrating the "new" multicolor France replaced customary digressions on French xenophobia. Political leaders were eager to drive the point home: on every possible occasion, President Chirac waxed lyrical about a soccer squad that, like the country it represented, was "both *tricolore* and *multicolore,*" while an embarrassed Jean-Marie Le Pen was reduced to arguing that Zinédine Zidane, who had scored the winning goal, was "a son of *Algérie Française.*"

24. A number of studies on Vichy and its aftermath in contemporary France and on issues of national identity both in the thirties and today have been published in the last three or four years alone in the United States. See, for example (and the list is not exhaustive), David Carroll, *French Literary Fascism: Nationalism, Anti-Semitism and the Ideology of Culture* (Princeton: Princeton University Press, 1995); Eugen Weber, *The Hollow Years: France in the 1930s* (New York: Norton, 1995); W. D. Hall, *Politics, Society and Christianity in Vichy France* (Oxford: Berg, 1995); S. Ungar and T. Conley, eds., *Identity Papers: Contested Nationhood in Twentieth-Century France* (Minneapolis: University of Minnesota Press, 1996); Richard Golsan, ed., *Memory, the Holocaust and French Justice: The Bousquet and Touvier Affairs* (Hanover, N.H.: University Press of New England, 1997); Melanie Hawthorne and Richard Golsan, eds., *Gender and Fascism in Modern France* (Hanover, N.H.: University Press of New England, 1997).

25. Fassin, *"Political Correctness."*

26. Richard Rorty, quoted in Fassin, *"Political Correctness"*; François Furet, "L'utopie démocratique à l'américaine," *Le Débat* 69 (1992): 83.

27. Fassin, *"Political Correctness,"* 34.

28. Quoted in Granjon, "Le Regard en biais," 23.

29. Kwame Anthony Appiah, "The Multiculturalist Misunderstanding," *The New York Review* (9 October 1997): 30–36.

30. The resistance to modernity, however conceived, is the source of many forms of nationalism, from the German Romanticism of the 1820s and 1830s to contemporary calls for popular mobilization against the "American Satan" in Iran, Algeria, or Serbia.

31. Michael Walzer, *On Toleration* (New Haven: Yale University Press, 1997).

1. FRENCH THEORY IN THE UNITED STATES

1. See Richard Hofstadter's classic study, *Anti-Intellectualism in American Life* (New York: Vintage, 1962), especially chapters 3–5. Hofstadter prefaced his analysis of the Evangelical spirit as a "religion of the heart" with the following remarks: "The American mind was shaped in the mold of early modern Protestantism. Religion was the first arena for American intellectual life, and thus the first arena for an anti-intellectual impulse" (55).

2. Kathy Trumpener and Richard Maxwell, "Forum on Cultural Studies and the Literary," *PMLA* 112, no. 2 (1997): 263.

3. Los Angeles-based screenwriter Mark Horowitz, reflecting on the French enthusiasm for movies starring Mickey Rourke, views the deconstruction debate as just another episode of the "constant war between the U.S. and France." In Horowitz's words, "we sent them Jerry Lewis, so they retaliated by sending us deconstruction and Jacques Derrida" (cited in David Lehman, *Signs of the Times: Deconstruction and the Fall of Paul de Man* [New York: Poseidon Press, 1991], 22).

4. David Lehman rightly notes that "deconstruction in America owes much to our starry-eyed reverence for French culture, based perhaps on a misguided notion of French culture. Deconstruction conforms to an American preconception of the cerebral French" (22). The resistance to French theory can be ascribed to the same preconception, valued inversely.

5. American feminist critics of Derrida, Lacan, and Foucault usually ground their rejection of part or the totality of these authors' views on their maleness rather than on their Frenchness, thereby disregarding most of what these various theorists owe to the specificity of the national context. Criticism of Foucault's writings from a feminist perspective generally falls into one or more of the following areas of contention: (1) Foucault's rejection of essentialism and

his fragmentary view of practice end up atomizing, and thereby weakening, women's struggles; (2) he does not distinguish sufficiently along gender lines, thereby erasing the specificity of women's oppression; (3) his views of history as discontinuous makes it impossible for women to think of patriarchal oppression in terms of its historical continuity; and (4) Foucault's work excludes any possibility of effective, global resistance against patriarchy. Most of these objections have been refuted, convincingly or not, by Foucault himself. My point, however, is that none of these criticisms is related specifically to the national origin of Foucault's thought. Few of his critics look at him as a *French* intellectual.

6. Antifoundationalism refutes all philosophical attempts to ground thought and action on transcendental or universal principles, such as human nature or transhistorical reason. By "neopragmatists" I mean philosophers and critics such as Richard Rorty and Stanley Fish, whose critiques of objectivism have contributed to the current revival of pragmatism in American academic circles. Their brand of pragmatism differs from that of Dewey, for example, in that they do not share his modernist faith in science, socialism, and in the universalization of democratic principles.

7. Richard Rorty, *Consequences of Pragmatism,* xxi.

8. See, for example, Jean-François Lyotard, *The Postmodern Condition: A Report on Knowledge,* trans. Brian Massumi (Minnesota: University of Minnesota Press, 1985), *The Differend: Phrases in Dispute,* trans. G. Van Den Abbeele (Minneapolis: University of Minnesota Press, 1988), and Jean Baudrillard, *America,* trans. Chris Turner (London: Verso, 1988).

9. As has often been remarked, the rapid proliferation of French contemporary theory in American departments of literature also had a lot to do with the legacy of New Criticism. Its proponents also prepared academic minds for poststructuralism by stressing the autonomy of the text in terms of both its author and the social conditions of its production, a conception of the status of literary works not unlike the views advanced by the French promoters of hypertextualism and the death of the author.

10. For recent examples of the extent to which French philosophers and social scientists are now borrowing from Anglo-American philosophies (and especially pragmatism), see Luc Boltanski and Laurent Thévenot, *Les Economies de la grandeur* (Paris: Presses Universitaires de France, 1987) and *De la justification* (Paris: Gallimard, 1991), as well as Bruno Latour, *Nous n'avons jamais été modernes* (Paris: La Découverte, 1991). See also Louis Quéré's remarks in the special issue of the journal *Espace-Temps* devoted to these (neo)pragmatist currents in contemporary French thought, *Espace-Temps* 49–50 (1992): 41–60.

11. Thomas Pavel makes an illuminating distinction between decentralized cultures (such as the United States), which are slow to adopt new interpretive regimes but equally reluctant to give them up, and centralized cultures (such as France), "which tend to speed up the renewal of ideas, and, by the same token,

sharpen the public's sensitivity to the elites' momentary frame of mind . . . [In the latter], cultural novelties take on a pleasant effervescent character, but often lead to a premature canonization of the ephemeral" ("Empires et paradigmes," *Le Débat* 50 [1989]: 175–76).

12. Michèle Lamont, "How to Become a Dominant French Philosopher: The Case of Jacques Derrida," *American Journal of Sociology* 3 (1987): 584–622.

13. Derrida's *Of Grammatology* appeared in 1977, *Speech and Phenomena* in 1980, and *Positions* and *Dissemination* in 1981, ten to fifteen years after their publication in France on the eve and in the immediate aftermath of May 68. It took eleven years for Lacan's *Ecrits,* first published in France in 1966, to appear in English. By then, the attraction of *le lacanisme* had waned in France, where it was limited to small circles of devotees. Foucault's books fared a little bit better: there was only a three-year lag in the case of *The Archaeology of Knowledge* (1969–1972) and a five-year delay for *The Order of Things* (1966–1971). The complexity of Derrida's and Lacan's prose, beyond issues of theoretical content and ideological-institutional power struggles, may account for the time between original publication and translation.

14. It is this high cultural strategy that recently backfired. Once the shot in the arm provided by French theory wore off, literary criticism found itself in the same situation as before the theoretical turn, and it was once again asked to show its social relevance. This time, however, the request did not come from the practitioners of traditional, empirical social science, as in the fifties, but from cultural and postcolonial studies theorists impatient with the politically demobilizing consequences of the new literary scholasticism.

15. Derrida has repeatedly stressed the commonality of views and objectives between deconstruction and the most radical forms of social and cultural critique in the United States. See, for example, his remark, quoted by Elaine Showalter, that "feminists or feminist scholars are to some extent interested in deconstruction" because "the struggle is the same" ("Critical Crossdressing and the Woman of the Year," in *Men in Feminism,* ed. Alice Jardine and Paul Smith [New York: Methuen, 1987], 196).

16. Blau's account of the transatlantic voyage of sixties radicalism (from America to France and back) has prompted Joan DeJean to argue for the American origin of French theory: "The ideology that Barthes portrays as the hallmark of the theory produced by Moderns was of American inspiration" (*Ancients against Moderns,* 27).

17. Blau's description of the transatlantic relation between practical, unreflexive American youth and theoretically savvy but libidinally exhausted French middle-aged thinkers is consistent with widespread identifications of America with nature, body, pulsion, desire, unconscious, and so on . . . and France with culture/civilization, mind, sublimation, intellect, consciousness, and so on . . .

in cross-cultural depictions of France and the United States at least since the Romantic Age. In Blau's account of the symbolic exchange of the rebellious sixties, American students provided the French with youthful libido while the French gave the American radicals the much-needed intellectual tools to make sense of their revolt. Reflecting on the reception of her work on American campuses in the aftermath of the sixties, Julia Kristeva declared that there was a natural fit between the students' "hysterical rebellion" and French theory because the latter could speak the *jouissance* of the American body: "Despite the naïveté, the American audience gives the European intellectual the impression that there is something he can do on the other side of the Atlantic, namely that he can speak in a place where it [ça] doesn't speak" (*The Kristeva Reader,* ed. Toril Moi [New York: Columbia University Press, 1986], 275).

On the American side, some have remarked that just as the Romantic German philosophers had fought the French Revolution in their minds since they could not wage it in the streets, so the French theorists of liberatory desire (Deleuze, Guattari, Lyotard, and so on) were forced to give a philosophical account of a revolutionary upheaval that could only take place, in its most radical, libidinal form, on American campuses, in rock festivals, and California communes.

18. Lacan's brand of psychoanalysis, a target of French feminism, owes a lot to Hegelian thought, which was anathema to the Nietzscheans Deleuze and Lyotard. As for Derrida and Foucault, they certainly shared more than misgivings regarding their respective theoretical enterprises, at least during Foucault's so-called structuralist moment. In his 1963 lecture on Foucault's *Madness and Civilization,* Derrida questioned the author's "naive" reading of Descartes and deplored his colleague's tendency to reinscribe philosophical texts in a "total historical project," claiming that Foucault's "structuralist totalitarianism would be responsible for an internment of the cogito similar to the violences of the classical age." Foucault replied years later that the true repressive political project was in fact Derridean deconstruction, since it ended up in restoring tradition and authority via a "systematic" reading constructed "so as not to have to analyze the ways in which the subject is implicated." The abusive "textualization" of discursive practices, Foucault went on, was nothing but "a thoroughly historically determined minor pedagogy." By teaching the pupil that "there is nothing outside the text" deconstruction "gives the teacher's voice that unlimited sovereignty which allows it to repeat the text indefinitely." On the Foucault-Derrida controversy, see Didier Eribon, *Michel Foucault,* trans. Betsy Wing (Cambridge: Harvard University Press, 1991): 120–21.

19. Pierre Bourdieu, *Homo academicus* (Paris: Minuit, 1984) and *Les Règles de l'art: Genèse et structure du champ littéraire* (Paris: Seuil, 1992), and Niilo Kauppi, *French Intellectual Nobility: Institutional and Symbolic Transformations in the Post-Sartrean Era* (Albany: State University of New York Press, 1996).

20. John Searle's well-known critique of Derridean deconstruction is paradigmatic of what practitioners of one form or another of Anglo-American philosophy find wrong with poststructuralism (see John Searle, "The Word Turned Upside Down," *New York Review of Books* [27 October 1983]).

21. See, for example, the Marxist critic Frank Lentricchia's characterization of Paul de Man's style as "the rhetoric of authority" (*After the New Criticism* [Chicago: University of Chicago Press], 283–84).

22. Showalter's reference to the French (Founding) *fathers* is quite significant in this context. The younger generation of Anglo-American male theorists seem to have their own Oedipal quarrel with their French predecessors. In another chapter in *Men in Feminism,* in response to a question concerning the difference between his generation and "the old French guys talking about the feminine," Paul Smith, a British cultural critic who teaches in the United States, remarked that "one of the successes of feminism has been to take the old white male French masters to task, and it's true that we can only learn from that" (Alice Jardine and Paul Smith, "A Conversation," 252).

23. Cited in Michèle Sarde, *Regard sur les Françaises: Xe–XXe siècles* (Paris: Stock, 1983), 644. The distaste for intellectualism in French feminist writings is not limited to recent authors. In the early seventies, Betty Friedan found that Simone de Beauvoir had grown both too radical in her advocacy of a feminism of difference and too abstract in her assessment of the situation of women. De Beauvoir's self-assurance was, Friedan noted, sterile, cold, an abstraction that had little to do with real lives. On the Friedan-de Beauvoir debate from a French perspective, see Sarde (629–32) and Mona Ozouf, *Women's Words: Essay on French Singularity,* trans. Jane Marie Todd (Chicago: University of Chicago Press, 1997), 392–94.

24. Richard Rorty, "Taking Philosophy Seriously," *The New Republic* (11 April 1988).

25. One notable exception is James Miller's biography of Foucault, which places the philosopher's experiments with the limits of pleasure, pain, and death at the core of his theoretical enterprise. See James Miller, *The Passion of Michel Foucault* (New York: Simon and Schuster, 1993).

26. Jacques Derrida, *L'Ecriture et la différence* (Paris: Seuil, 1967); Paul de Man, *Allegories of Reading: Figural Language in Rousseau, Nietzsche, Rilke and Proust* (New Haven: Yale University Press, 1979); and Barbara Johnson, *Défigurations du langage poétique: La seconde révolution baudelairienne* (Paris, 1979).

27. This difference in emphasis, to the extent that it is so clear-cut, could be taken to illustrate the elitism, both social and theoretical, of the French feminist discourse. Elite women, in the love courts as well as in the salons, felt culturally repressed rather than economically oppressed. The articulation of a discourse of oppression appears later, as a product of the age of democracy.

28. Ozouf, *Women's Words.*

29. The French school system played an institutional role in the promotion of women's rights similar to that of the United States Army in the integration of minorities.

30. As exemplified by Stanislas de Clermont-Tonnerre's famous declaration during the 1791 Legislative Assembly's debate over the emancipation of the Jews: "One must refuse everything to the Jews as a nation, and give everything to the Jews as individuals" (cited in Walzer, *On Toleration*, 39).

31. Compare Michèle Sarde's conclusion: "Will there still be French women in the twenty-first century?" (*Regard sur les Françaises*, 647).

32. I am thinking here of works in the new paradigm of (British, Australian, and American) cultural studies. Although their political and theoretical premises differ greatly from those of Paglia, critics such as Andrew Ross, Larry Grossberg, Meaghan Morris, and John Frow are similarly very critical of the elitism of Old World intellectuals as they attempt to valorize popular forms of cultural practice.

2. THE FRENCH REVOLUTION AT TWO HUNDRED

1. One of the best-known verses of *L'Internationale* reads: "Du passé, faisons table rase!" (Let's make a clean sweep of the past!).

2. The fundamental naturalism of the dominant English self-image, evident in Burke's political conceptions, equally pervades the following passage from Shaftesbury's *Characteristics of Men, Manners, Opinions, Times* (New York: Bobbs-Merrill, 1964): "And 'tis in this that the very worst of poets may justly be preferred to the generality of modern philosophers or other formal writers of a yet more specious name . . . They follow Nature. They move chiefly as she moves in them, without thought of disguising her free motions and genuine operations, for the sake of any scheme or hypothesis they have formed at leisure and in particular narrow views" (347). Both the poet and the scientist "follow Nature," both stand in opposition to the theorist (or modern philosopher), enamored of idle speculations, abstractions, and generalities.

3. Hartz was quite aware of the problems raised by his use of the word "feudalism" to describe seventeenth-century Europe and "nonfeudal" society to refer to the colonial United States: "I know that I am using broad terms broadly here. 'Feudalism' refers technically to the institutions of the medieval era, and it is well known that aspects of the decadent feudalism of the later period . . . were present in America even in the eighteenth century. 'Liberalism' is an even vaguer term . . . But these are the liabilities of any large generalizations, danger points but not insuperable barriers" (*The American Liberal Tradition* [New York: Harcourt, 1955], 4).

4. Pierre Manent, for his part, has remarked that although the debate between Burke and Paine may be considered as "the emblematic figure of subsequent

conflicts between 'the right' and 'the left' in liberal societies or in societies in search of liberal institutions," neither of the two protagonists stepped outside of the circle of liberalism: "Neither Burke, on the right, renounces liberalism to favor a 'restoration' of the preliberal order, as the continental European right will do for a long time, nor does Paine, on the left, in order to propose a 'surpassing' of liberal individualism, as the socialists will do even in England. Burke is as 'conservative' and 'aristocratic' as a liberal can be without ceasing to be a liberal, and Paine is as 'progressive' and 'democratic' as a liberal can be without ceasing to be liberal" (*Les libéraux* [Paris: Hachette, 1986], 10).

5. See, for example, Dorothy Ross, "The Liberal Tradition Revisited and the Republican Tradition Addressed," in *New Directions in American Intellectual History,* ed. John Higham and Paul K. Conkin (Baltimore: Johns Hopkins University Press, 1979) and Robert N. Bellah et al., *Habits of the Heart: Individualism and Commitment in American Life* (New York: Harper and Row, 1985). Although the authors of *Habits of the Heart* stress the multiple strands (biblical, republican, utilitarian individualistic, and expressive individualistic) that make up the American cultural tradition, they ultimately grant individualism the same all-encompassing reach as Hartz did liberalism. "Individualism lies at the very core of American culture. Every one of the four traditions we have singled out is in a profound sense individualistic" (142). In fact, what Bellah and his colleagues find wrong with individualism is in many cases quite similar to what Hartz found objectionable in the "American liberal intelligence": the pressure to conform and the "unwritten tyrannical compulsion it contains" (Hartz, *American Liberal Tradition,* 12). Compare with the following passage (from *Habits of the Heart*): "As Tocqueville observed, when one can no longer rely on tradition or authority, one inevitably looks to others for confirmation of one's judgments. Refusal to accept established opinion and anxious conformity to the opinions of one's peers turn out to be two sides of the same coin" (148).

The centrality of anti-individualism in Bellah's (and other communitarians') argument, and his celebration of civic and republican conceptions of citizenship, is reminiscent of recent French neo-Jacobin critiques of (American) liberalism. On the homology between these two intellectual currents and the role of anti-individualism both in the French republican philosophical tradition and in recent forms of communitarianism in the United States, see further, chapter 5).

6. Letter to Samuel Moore, 5 November 1789, cited in Jean-Pierre Dormois and Simon P. Newman, *Vue d'Amérique: La Révolution française jugée par les Américains* (Paris: Ed. France-Empire, 1989), 39.

7. Cited in Dormois and Newman, *Vue d'Amérique,* 83.

8. Cited in Dormois and Newman, *Vue d'Amérique,* 164.

9. Jefferson, by contrast, was confident twenty years after the Terror that the mistakes made "in good faith" by the French patriots, and even the crimes of Danton and Robespierre, would soon be forgotten (letter to Benjamin Gallo-

way, 2 December 1812, in *The Writings of Thomas Jefferson,* vol. 9, ed. A. A. Lipscomb [Washington, 1903]).

10. Judt writes: "Some of the themes of French intellectual discourse that helped pave the way for the political positions I shall be describing—the attraction to violence, the uninterest in morality as a category of public behavior, the curious and repeated addiction to German philosophical style—could be traced readily back to Victor Cousin, 1793, Voltaire, and doubtless beyond. The *longue durée,* already hard to justify in social history, explains very little if anything in the history of public language and its political deployment" (*Past Imperfect,* 7).

11. The ambiguities of Comte's philosophy, a mixture of progressive belief in science as emancipatory power and conservative appeal to social organicism, explains that his views influenced both the Republicans, who relished his rationalism and faith in the scientific improvement of society, and the reactionary Right, bent on opposing the concrete communities of blood and soil to the abstract principles of Enlightenment universalism. In the American context, the influence of Comtism on late nineteenth-century Progressives contributed to the transformation of American liberalism from a theory of limited government to an ideology of corrective state intervention, closer to French republicanism than to *laissez-faire* Whiggism (see Gillis J. Harp, *Positivist Republic: Auguste Comte and the Reconstruction of American Liberalism, 1865–1920* [University Park: Pennsylvania State University Press, 1995]).

12. Harp argues that a similar evolution of liberalism, from a doctrine hostile to governmental intervention in social and economic life to current (embattled) notions of welfare state liberalism, was also under way at the same time in the United States, under the influence of positivist principles imported from . . . France!

13. See, for example, Berlin on epistemological pluralism, empirical diversity, and the tolerance of ambiguity: "For every rationalist metaphysician, from Plato to the last disciples of Hegel and Marx, this abandonment of the notion of a final harmony in which all riddles are solved, all contradictions reconciled, is a piece of crude empiricism, abdication before brute facts, intolerable bankruptcy of reason before things as they are, failure to explain and justify, to reduce everything to a system, which 'reason' indignantly rejects. But if we are not armed with an a priori guarantee of the proposition that a total harmony of true values is somewhat to be found . . . we must fall back on the ordinary resources of empirical observation and ordinary human knowledge . . . If, as I believe, the ends of men are many, and not all of them are in principle, compatible with each other, then the possibility of conflict—and of tragedy—can never wholly be eliminated from human life, either personal or social . . . Pluralism, with the measure of 'negative' liberty it entails, seems to me a truer and more humane ideal than the goals of those who seek in the great, disciplined, authoritarian

structures of the ideal of 'positive' self-mastery by classes, or peoples, or the whole of mankind. It is truer because it does, at least, recognize the fact that human goals are many, not all of them commensurable, and in perpetual rivalry with one another" (*Four Essays on Liberty* [Oxford: Oxford University Press, 1990], 168–69, 171).

14. Alexis Philonenko, *Jean-Jacques Rousseau et la pensée du malheur* (Paris: Vrin, 1984).

15. On the "responsibility" of Rousseau's thought in revolutionary excesses, see also François Furet, *Interpreting the French Revolution,* trans. Elborg Forster (Cambridge: Cambridge University Press, 1981): "Rousseau may well have been the most far-sighted genius ever to appear in intellectual history, for he invented, or sensed, so many of the problems that were to obsess the nineteenth and twentieth centuries. His political thought set up well in advance the conceptual framework of what was to become Jacobinism and the language of the Revolution, both in his philosophical premises (the fulfillment of the individual through politics) and because the radical character of the new consciousness of historical action is in keeping with his rigorous theoretical analysis of the conditions necessary for the exercise of popular sovereignty. Rousseau is hardly 're-sponsible' for the French Revolution, yet he unwittingly assembled the cultural materials that went into revolutionary consciousness and practice. It is an ironic twist of history that at the very moment when the Revolution believed it was implementing Jean-Jacques' ideas, it demonstrated, on the contrary, the validity of Rousseau's pessimism, that is to say the infinite distance between the rule of law and the rule of force, democracy's inability to follow its own theory in practice" (32).

16. The right wing of the historical profession was also quick to denounce the American roots of the revisionist school. Jean Tulard, a professor at the Sorbonne, complained that Furet's views of a consensual France were out of touch with the realities and feelings of *la France profonde*. The problem with Furet's view of the French Revolution, Tulard said, was that "he sees it from Chicago" (cited in Steven L. Kaplan, *Farewell, Revolution* [Ithaca: Cornell University Press], 2:128). Tulard's remarks combine the widespread *ressentiment* in the French professoriate against colleagues who hold (lucrative) visiting faculty positions in prestigious American universities, with the traditionalist's rejection of the United States as a desirable cultural model.

17. The fact that the question of liberalism was at the heart of the new quarrel of the intellectuals does not mean, as we shall see, that the field of French thought is now dominated by authors of liberal or neoliberal persuasion. The term is highly polysemic and the notion of liberalism is a very complex one, as witnessed by the different use of the term on the continent and in the United States. In France, liberalism, central as it was to the first phase of the Revolution

(the principles of 89) soon came to be associated with the moderate bourgeoisie's attempt to secure its social and economic gains after the fall of the Jacobins, and later (1830–48) to establish a British-style constitutional regime in the country. In the eyes of the Left after 1848, liberals were simply conservatives bent on denying the people access to universal suffrage and social and economic democracy. Similarly, in Italy and Germany, liberalism came to mean "the political organization and ideas of the industrial and commercial elites," as Tony Judt puts it (*Past Imperfect*, 232).

Today, when the French Socialists denounce the liberalism of the Right, they refer to their opponents' attachment to a free-market economy and the limitations of state intervention in economic and social matters, in short, the ideology of American *conservatives*. As a matter of fact, the French Left in the 1980s faulted both the Gaullist and centrist parties for their uncritical praise of Reaganomics, perceived as the latest form of "le libéralisme." The gradual dissociation of American liberalism from its original, classical nineteenth-century version (in the absence of a strong reactionary, antiliberal political tradition in the United States) means that to be a liberal in America today implies, paradoxically for Europeans, expanding the role of government and limiting the effects of a free-market economy. American libertarianism, in this respect, is closer to the individualistic, free-market, antistatist ideology the European Left usually means by "liberalism."

The widely divergent meanings of "liberalism" on both sides of the Atlantic show that there are many kinds of liberalism—social, political, and economic—according to the variety in the national structural contexts of appropriation of liberal ideas (especially in terms of the differential position and power of the various national bourgeoisies in those contexts, along a continuum marked by the two extremes of Britain and the United States on the one hand, and Germany on the other). Throughout the remainder of this book I will deliberately keep the different meanings of "liberalism" open. This tolerance of ambiguity is, I think, an adequate response to the fact that the question of liberalism is still a contested one today, and that the debate often involves misreadings by intellectuals trained in specific national traditions of what constitutes liberalism, and illiberalism, in other cultures.

18. See, for example, Sunil Khilnani, *Arguing Revolution: The Intellectual Left in Postwar France* (New Haven: Yale University Press, 1993), chapters 5 and 6; Jacques Julliard, "La course au centre," in François Furet, Jacques Julliard, and Pierre Rosanvallon, *La République du Centre* (Paris: Calmann-Lévy, 1988); and Marc Lilla, "The Legitimacy of the Liberal Age," in *New French Thought: Political Philosophy* (Princeton: Princeton University Press, 1994).

19. See, for example, Louis Dumont, *Essays on Individualism: Modern Ideology in Anthropological Perspective* (Chicago: University of Chicago Press, 1986);

Furet, *Interpreting the French Revolution;* and Gilles Lipovetsky, *L'Ere du vide: Essai sur l'individualisme contemporain* (Paris: Gallimard, 1983).

20. A sign of the deep symbolic rupture effected by the creation of *Le Débat:* Michel Foucault was greatly upset by the tone and content of the first issue, which he perceived, *quite accurately,* as a genuine declaration of war against the class of 68, on the level of theory as well as practice. The friendship between Foucault and Nora quickly soured. On this point, see Eribon, *Michel Foucault,* 292–93.

3. BACK TO LA RÉPUBLIQUE

1. The Socialists' rise to power and the question of the future of the institutions of the Fifth Republic (established by de Gaulle in 1958) also revived the discussion on the native political tradition, a reflection often tinged with anxiety in the context of a national identity weakened by the triple threat of Americanization, immigration, and European integration. Claude Nicolet, one of the best historians of the Republic, remarks that "the power changeover finally achieved in 1981 (with its expected misfortunes such as the 'cohabitation' [power-sharing between a socialist president and a conservative prime minister, as in 1986–1988] undoubtedly brought about a renewal of the various reflections, all beneficial after all, on the foundations of the French republican tradition" (*La République en France: Etat des lieux* [Paris: Seuil, 1992], 11).

Among the many studies published on this topic before and after the Bicentennial, see also Nicolet's *L'Idée républicaine en France* (Paris: Gallimard, 1992), as well as the edited volume by S. Berstein and O. Rudelle, *Le Modèle républicain* (Paris: Presses Universitaires de France, 1992). The title of another notable publication (by R. Huart, R. Martelli, C. Nicolet, and M. Vovelle), *La Passion de la République: Un itinéraire français* (Paris: Editions Sociales, 1992), shows to what extent the revaluation of the republican tradition dovetails with the theme of French exceptionalism.

On the ceremonies of the bicentennial and the debates surrounding the celebration, see Steven L. Kaplan's remarkably comprehensive and detailed study, *Farewell, Revolution.*

2. Benjamin Barber, *Jihad vs. McWorld: How the Planet Is Falling Apart and Coming Together* (New York: Ballantine, 1995). The French translation was widely, and mostly approvingly, reviewed in the French media.

3. Liberalism paradoxically shares the view of history as the self-deployment of immanent forces (most emphatically expressed in the workings of the economic market) with most socialist theories.

4. On the tension between idealistic and positivistic components of the republican ideology during the Second Empire and in the early years of the

Third Republic, see Mona Ozouf, "Entre l'esprit des Lumières et la lettre positiviste: Les républicains sous l'Empire," in *Le Siècle de l'avènement républicain,* ed. François Furet and Mona Ozouf (Paris: Gallimard, 1993).

5. On the philosophical absolutism of many contemporary French conceptions of the relationship of rights, ethics, and history viewed from an Anglo-American perspective, see Charles Larmore's assessment of their inability to conceive of a Reason steeped in history and yet not entirely determined by empirical processes, in "Histoire et raison en philosophie politique," *Stanford French Review* 15, nos. 1–2 (1991): 183–206.

6. See, for example, Touraine's emphatic homage to Isaiah Berlin, commended for upholding a pluralism of values and attempting "to resist both the arrogance of French Enlightenment thought and the dangers of German Romanticism" (*Critique of Modernity,* 343). Contemporary debates on multiculturalism and national identity are almost always framed in terms of a triangular configuration of cultural traditions, French, German, and Anglo-American, conceived as national expressions of, respectively, Enlightenment rationalism (civic nationalism), Romanticism (the ethnic definition of the nation), and liberalism (pluralistic federalism and liberalism).

7. Ferry and Renaut point to what they call the ambiguities of the French tradition of democratic socialism, which, in many ways, was "a deepening of the idea of the republic," as Blum said of Jaurès's thought. They argue that both Jaurès and Blum, although they reject at times the notion of the dictatorship of the proletariat, were very critical of the reformism of their German social-democratic counterparts. "We are forced to admit that French democratic socialism, especially beginning with Blum, has had little success becoming doctrinally clear about the problem of the status of permissions [*droits-libertés*] (even when we grant that it does not in fact think of suspending them even temporarily)" (Luc Ferry and Alain Renaut, *French Philosophy of the Sixties: An Essay on Antihumanism,* trans. Mary H. S. Cattani [Amherst: University of Massachusetts Press, 1990], 117).

8. The Yugoslavian tragedy prompted a spate of essays from prominent players on the Parisian scene, most of them supporting the Bosnian cause, others the Croatian side. See Alain Finkielkraut, *Comment peut-on être croate?* (Paris: Gallimard, 1992); Jacques Julliard, *Ce fascisme qui vient* (Paris: Seuil, 1994); Pascal Bruckner, *La Tentation de l'innocence* (Paris: Grasset, 1995); Bernard-Henri Lévy, *Le Lys et la cendre: Journal d'un écrivain au temps de la guerre de Bosnie* (Paris: Grasset, 1996).

9. See, for example, Christophe Prochasson's remark that "the Dreyfusard intellectual is back" (*Les Intellectuels, le socialisme et la guerre 1900–1938* [Paris: Seuil, 1993], 265).

10. A position that may seem quite paradoxical on the part of scholars other-

wise inclined to celebrate the Kantian roots of their own thinking. But, of course, Heidegger is not "German" in the way Kant is.

11. For Ferry and Renaut, there is no going back to the rationalistic beliefs of a bygone, pre-Nietzschean past. In the same way as the return to the Republic cannot mean that one simply harks back to the roots of a doctrinaire, assimilationist, and universalistic Jacobinism, it is philosophically impossible, in their own words, "to return, after Marx, Nietzsche, Freud, and Heidegger, to the idea that man is the master and possessor of the totality of his actions and ideas" (*French Philosophy*, xvi). They define their own project as an attempt to "rethink the question of the subject, after his critique [by the philosophies of suspicion], and not only against it" (xvi). Paraphrasing this formulation, one could venture to say that the revival of the republican project in France today is an effort to rethink the postimperial national community *after* the critique of the authoritarian, statist, and imperialistic components of the Jacobin tradition (by Marxists and "neo-Tocquevillians" alike) and not only *against* it.

12. On the comparative history of the French and German ideas of the nation, see Rogers Brubaker, *Citizenship and Nationhood in France and Germany* (Cambridge: Harvard University Press, 1992) and Louis Dumont, *German Ideology: From France to Germany and Back* (Chicago: Chicago University Press, 1994).

13. Benda concluded that "in the world of spiritual things the victory of Germany is now complete" (58). In a footnote to the 1946 (French) edition of his book, the French essayist noted that history had borne out his earlier assertion. Anticipating Ferry and Renaut's critique of the Germanization of French thought, Benda remarked: "How much truer today. With our (surrealist) poets whose acknowledged masters are Novalis and Hölderlin, our (existentialist) philosophers who take their inspiration from Husserl and Heidegger, with Nietzscheism whose triumph is properly worldwide" (*La Trahison des clercs* [Paris: Grasset, 1975], 140).

14. On the centrality of the Eliasian opposition between culture *(Kultur)* and civilization both in the contemporary Battle of the Books and in the seventeenth-century French *Querelle des Anciens et des Modernes*, see Joan DeJean, *Ancients against Moderns*, 139–50.

15. I develop this point in chapter 5.

16. The first article of the American Anthropological Association's proposal to the United Nations reads as follows: "The individual realizes his personality through his culture, hence respect for individual differences entails a respect for cultural differences" (cited in Finkielkraut, *Defeat of the Mind*, 75).

17. Historians objected to Debray's neat philosophical packaging of transhistorical totalities such as republic and democracy, whose conceptual and empirical boundaries were never so clearly delineated as Debray would have the reader believe. In *Le Débat*, Jacques Le Goff worried that the equation between the State, the Republic, and Reason (or, worse, Reason of State) could prove as

intolerant and as divisive as the religious and ethnic fundamentalisms it was supposed to discredit ("Derrière le foulard, l'histoire," *Le Débat* 58 [1990]: 32). He also questioned Debray's paralogical logic, which "starts from an erroneous premise and draws from it consequences that can only be so" (31). Jacques Julliard, for his part, pointed out in *Le Nouvel Observateur* that "the abstract universalism borrowed from Rousseau and the principles of 1789 was throughout the history of the Republic a convenient smokescreen behind which to hide the domination of those in power and their social conservatism" ("Où est-elle, votre République?" *Le Nouvel Observateur* [7–13 December 1989]: 50–51).

One way to deconstruct Debray's neat binary categories would be to point out that liberal currents have been contesting the dominance of the republican model ever since the French Revolution, even though they were largely consigned after 1848 to the margins of the political arena. In the same way, the current critique of liberalism brought forward by American communitarians attests to the survival of the republican civic tradition in the United States. While the republican discourse has been dominant in France, and the liberal one in America, countertraditions and lines of resistance have always been present within each cultural formation.

18. Those familiar with the writings of Alain Finkielkraut will recognize in this two-pronged attack the rhetorical structure of his indictment of our present cultural malaise in *The Defeat of the Mind* and other related essays. On Finkielkraut's critique of relativism and multiculturalism, see chapter 4.

19. On the widespread opinion among supporters of the Republic that consumerism and multiculturalism (or cultural relativism) are related as powerful solvents of the national idea, consider, for example, Maurice Agulhon's position during the 1989 Bicentennial debate. According to Steven L. Kaplan, Agulhon, whose leftist proclivities were no secret, worried "about the powerful forces that had gradually blunted one's sense of republican Frenchness: the leveling impact of an Americanized media, the ethic of 'culturalism,' fortified by the massive influx of immigrants, that celebrated differences to the detriment of common foundations (the prospect of a 'Lebanonization' of France haunted the historian), the erosion of the history curriculum in the schools, the disintegrating impact of economic competition and other manifestations of acute individualism" (Kaplan, *Farewell, Revolution,* 2:25).

4. CULTURAL STUDIES, POSTCOLONIALISM, AND THE FRENCH NATIONAL IDEA

1. Throughout this chapter, Islamism (like the French *Islamisme*) refers to the particular use and interpretation of Muslim religion and culture by radical movements that, following Khomeinist doctrine, support the establishment of theocracies based on a strict application of Koranic Law. Islam, as a complex

system of practices, beliefs, and representations, should not be reduced to the intolerant, antimodernist ideology of some of its most radical proponents. Moderate Muslims argue that there is no prescription regarding the veil in the Qu'ran.

2. Elizabeth Badinter, Régis Debray, Alain Finkielkraut, Elizabeth de Fontenay, and Catherine Kintzler, "Profs, ne capitulons pas!" (Teachers, let's not surrender!), *Le Nouvel Observateur* (2–8 November 1989): 30–31.

3. The argument of the "universalists" on both sides of the Atlantic is well known: one cannot place group solidarities above individual freedom without threatening the very basis of the democratic order. In the case of the Islamic veil, the implication was that one should not welcome in public institutions, even in the name of pluralism and diversity, symbols of archaic religious practices and premodern ritual codes that legitimize patriarchal structures and deny the daughters of immigrants the same rights and liberties accorded to other French women. In this view, the republican state, far from being an oppressive institution that destroys traditional cultures and silences minorities, in fact protects the daughters who refuse to wear the hidjab from the fathers and older brothers who want to impose it on them. More generally, the debate opens up the question of the ambiguous nature of the democratic state from a leftist perspective, since the capitalist state both guarantees civil liberties and reinforces economic inequalities. In the same way, representatives of the modernist Left such as Pierre Bourdieu now defend the republican schools as historical vehicles of democratic achievements after having attacked them as instruments of the "reproduction" of social and cultural inequalities.

4. Mohammed Harbi, "Il est permis d'interdire," *Le Nouvel Observateur* (26 October–1 November 1989): 39.

5. Habib Boularès, "Non à l'uniforme politique!" *Le Nouvel Observateur* (2–8 November 1989): 36.

6. Haytham Manna, "L'imposture du voile," *Le Nouvel Observateur* (2–8 November 1989): 38.

7. See Françoise Gaspard and Farhad Khosrokhavar, *Le Foulard et la République* (Paris: La Découverte, 1995).

8. On this point, see Gaspard and Khosrokhavar, *Le Foulard,* chapter 2.

9. Foreign observers were usually astonished at the violence of the controversy surrounding the Islamic veil, and many thought the French were making a mountain out of a molehill. The violence of the debate is symptomatic of the degree of *anomie* confronting "liberalized" French society today and of the magnitude of the ideological charge invested in the national mythologies in the course of two hundred years of republican politics.

10. For a critique of Ross's book as "the kind of scholarship French cultural studies based on the Anglo-American model can produce," see Marie-Pierre Le Hir, "French Cultural Studies in the United States: A Case Study," *Sites* 1, no. 1

(spring 1997): 171–90. Le Hir argues that one of the major flaws of Ross's account is that "it contributes to reinforcing static concepts of national identity when cultural studies is supposed to be 'a brutal assault' on them" (187). Generalizations about good Algerians and bad French people enable Ross's narrative to seductively "erase all traces of political divisions among the French and among Algerians," contributing to what John Guillory has called "the very powerful fiction of the cultural homogeneity of the West" (cited in Le Hir, 188).

11. Michèle Tribalat, "Mobilité géographique et insertion sociale," cited in Emmanuel Todd, *Le Destin des immigrés: Assimilation et ségrégation dans les démocraties occidentales* (Paris: Seuil, 1994), 298.

12. Todd, *Le Destin,* 303.

13. Gouvernement général de l'Algérie, *Etat de l'Algérie* (1880) and *Annuaire statistique de l'Algérie* (1955). Figures cited in Todd, *Le Destin,* 296.

14. France has a relatively high rate of interracial marriage compared to other Western nations. In Britain during the period 1985–88, 16 percent of second-generation Indian males and 19 percent of British-born Pakistani males had a "white" spouse or partner. In Germany in 1985, 24 percent of Turkish men had a "German" spouse (only 7 percent of women were married outside the Turkish community). In the United States in 1980, 10 percent of black males and 3 percent of black women were married to nonblacks, whereas .5 percent of black married women or unwed mothers had a white spouse in 1970 (1.2 percent in 1992). The figures for African American women married to Hispanic men were similar. Sources for the United States are from Bureau of the Census, *Household and Family Characteristics,* March 1992; figures for Britain and Germany are cited in Todd, *Le Destin,* 127, 130, 132.

15. Todd rightly points out that, if the endogamous and patrilinear North African kinship system is considered unacceptable by most French nationals, the rejection cuts both ways: "Symmetrically, the French system . . . is in the eyes of the Arab the very expression of barbarity," especially with regard to the status, independence, and sexual freedom of women (*Le Destin,* 294).

16. "La société française reste taraudée par le racisme," *Le Monde* (2 July 1998): 14–15.

17. See James G. Gimpel and James R. Edwards Jr., *The Congressional Politics of Immigration Reform* (Boston: Allyn and Bacon, 1998).

18. Commission consultative des droits de l'homme, *Rapport 1992. La lutte contre le racisme et la xénophobie* (Paris: La Documentation française, 1993): 62.

19. The phrase is from Rosemarie Scullion's essay, "Vicious Circles: Immigration and National Identity in Twentieth-Century France," *SubStance* 76/77 (1995): 30–48. The author contends that in twentieth-century France "the wars of cultural identity . . . continue to pit principles of multi-culturalism against the hegemonic paradigm Herman Lebovics calls 'True France,' a monolithic model of national identity formation 'hold[ing] that there is only one way to

participate in the culture of a country and only one natural political organization that fits the society'" (35).

20. The pessimistic version of immigration dominated the first half of the twentieth century, casting the problem in terms of an inescapable dilemma, a no-win situation regarding the possibility of assimilating the other. In the words of Gérard Noiriel, "either the waves of immigrants 'flooding' into France would integrate themselves, thus causing the French population to lose its 'identity' . . . or the immigrants would not be assimilated, thus putting the political unity of France at risk by the formation of 'national minorities'" (see Gérard Noiriel, "Difficulties in French Historical Research on Immigration," *Immigrants in Two Democracies: French and American Experience,* ed. D. L. Horowitz and Gérard Noiriel [New York: New York University Press, 1992], 74). The theme of the moral and vital decadence brought about by assimilation and miscegenation was formulated in the following way in 1883 by a critic of the melting pot: "A population that recruits from abroad will quickly lose its character, its morals, its own force; it will lose with time that which is most precious: its nationality" (cited in Noiriel, 74).

21. Tony Judt, to give a recent example, describes totalitarianism as "a logical and historical derivative of precisely that universalistic vision of republican democracy that still bedazzles so many French thinkers" (*Past Imperfect,* 313).

22. Many interpreters of French universalism have noted the paradox (see Paul Valéry's remark, cited as an epigraph). Pierre Bourdieu for his part notes that "to be French is to feel one is entitled to universalize one's particular interest, that national interest which has its peculiarity to be universal" (cited in Schor, *Bad Objects,* 5). That French universalism is so guilt-free and French imperialism "can deploy itself in all good conscience" is particularly irritating to Schor and other American critics of French colonialism (5–6).

23. Joan DeJean and Nancy K. Miller, eds., *Displacements* (Baltimore: Johns Hopkins University Press, 1991), viii.

24. The problem with representing the legacy of the early Third Republic simply as internal colonialism (as Breton or Occitan independence movements in the 1970s did) is that this legacy is part and parcel of the global movement of democratization and modernization of French society during the years 1871–1914. That is also why a reading of the Dreyfus affair that limits itself to the rise of anti-Semitism and intolerance is bound to ignore the fact that a Jew, otherwise thoroughly secularized, assimilated, and hence "republicanized," could be an officer in the French military. In many ways, fin-de-siècle anti-Semitism and nascent Zionism were opposite *responses* to the successful integration of a growing fraction of the Jewish bourgeoisie.

25. In the African context, Kwame Anthony Appiah makes a similar point, arguing that early Pan-African nationalisms, and some of today's postcolonial studies, have a tendency to overstate the impact of colonialism on native cul-

tures, embracing the colonizers' self-interested delusion: "The experience of the vast majority of the citizens of Europe's African colonies was one of an essentially shallow penetration by the colonizer . . . The colonizers overrate the extent of their cultural penetration . . . Indeed to speak of 'resistance' . . . is already to overstate the ways in which the colonial state was invasive . . . As Camara Laye showed in *L'Enfant noir,* colonial pedagogy failed as notably in francophone and anglophone Africa to fully deracinate its objects" (*In My Father's House: Africa in the Philosophy of Culture* [Oxford University Press, 1992], passim, and 7–9).

26. Jules Ferry, one of the leaders of the Republican party, declared in a speech before the Assemblée nationale that "our colonial policy is the daughter of our industrial policy."

27. A passing remark at the beginning of Lebovics's study is quite revelatory of the theoretical and cultural divide I have been documenting in this book. The author thanks two of his colleagues for reassuring him that "what I was writing might make sense to French readers" (*True France: The Wars over Cultural Identity, 1900–1945* [Ithaca: Cornell University Press, 1992], xviii). In other words, a thorough postmodernist critique of French nativistic discourse during the interwar period, quite de rigueur in the American academic context, may encounter strong resistance in the French intellectual community and reading public because of the incommensurability of both conceptual (and political) universes. Presumably, the inability of the French to "make sense" of the critique is predicated upon the unshakable grip that the integrationist view of the national community and the sacred reverence for the national past as a civilizing process continue to hold on many French minds.

28. Lebovics is quite aware of the predicament, writing that "analyses of hegemonic relations are dangerous when they focus primarily on differences and the right to differences of the dominated in emancipation struggles . . . Today, for example, Jean-Marie Le Pen and other French racists use the ways immigrants are different and the uniqueness of their cultures to argue that they can never become part of French national life" (*True France,* 125). Indeed, the New Right in France is quite supportive of ethnic or racial separatism and pluralistic critiques of the melting pot: they reinforce a belief in the impossibility of a multicultural society. See Pierre-André Taguieff, *Sur la Nouvelle droite: Jalons d'une analyse critique* (Paris: Descartes and Cie), 1994.

29. On the role of colonial elites and *indigenista* intelligentsias in the rise of nationalism and anticolonial struggles, see Benedict Anderson, *Imagined Communities: Reflections on the Origin and Spread of Nationalism* (London: Verso, 1991), esp. chapters 4 and 7.

30. Lebovics resorts to the Marcusean concept of repressive tolerance to account for the fact that some colonials eventually gained the "right" to attend elite higher educational institutions. They were forbidden, he writes, to study colonial administration and military science. However, all of this did not pre-

vent some of them from becoming the new cadres of the anticolonial struggle in the postwar period. The contradictions of the modernization project give rise to an unending process of ideological and social *bricolage,* a series of temporary compromises between the accelerated circulation of peoples, goods, and ideas and the ultimately self-defeating desires of the dominant social groups to stabilize a movement that their own welfare demands while it threatens their dominance at every turn. That is why all attempts at conserving the social order, or turning back the clock, are bound to fail, notwithstanding the human tragedies such attempts often bring in their wake. The Nazis could not maintain an authoritarian, organicist order based on the proliferation of technological innovation, military or otherwise; they could not reinscribe the idiom of modernization in the old preindustrial culture of the *Gemeinschaft.* Today, Chinese Communists have a hard time containing the consequences of the computer revolution, while conservatives, in the United States as in Europe, are faced with the challenge of upholding traditional, largely premodern, moral and "family" values at the same time that they support a market economy and, by implication, a consumerist culture that is largely responsible for the breakup of traditional communities and the dissolution of some of the very values they wish to safeguard.

31. Brett C. Bowles, "La République régionale," *The French Review* 69 (1995): 103–17.

32. Caroline Ford, *Creating the Nation in Provincial France: Religion and Political Identity in Brittany* (Princeton: Princeton University Press, 1993).

33. Barère, a Jacobin, is famous for his denunciations of the use of Basque, Breton, Italian, and German in some parts of the nation as the surest way to perpetuate "the reign of fanaticism and superstition" and the domination of priests and aristocrats over the minds of the rural masses. Barère urged his fellow revolutionaries to complete the eradication of clericalism and linguistic diversity: "You have taken the saints away from these erring fanatics through the calendar of the republic, take from them the empire of priests through the teaching of the French language" (cited in Ford, *Provincial France,* 14). Again, the hostility to linguistic pluralism as an ideological program does not make it a historical reality. The wishes of the rationalistic, secularized elites need to be distinguished from the actual implementation of their policies in rural areas.

34. On the notion of transculturation, see Mary Louise Pratt, *Imperial Eyes: Travel Writing and Transculturation* (London: Routledge, 1992): "Ethnographers have used this term to describe how subordinated or marginal groups select and invent from materials transmitted to them by a dominant or metropolitan culture. While subjugated peoples cannot readily control what emanates from the dominant culture, they do determine to varying extents what they absorb into their own, and what they use it for" (6). Pratt suggests that transculturation works both ways: "With respect to representation, how does one speak

of transculturation from the colonies to the metropolis . . . Borders and all, the entity called Europe was constructed from the outside in as much as from the inside out" (6).

35. An amusing illustration of the fact that the republicanization of the French peasantry did not entail only ruthless policies of forced eradication of local cultural and linguistic identities can be found in the following piece of patriotic advice, from the *Tour de la France par deux enfants,* a central piece in the whole republican pedagogical setup (it was taught to generations of schoolchildren). Note the metaphorical motif reminiscent of the *e pluribus unum* of American federalism: "Just ask a gardener which is the prettiest flower, and he will be very embarrassed; but on the other hand he will tell you that the most beautiful garden of all is the one that has the most species of flowers and the prettiest. Well, child, France is this garden. Her provinces are like flowers of all kinds among which it is hard to choose, but that together form the most beautiful country, the sweetest to live in, our beloved fatherland" (cited in Bowles, "La République régionale," 106).

5. MULTICULTURALISM AND ITS DISCONTENTS

1. Conversely, for American multiculturalists, the French perception of ethnic pluralism in the United States is nothing but a caricature, a gross misconception produced by a particular kind of historical blindness that prevents the French from conceiving of diversity other than as the clash of separatist forces driven by racism and fanaticism. For these critics, the weight of a centralist and universalistic local tradition going back to ancien regime absolutism makes a liberal-democratic response to the challenge of cultural pluralism highly improbable in the French context.

2. Via the critique of 1960s French antihumanism, the debate on multiculturalism links up with earlier disputes regarding theory.

3. Roger Kimball, "The Treason of the Intellectuals and 'The Undoing of Thought,'" *New Criterion* 11 (December 1992): 13.

4. Harold Bloom, not surprisingly, has only praise for Finkielkraut's views, which he, too, reinscribes in the continuity of the French national idiom: "*The Defeat of the Mind* is one of the final flowerings of the spirit of Diderot. It teaches again the truths that ignorance cannot foster freedom, that Shakespeare is of a different order than a pair of boots, and that rock religion is suicide."

5. Cited in Noiriel, "Difficulties," 74.

6. Cited in Panivong Norindr, "La Plus Grande France: French Cultural Identity and Nation Building under Mitterrand," in *Identity Papers: Contested Nationhood in Twentieth-Century France* (Minneapolis: University of Minnesota Press, 1996): 248. Norindr is very suspicious of the inclusive rhetoric of the Left and views *intégration* as an updated, euphemistic, postimperial version of

cultural assimilation: "Mitterrand's cultural project wants to cement and unify *(rassembler)* the peoples of France. But it also means absorbing and neutralizing difference by coercing the immigrants into assuming the identity and values of the French, by forcing them to become fully integrated and productive members of the French community of citizens, in short by exerting considerable cultural pressure. It is therefore 'democratic' only if we believe that immigrants willingly reject their own native customs and traditions in order to become fullfledged citizens, and wait enthusiastically to be incorporated and transformed into acquiescing members of the French body politic" (249).

7. Tzvetan Todorov, *On Human Diversity: Nationalism, Racism, and Exoticism in French Thought,* trans. Catherine Porter (Cambridge: Harvard University Press, 1993). The fact that both Kristeva and Todorov are foreigners perfectly acculturated to French intellectual life, exiled in the language of the Other, but skillful masters of its syntax like Cioran or Beckett before them, affords them a unique perspective on the French national tradition. Both authors make their own relationship of estranged closeness or distanced adherence to their adoptive culture the object of their theorizing, Kristeva in *Strangers to Ourselves* (in which literature becomes the space of the interplay between the same and the other), and Todorov in his reading of the double movement of distancing and *rapprochement* in Lévi-Strauss's anthropology (in *Diversity,* 82). Both intellectual *émigrés* share with the anthropologist a "distanced gaze" on a national culture they end up appropriating for themselves (on its universalist side). See Julia Kristeva, *Strangers to Ourselves,* trans. Leon S. Koudiez (New York: Columbia University Press, 1991).

8. Ironically enough, the same German model would be used by the nationalistic (and hence, anti-Prussian) opponents of the Republic to denounce Jewish cosmopolitanism and the degeneration of the French "race" in the heyday of the Dreyfus affair.

9. The current French critique of American multiculturalism as the product of a convergence between (British) radical pluralism and (German) romantic culturalism is reminiscent of Allan Bloom's charge (in *The Closing of the American Mind: How Higher Education Has Failed Democracy and Impoverished the Souls of Today's Students* [New York: Simon and Schuster, 1987]) that the triumph of relativism in the contemporary United States is the direct result of the unfortunate postwar "Germanization" of American culture.

10. For a discussion of similar moves on this side of the Atlantic, see Naomi Schor, "French Feminism is a Universalism," in *Bad Objects: Essays Popular and Unpopular* (Durham: Duke University Press, 1995), and Amanda Anderson, "Cosmopolitanism, Universalism, and the Divided Legacies of Modernity," in *Cosmopolitics: Thinking and Feeling beyond the Nation,* ed. Pheng Cheah and Bruce Robbins (Minneapolis: University of Minnesota Press, 1998). Citing a number of French and American critics who are reluctant to do away with all

forms of universalism, in both the aesthetic and political realms, Schor argues for "a new universal that would include all those who wish to be included and that would above all afford them the opportunity to speak universal while not relinquishing their difference(s)" (27). Such a plea for inclusion resonates with what some French authors today call *intégration* (as opposed to the now discredited notion of assimilation). In fact, the term "assimilation" (in its nineteenth-century meaning) did not imply a total obliteration of all cultural and linguistic identities on the part of "minorities." For example, "assimilated" Jews in France apparently did not feel any contradiction between their ideological attachment to the Republic and their membership in the Alliance israélite universelle, an organization devoted to the promotion of Jewish values and culture throughout the world. The notion of *laïcité* applied to public education similarly did not deny religious pluralism or freedom of religion, but limited the expression of religious convictions to the "private" sphere, that is, to those spaces in social life that were not under the jurisdiction of the government of the Republic.

11. Kristeva's cosmopolitanism is not incompatible with a reassertion of France's *mission civilisatrice* via a defense of universalism, albeit in a revised, less absolutist manner. Many passages in *Nations without Nationalism* point to the central role of culture in the definition of the French identity, call for the rebirth of the French national spirit beset by doubts and the self-contempt of the intellectuals, and suggest that France must play a leading role in the establishment of a "Mediterranean peace" *(pax mediterranea?)* based on Enlightenment secularism as an antidote to radical Islamism.

12. I am grateful to Kevin Doak for pointing out this crucial distinction to me.

13. See Etienne Balibar, *La Crainte des masses* (Paris: Galilée, 1997), and Jacques Rancière, *La Mésentente: Politique et philosophie* (Paris: Galilée, 1995).

14. Slavoj Žižek, *The Ticklish Subject: The Absent Center of Political Ontology* (London: Verso, 1999), 216. For a similar argument regarding the collusion between capitalism and multiculturalism on the American side, see David Rieff, "Multiculturalism's Silent Partner," *Harper's* (August 1993): 62–63.

15. Charles Taylor, "Cross-Purposes: The Liberal-Communitarian Debate," in *Liberalism and the Moral Life,* ed. N. Rosenblum (Cambridge: Harvard University Press, 1989), 159–82.

16. Kallen and his followers were reacting to the excesses of the forced Americanization of newcomers after World War I rather than advocating the breakup of the United States into separate enclaves. Kallen's pluralism was a call for tolerance and diversity within the unitary framework of the American nation. Because separatism was not as widespread an option then as it is now, allowing the diversity of cultural practices to flourish was not perceived as it is today as a threat to national unity.

17. See Gérard Noiriel, *The French Melting-Pot: Immigration, Citizenship and National Identity* (Minneapolis: University of Minnesota Press, 1996), 335.

18. "Public proclamations notwithstanding, the few statistics that we have at our disposal all point to a decline of identity-based claims between the second and third generations . . . The tendency among scholars with foreign origins to overestimate the 'resistance' of immigrant communities to the norms of the dominant society illustrates the inherent risk in any research endeavor whose implicit goal is to rehabilitate one's own group" (Noiriel, *Melting-Pot*, 185, 187). The author suggests that "it may be useful to look at the US example, which is more similar to the French—at least in this respect—than is often believed" (186). On the American side, see Stephen Steinberg, *The Ethnic Myth: Race, Ethnicity and Class in America* (New York: Atheneum, 1981), who relies on Herbert Gans's concept of "symbolic ethnicity" to describe the quest for lost ethnic roots among third- or fourth-generation Americans.

CONCLUSION

1. Todd, *Le Destin*.

2. On the role of inheritance practices and kinship rules in the genesis of English individualism, see Alan Macfarlane, *The Origins of English Individualism: The Family, Property and Social Transition* (Cambridge: Cambridge University Press, 1978). Macfarlane reminds his readers that by Common Law, "the wife had rights to one third of the husband's estate, including goods, but the children had no rights in their parents' goods" (81). As a consequence, women could own land and children could be disinherited (right of alienation) and forced to find employment elsewhere as hired labor. Such inheritance practices of course meant that a traditional peasant society, in which the heirs do not inherit the land, but are inherited by it, was impossible in the English context.

Individualism was viewed by its supporters, then as now, not as a social catastrophe responsible for the collapse of extended families as viable economic units, but as moral progress, as an incentive to the enterprising spirit, altogether a good thing, as in the following assessment of life in mid-thirteenth-century England in Bracton's *On the Laws and Customs of England*: "A citizen could scarcely be found who would undertake a great enterprise in his lifetime if, at his death, he was compelled against his will to leave his estate to ignorant and extravagant children and undeserving wives. Thus it is very necessary that freedom of action be given him in this respect, for thereby he will curb misconduct, encourage virtue, and put in the way of both wives and children an occasion for good behavior, which indeed might not come about if they knew without doubt that they would obtain a certain share irrespective of the testator's wishes" (quoted in Macfarlane, 103). That such arguments (six centuries old!) closely resemble current opinions on the deleterious effects of the welfare system in the

United States testifies to the resiliency of moral conceptions of the self in society within the tradition of liberal individualism.

Macfarlane's arguments are reminiscent of earlier descriptions of the English difference among French liberals themselves. Montesquieu intimated that English exceptionalism existed from time immemorial, and linked England's prosperity to the difference of laws. Tocqueville ascribed the peculiarities of the country's laws, spirit, and history to the fact that "England was the only country in which the system of caste had not been changed but effectively destroyed," opening the way to acquisitive individualism and the fusion of the nobility and the bourgeoisie into one single elite group (quoted in Macfarlane, 167). As for English writers familiar with life on the Continent or in Ireland, they were quick to point out that the main difference between the two social worlds rested in matters of customary law and kinship systems. Sir John Davies (in 1612) attributed the prosperity of England, when compared to the lot of the Irish, to the rules of primogeniture and impartible inheritance. Sir John Fortescue, contrasting England and France in 1461, insisted on the political consequences of the difference between English Common Law and Civil (Roman) Law. In Macfarlane's words, the difference rested in "the methods of trial, the use of juries, the absence of torture in England, the use of sheriffs in the legal process" (180). Similarly, the uses and abuses of absolutism were rooted in the legal system.

3. Quoting an unnamed French historian ("There is no cause for blushing in having been born a Frenchman, for it is a matter of chance"), Louis Dumont comments: "Who but a Frenchman can imagine he could possibly have been both himself and other than French? Only ask a Japanese, or an Iranian. These men know that their personal identity is inseparable from a collective identity, from what we shall call here a culture" (*German Ideology*, 3). French universalism comforts the unnamed historian's belief that national identity is a matter of chance: "I am a man by nature," he seems to say, "and a Frenchman by accident."

4. The Ligue Savoisienne is a recently formed political party inspired by the successes of the northern Italian Lombard League; it advocates the economic and political sovereignty of the Savoie region in the French Alps.

5. The same can be said of the United States, in view of the idealistic nature of the nation's dominant political creed. But the interpretation of what American democracy is and should be about is precisely what is in question in American politics. Beyond a general agreement on democratic principles, there is no consensus on what constitutes the country's proper commitment to human, civil, or individual rights.

6. Barbara Christian, *Black Feminist Criticism: Perspectives on Black Women Writers* (Elmsford, N.Y.: Pergamon Press, 1985), 260.

7. Kwame Anthony Appiah, "Cosmopolitan Patriots," in *Cosmopolitics: Thinking and Feeling beyond the Nation,* ed. Pheng Cheah and Bruce Robbins (Minneapolis: University of Minnesota Press, 1998), 102.

8. Paul Veyne, "Foucault révolutionne l'histoire," in *Comment on écrit l'histoire* (Paris: Seuil, 1971), 204.

9. Even a cursory reading of the current debates surrounding the national question reveals at least three major sets of positions on the issue, usually subsumed under the three headings of nationalism, universalism, and cosmopolitanism. Each of these doctrinal positions in turn harbors different kinds of nationalism, universalism, and cosmopolitanism. On the complexity of the philosophical positions involved in contemporary discussions, see, for example, the extreme diversity of the essays collected in *Cosmopolitics.*

Bibliography

❧ ❧ ❧

Agulhon, Maurice. *La République au village*. Paris: Plon, 1970.

Ahmad, Aijaz. *In Theory: Classes, Nations, Literatures*. London: Verso, 1992.

Anderson, Benedict. *Imagined Communities: Reflections on the Origin and Spread of Nationalism*. London: Verso, 1991.

Appiah, Kwame Anthony. *In My Father's House: Africa in the Philosophy of Culture*. Oxford: Oxford University Press, 1992.

————. "The Multiculturalist Misunderstanding." *The New York Review* (9 October 1997): 30–36.

Badinter, Elizabeth, Régis Debray, Alain Finkielkraut, E. de Fontenay, and C. Kintzler. "Profs, ne capitulons pas!" *Le Nouvel Observateur* (2–8 November 1989).

Bell, David A. "Forgotten Frenchmen." *Times Literary Supplement* (24 January 1997): 7.

————. Review of *Realms of Memory: The Construction of the French Past, Volume 1*, ed. Lawrence D. Kritzman. *The New Republic* (1 September 1997): 32–36.

Bellah, Robert N., et al. *Habits of the Heart: Individualism and Commitment in American Life*. New York: Harper and Row, 1985.

Benda, Julien. *La Trahison des clercs*. Paris: Grasset, 1975.

————. *The Treason of the Intellectuals*. Trans. Richard Aldington. New York: Norton, 1969.

Berlin, Isaiah. *Four Essays on Liberty*. Oxford: Oxford University Press, 1990.

Bernstein, Richard. *Fragile Glory: A Portrait of France and the French*. New York: Knopf, 1990.

Blau, Herbert. *The Eye of Prey: Subversions of the Postmodern*. Bloomington: Indiana University Press, 1987.

Bloom, Allan. *The Closing of the American Mind: How Higher Education Has Failed Democracy and Impoverished the Souls of Today's Students*. New York: Simon and Schuster, 1987.

Boorstin, Daniel J. *The Americans: The Colonial Experience*. Harmondsworth: Penguin, 1965.

Bourdieu, Pierre. *Les Règles de l'art: Genèse et structure du champ littéraire.* Paris: Seuil, 1992.

Bowles, Brett C. "La République régionale." *The French Review* 69 (1995): 103–17.

Bramsted, E. K., and K. J. Melhuish. *Western Liberalism: A History in Documents from Locke to Croce.* London: Longman, 1978.

Brubaker, Rogers. *Citizenship and Nationhood in France and Germany.* Cambridge: Harvard University Press, 1992.

Burke, Edmund. *Reflections on the Revolution in France.* New York: Doubleday, 1989.

Camus, Albert. *The Rebel: An Essay on Man in Revolt.* New York: Knopf, 1961.

Carroll, David. *French Literary Fascism: Nationalism, Anti-Semitism and the Ideology of Culture.* Princeton: Princeton University Press, 1995.

Carroll, Raymonde. *Cultural Misunderstandings: The French-American Experience.* Trans. Carol Volk. Chicago: University of Chicago Press, 1990.

Cohen, Roger. "France's Allegiance: To Things French, Like Hypocrisy." *The New York Times* (24 August 1997).

Constant, Benjamin. "The Liberty of the Ancients Compared with That of the Moderns." In *Political Writings.* Trans. Biancamaria Fontana. Cambridge: Cambridge University Press, 1988.

Curtius, Ernst Robert. *The Civilization of France: An Introduction.* Trans. Olive Wyon. New York: Macmillan, 1932.

Debray, Régis. *Contretemps: Eloge des idéaux perdus.* Paris: Gallimard, 1992.

———. *A demain De Gaulle.* Paris: Gallimard, 1990.

DeJean, Joan. *Ancients against Moderns: Culture Wars and the Making of a Fin de Siècle.* Chicago: University of Chicago Press. 1997.

———, and Nancy K. Miller, eds. *Displacements.* Baltimore: Johns Hopkins University Press, 1991.

de Man, Paul. *Allegories of Reading: Figural Language in Rousseau, Nietzsche, Rilke and Proust.* New Haven: Yale University Press, 1979.

Derrida, Jacques. *The Other Heading: Reflections on Today's Europe.* Trans. P.-A. Brault and M. B. Naas. Bloomington: Indiana University Press, 1992.

———. "Racism's Last Word." Trans. Peggy Kamuf. *Critical Inquiry* 12 (1985): 290–99.

Descombes, Vincent. "Je m'en Foucault." *London Review of Books* (5 March 1987): 20–21.

Dormois, Jean-Pierre, and Simon P. Newman. *Vue d'Amérique: La Révolution française jugée par les Américains.* Paris: Ed. France-Empire, 1989.

Dulany, Daniel. "Considerations on the Propriety of Raising Taxes in the British Colonies" (1765). In vol. 1 of *Pamphlets of the American Revolution 1750–1776,* ed. Bernard Bailyn. Cambridge: The Belknap Press of Harvard University Press.

Dumont, Louis. *Essays on Individualism: Modern Ideology in Anthropological Perspective.* Chicago: University of Chicago Press, 1986.

———. *German Ideology: From France to Germany and Back.* Chicago: Chicago University Press, 1994.

Etzioni, Amitai. *The Spirit of Community: Rights, Responsibilities and the Communitarian Agenda.* New York: Crown, 1993.

Fassin, Eric. "La chaire et le canon: Les intellectuels, la politique et l'université aux Etats-Unis." *Annales ESC* (March–April 1993): 265–301.

———. "*Political Correctness* en version originale et en version française: Un malentendu révélateur." *Vingtième siècle. Revue d'histoire* 43 (July–September 1994): 30–42.

Ferry, Luc, and Alain Renaut. *French Philosophy of the Sixties: An Essay on Antihumanism.* Trans. Mary H. S. Cattani. Amherst: University of Massachusetts Press, 1990.

———. *Political Philosophy III: From the Rights of Man to the Republican Idea.* Trans. F. Philip. Chicago: University of Chicago Press, 1992.

Finkielkraut, Alain. *The Defeat of the Mind.* Trans. Judith Friedlander. New York: Columbia University Press, 1995.

Ford, Caroline. *Creating the Nation in Provincial France: Religion and Political Identity in Brittany.* Princeton: Princeton University Press, 1993.

Fourny, Jean-François. "The Maastricht Treaty and France's 'Great Design.'" *SubStance* 76/77 (1995): 49–61.

Fumaroli, Marc. *L'Etat culturel: Une religion moderne.* Paris: Ed. de Fallois, 1991.

———. "The State, Culture and 'L'Esprit.'" *SubStance* 76/77 (1995): 126–36.

Furet, François. *Interpreting the French Revolution.* Trans. Elborg Forster. Cambridge: Cambridge University Press, 1981.

———. *Le Passé d'une illusion: Essai sur l'idée communiste au XXe siècle.* Paris: Laffont-Calmann Lévy, 1995.

Furet, François, Jacques Julliard, and Pierre Rosanvallon. *La République du centre.* Paris: Calmann-Lévy, 1988.

Gaspard, Françoise, and Farhad Khosrokhavar. *Le Foulard et la République.* Paris: La Découverte, 1995.

Gates, Henry Louis, Jr. "Critical Fanonism." *Critical Inquiry* 17 (1991): 457–70.

Gauchet, Marcel. *La Révolution des droits de l'homme.* Paris: Gallimard, 1989.

Gellner, Ernst. *Nations and Nationalism.* Ithaca: Cornell University Press, 1983.

Genovese, Eugene D. "Heresy, Yes—Sensitivity, No." Review of *Illiberal Education: The Politics of Race and Sex on Campus,* by Dinesh D'Souza. *The New Republic* (15 April 1991): 30–35.

Girard, Louis. *Les Libéraux français, 1814–1875.* Paris: Aubier, 1985.

Granjon, Marie-Christine. "Le regard en biais: Attitudes françaises du multiculturalisme américain (1990–1993). *Vingtième siècle. Revue d'histoire* 43 (July–September 1994): 18–29.

Greenfeld, Liah. *Nationalism: Five Roads to Modernity*. Cambridge: Harvard University Press, 1992.

Habermas, Jürgen. "Natural Law and Revolution." In *Theory and Practice*, trans. John Viertel. Boston: Beacon Press, 1973.

Hall, A. Rupert, and Marie Boas Hall, eds. *The Correspondence of Henry Oldenburg*. Madison: University of Wisconsin Press, 1966–1973.

Hamilton, Alexander. *The Papers of Alexander Hamilton*. Vol. 14, ed. Harold Syrett. New York: Columbia University Press, 1969.

Harp, Gillis J. *Positivist Republic: Auguste Comte and the Reconstruction of American Liberalism, 1865–1920*. University Park: Pennsylvania State University Press, 1995.

Hartz, Louis. *The American Liberal Tradition*. New York: Harcourt, 1955.

Hill, Christopher. *Intellectual Origins of the English Revolution*. Oxford: Oxford University Press, 1965.

Hobsbawn, Eric J. *Nations and Nationalism Since 1780: Programme, Myth, Reality*. Cambridge: Cambridge University Press, 1990.

Hofstadter, Richard. *Anti-Intellectualism in American Life*. New York: Vintage, 1962.

Jacoby, Russell. "Marginal Returns: The Trouble with Post-Colonial Theory." *Lingua Franca* (September/October 1995): 30–37.

Jardine, Alice. *Gynesis: Configurations of Woman and Modernity*. Ithaca: Cornell University Press, 1985.

Jefferson, Thomas. *The Writings of Thomas Jefferson*. Vol. 9, ed. A. A. Lipscomb. Washington, D.C., 1903.

Jolly, Rosemary. "Rehearsals of Liberation: Contemporary Postcolonial Discourse and the New South Africa." *PMLA* 110, no. 1 (January 1995): 17–29.

Jospin, Lionel. "Le moment ou jamais." *Le Débat* 58 (1990): 3–19.

Judt, Tony. *Past Imperfect: French Intellectuals, 1944–1956*. Berkeley: University of California Press, 1993.

Julliard, Jacques. "Où est-elle, votre République?" *Le Nouvel Observateur* (7–13 December 1989): 50–51.

Kallen, Horace. *Culture and Democracy in the United States*. New York, 1924.

Kaplan, Steven L. *Farewell, Revolution*. 2 vols. Ithaca: Cornell University Press, 1995.

Khilnani, Sunil. *Arguing Revolution: The Intellectual Left in Postwar France*. New Haven: Yale University Press, 1993.

Kimball, Roger. "The Treason of the Intellectuals and 'The Undoing of Thought.'" *New Criterion* 11 (December 1992): 10–16.

Kohn, Hans. *Nationalism: Its Meaning and History*. Malabar: Krieger, 1965.

Kristeva, Julia. *Nations without Nationalism*. New York: Columbia University Press, 1993.

Kritzman, Lawrence. "Identity Crises: France, Culture and the Idea of the Nation." *SubStance* 76/77 (1995): 5–19.

Kuisel, Richard. *Seducing the French: The Dilemma of Americanization.* Berkeley: University of California Press, 1993.

Lamont, Michèle. "How to Become a Dominant French Philosopher: The Case of Jacques Derrida." *American Journal of Sociology* 3 (1987): 584–622.

———. *Money, Morals, and Manners: The Culture of the French and American Upper-Middle Class.* Chicago: University of Chicago Press, 1990.

Lamont, Michèle, and Marsha Witten. "Surveying the Continental Drift: The Diffusion of French Social and Literary Theory in the United States." *French Politics and Society* 6, no. 3 (1988): 17–23.

Larmore, Charles. "Histoire et raison en philosophie politique." *Stanford French Review* 15, nos. 1–2 (1991): 183–206.

Lebovics, Herman. *True France: The Wars over Cultural Identity, 1900–1945.* Ithaca: Cornell University Press, 1992.

Le Bras, Hervé, and Emmanuel Todd. *L'Invention de la France.* Paris: Hachette, 1981.

Le Goff, Jacques. "Derrière le foulard, l'histoire." *Le Débat* 58 (1990): 21–33.

Le Hir, Marie-Pierre. "French Cultural Studies in the United States: A Case Study." *Sites* 1, no. 1 (spring 1997): 171–90.

Lehman, David. *Signs of the Times: Deconstruction and the Fall of Paul de Man.* New York: Poseidon Press, 1991.

Lentricchia, Frank. *After the New Criticism.* Chicago: University of Chicago Press, 1980.

Lilla, Marc. "The Legitimacy of the Liberal Age." In *New French Thought: Political Philosophy.* Princeton: Princeton University Press, 1994.

Logue, William. *From Philosophy to Sociology: The Evolution of French Liberalism, 1870–1914.* Dekalb: Northern Illinois University Press, 1985.

Macfarlane, Alan. *The Origins of English Individualism: The Family, Property and Social Transition.* Cambridge: Cambridge University Press, 1978.

Manent, Pierre. *Les libéraux.* Vol. 2. Paris: Hachette, 1986.

Martin, Marie-Madeleine. *The Making of France.* London: Eyre and Soffiswode, 1951.

McClintock, Anne, and Rob Nixon. "No Names Apart: The Separation of Word and History in Derrida's 'Le dernier mot du racisme.'" *Critical Inquiry* 13 (1986): 140–54.

Mongin, Olivier. "Retour sur une controverse: Du 'politiquement correct' au multiculturalisme." *Esprit* (June 1995): 83–87.

Morris, Gouverneur. *A Diary of the French Revolution, 1789–1793.* Vol. 1, ed. Beatrix Davenport. Boston: Houghton Mifflin, 1939.

Nicolet, Claude. *L'Idée républicaine en France (1789–1924): Essai d'histoire critique.* Paris: Gallimard, 1982.

———. *La République en France: Etat des lieux.* Paris: Seuil, 1992.

Noiriel, Gérard. "Difficulties in French Historical Research on Immigration." *Immigrants in Two Democracies: French and American Experience.* Ed. D. L. Horowitz and Gérard Noiriel. New York: New York University Press, 1992.

———. *The French Melting-Pot: Immigration, Citizenship and National Identity.* Minneapolis: University of Minnesota Press, 1996.

Ozouf, Mona. *Women's Words: Essay on French Singularity.* Trans. Jane Marie Todd. Chicago: University of Chicago Press, 1997.

Paglia, Camille. "Junk Bonds and Corporate Raiders." *Arion* (spring 1991): 173–98.

———. "Ninnies, Tyrants, Pedants and Other Academics." *New York Times Book Review* (5 May 1991): 29, 31.

Pavel, Thomas. "Empires et paradigmes." *Le Débat* 50 (1989): 175–76.

———. "Lettre d'Amérique. La liberté de parole en question." *Commentaire* (spring 1995): 163–73.

Petrey, Sandy. "French Studies/Cultural Studies: Reciprocal Invigoration or Mutual Destruction?" *The French Review* 69, no. 3 (1995): 389–90.

Philonenko, Alexis. *Jean-Jacques Rousseau et la pensée du malheur.* Paris: Vrin, 1984.

Prochaska, David. *Making Algeria French: Colonialism in Bône, 1870–1920.* Cambridge: Cambridge University Press, 1990.

Prochasson, Christophe. *Les Intellectuels, le socialisme et la guerre, 1900–1938.* Paris: Seuil, 1993.

Riding, Alan. "Where Is the Glory That Was France?" *The New York Times* (14 January 1996).

Roman, Joël. "Un multiculturalisme à la française?" *Esprit* (June 1995): 145–60.

Rorty, Richard. *Consequences of Pragmatism.* Minneapolis: University of Minnesota Press, 1982.

———. "Cosmopolitanism without Emancipation: A Response to Jean-François Lyotard." In *Objectivity, Relativism and Truth.* Cambridge: Cambridge University Press, 1991.

———. "Taking Philosophy Seriously." *The New Republic* (11 April 1988).

———. "Trotsky and the Wild Orchids." *Common Knowledge* 1, no. 3 (1992): 140–53.

Rosanvallon, Pierre. *Le Sacre du citoyen: Histoire du suffrage universel en France.* Paris: Gallimard, 1992.

Ross, Dorothy. "The Liberal Tradition Revisited and the Republican Tradition Addressed." In *New Directions in American Intellectual History,* ed. John Higham and Paul K. Conkin. Baltimore: Johns Hopkins University Press, 1979.

Ross, Kristin. *Fast Cars, Clean Bodies: Decolonization and the Reordering of French Culture.* Cambridge: MIT Press, 1995.

Rousseau, Jean-Jacques. *Political Writings.* Ed. Frederick Watkins. Edinburgh: Nelson, 1954.

Sarde, Michèle. *Regard sur les Françaises: Xe–XXe siècles.* Paris: Stock, 1983.

Schlesinger, Arthur. *The Disuniting of America: Reflections on a Multicultural Society.* New York: Norton, 1992.

Scullion, Rosemarie. "Vicious Circles: Immigration and National Identity in Twentieth-Century France." *SubStance* 76/77 (1995): 30–48.

Searle, John. "The Word Turned Upside Down." *New York Review of Books* (27 October 1983).

Serres, Michel. "Qu'est-ce que l'identité?" *Le Monde de l'éducation, de la culture et de la formation* (January 1997): 6.

Shaftesbury, Anthony Ashley Cooper. *Characteristics of Men, Manners, Opinions, Times.* Ed. John M. Robertson. New York: Bobbs-Merrill, 1964.

Shils, Edward. "British Intellectuals." In *The Intellectuals and the Powers and Other Essays.* Chicago: University of Chicago Press, 1972.

Showalter, Elaine. "Critical Crossdressing and the Woman of the Year." In *Men in Feminism,* ed. Alice Jardine and Paul Smith. New York: Methuen, 1987.

Simpson, David. *Nationalism, Romanticism and the Revolt against Theory.* Chicago: University of Chicago Press, 1993.

Soltau, Roger Henry. *French Political Thought in the Nineteenth Century.* New York: Russell & Russell, 1959.

Spivak, Gayatri. *The Post-Colonial Critic: Interviews, Strategies, Dialogues.* Ed. Sarah Harasym. London: Routledge, 1990.

Sprat, Thomas. *Observations on Mons. de Sorbiere's Voyage into England.* London, 1709.

Steinberg, Stephen. *The Ethnic Myth: Race, Ethnicity and Class in America.* New York: Atheneum, 1981.

Stora, Benjamin. "La fin de l'homogénéité républicaine." *Libération* (30 August 1996): 4.

Taguieff, Pierre-André. *La Force du préjugé: Essai sur le racisme et ses doubles.* Paris: La Découverte, 1988.

———. *Sur la Nouvelle droite: Jalons d'une analyse critique.* Paris: Descartes and Cie, 1994.

Taylor, Charles. "Cross-Purposes: The Liberal-Communitarian Debate." In *Liberalism and the Moral Life,* ed. N. Rosenblum. Cambridge: Harvard University Press, 1989. 159–82.

———. "The Politics of Recognition." In *Multiculturalism: Examining the Politics of Recognition,* ed. A. Gutmann. Princeton: Princeton University Press, 1994.

Thompson, E. P. *The Poverty of Theory and Other Essays.* New York: Monthly Review Press, 1978.

Bibliography

Tocqueville, Alexis de. *Democracy in America*. Vol. 2, trans. Henry Reeve. New York: Knopf, 1945.

Todorov, Tzvetan. *On Human Diversity: Nationalism, Racism, and Exoticism in French Thought*. Trans. Catherine Porter. Cambridge: Harvard University Press, 1993.

Touraine, Alain. *Critique of Modernity*. Trans. David Macey. Oxford: Blackwell, 1995.

Trilling, Lionel. "On the Teaching of Modern Literature." In *Beyond Culture*. New York: Harcourt Brace Jovanovich, 1979.

Walzer, Michael. *On Toleration*. New Haven: Yale University Press, 1997.

Weber, Eugen. *Peasants into Frenchmen: The Modernization of Rural France 1870–1914*. Stanford: Stanford University Press, 1976.

Zeldin, Theodore. *The French*. New York: Pantheon, 1982.

Index

JEAN-PHILIPPE MATHY is associate professor of French
and acting director of the Program in Comparative Literature
at the University of Illinois–Urbana. He is the author of
Extrême-Occident: French Intellectuals and America.